WONDERFUL
THINGS...

WONDERFUL
THINGS

UNCOVERING
THE WORLD'S GREAT
ARCHAEOLOGICAL
TREASURES

EDITOR
PAUL G. BAHN

SEVEN DIALS

CONTENTS

6　PREFACE

10　TREASURES OF AFRICA
12　Africa's Oldest Dated Rock Art
　　by Anne Thackeray
14　The Hetepheres Treasures *by Steven Snape*
16　The Tomb of Hemaka *by Steven Snape*
18　The 'Main Deposit' from Hierakonpolis
　　by Steven Snape
20　The Statues of Menkaure *by Steven Snape*
24　The Tod Treasure *by Steven Snape and
　　Louise Steel*
26　The Tomb of Kha *by Steven Snape*
28　The Amarna Letters *by Steven Snape*
30　Tutankhamen *by Steven Snape*
34　Tanis *by Steven Snape*
36　The Rosetta Stone *by Steven Snape*
38　Nigerian Sculpture *by Anne Thackeray*
44　The Lydenburg Heads *by Anne Thackeray*
46　Gold from Mapungubwe *by Anne Thackeray*
48　Birds from Great Zimbabwe
　　by Anne Thackeray
50　The Royal Graves of Thulamela
　　by Anne Thackeray

52　TREASURES OF ASIA
54　'Ain Ghazal *by Chris Edens*
56　The Uruk 'Sammelfund' *by Chris Edens*
58　The Mishmar Treasure *by Chris Edens*
60　The 'Royal' Tomb at Maikop
　　by Peter Bogucki
62　Tell Asmar *by Chris Edens*
64　The Gold of Troy *by Louise Steel*
68　Royal Treasures at Ur *by Chris Edens*
72　The Luristan Bronzes *by Chris Edens*
76　Bronze Age Treasures of Bactria
　　by Chris Edens
80　Alaca Höyük *by Chris Edens*
82　The Gold from Tell el-Ajjul *by Louise Steel*
84　The Burial Pits at Sanxingdui
　　by Simon Kaner
88　The Megiddo Ivories *by Chris Edens*
90　The Splendours of Prehistoric Japanese
　　Pottery *by Simon Kaner*
92　Scythian Treasures of the Steppes
　　by Peter Bogucki
96　Musical Treasures from Ancient China
　　by Simon Kaner
98　The Golden Hoard of Tillya Tepe
　　by Chris Edens
100　Bronze Bells of Yayoi *by Mark Hudson*

102　Treasures of Zhongshan
　　by Simon Kaner
106　Ancient Scripts from East Asia
　　by Simon Kaner
108　The Funeral Masks of Tashtyk
　　by Paul G. Bahn
110　The Dead Sea Scrolls *by Steven Snape*
112　Treasures from Early Korean Royal
　　Tombs *by Simon Kaner*
114　The Treasure House of Ancient Japan
　　by Mark Hudson
116　*Ikor* and the Ainu Bear Ceremony
　　by Mark Hudson

118　TREASURES
　　OF AUSTRALASIA
120　Valuable Goods in Australia and the
　　Pacific *by Caroline Bird*
122　Wooden Combs from Kauri Point
　　Swamp *by Caroline Bird*

124　TREASURES OF EUROPE
126　Early Ice Age Masterpieces
　　by John Hoffecker and Paul G. Bahn
128　Art Treasures of the Ice Age Steppe
　　by John Hoffecker
130　Power, Prestige and Gold at Varna
　　by Peter Bogucki
134　Prepalatial Jewellery from Mochlos
　　by Louise Steel
136　Amber and Jet: Treasured Accessories
　　from Prehistoric Europe
　　by Simon Kaner
138　Bush Barrow and the Treasures of
　　Bronze Age Goldwork *by Simon Kaner*
140　Bronze Age Hoards of the Carpathian
　　Basin *by Peter Bogucki*
142　The Aegina Treasure *by Louise Steel*
146　Mycenae 'Rich in Gold' *by Louise Steel*
148　Dowris and the Irish Goldsmiths
　　by Simon Kaner
150　Vix and Treasures of the European Iron
　　Age *by Simon Kaner*
152　Ancient Classical Sculptures
　　by David Gill
158　Celtic Prince *by Paul G. Bahn*
159　Celtic Torcs *by Paul G. Bahn*
160　The Lady of Elche *by Paul G. Bahn*
162　The Panagyurishté Treasure
　　by David Gill
164　The Rogozen Treasure *by David Gill*
166　Etruscan Tombs *by David Gill*
168　The Hildesheim Treasure *by David Gill*
170　Hoards from Pompeii *by David Gill*
176　The Boscoreale Treasure *by David Gill*
178　Mosaics from Roman Britain
　　by David Gill

182 Vindolanda: Letters from
Rome *by Paul G. Bahn*

186 The Treasure of the Spring at
Bad Pyrmont *by Peter Bogucki*

188 The Portland Vase
by David Gill

190 The Water Newton Hoard
by David Gill

192 The Mildenhall Treasure
by David Gill

194 The Esquiline Treasure *by David Gill*

196 The Hoxne Treasure *by David Gill*

198 The Golden Age of Scandinavia
by Peter Bogucki

200 Sutton Hoo *by Simon Kaner*

202 Medieval Buried Treasure at Środa
Śląska *by Peter Bogucki*

204 TREASURES OF NORTH
AND CENTRAL AMERICA

206 The Richey-Roberts Clovis Cache
by Philip Duke

208 The Olmec 'Fort Knox'
by Geoffrey McCafferty

210 Tomb 7: Shrine of a Mixtec Earth
Goddess *by Geoffrey McCafferty*

212 Ancient Treasures of Florida
by Philip Duke

214 The Funerary Mask of Pacal
by Constance Cortez

216 The Sacred Cenote of Chichén Itzá
by Geoffrey McCafferty

218 Treasures of the American Desert
by Philip Duke

220 Ancient Treasures of Ozette
by Philip Duke

224 TREASURES OF SOUTH
AMERICA

226 Ancient Textiles of the Andes
by Karen Wise

228 Paracas Textiles *by Karen Wise*

230 The Tombs of Sipán *by Karen Wise*

232 Laguna de los Condores and the
Chachapoyas *by Karen Wise*

234 The Gold of El Dorado
by Karen Wise

238 TREASURE MAPS OF THE
WORLD

246 BIBLIOGRAPHY

250 INDEX

256 LIST OF CONTRIBUTORS

PREFACE

What is a 'treasure'? Is it an object, a hoard, a precious metal or stone? The term is as vague as the range of material it encompasses is vast. After all, one person's treasure – for example, a family heirloom or a token of love – is another person's piece of worthless junk!

It is obvious that some raw materials such as gold, silver or jade have been highly prized in many ancient cultures, and they are well represented in this book. But equally, a whole gamut of other materials seems to have been of great value in the past, such as amber, copper, bronze and iron; faience and glass; fine ceramics; fossils and seashells; and various kinds of fine stone or even hardwood.

To the archaeologist almost any surviving scrap from the ancient past may represent a treasure, in that it can provide valuable information or represent a tangible link with our ancestors – it is hard to describe the emotion and excitement involved in unearthing an object that was last touched by human hands some centuries, millennia or even tens of millennia before the present.

In this book we have tried to include a representative selection of 'treasures' from around the world. Since the term is so general, this was the most difficult set of choices that we have had to face so far in this series of volumes. Think of the quantities of statuary and jewellery that survive from Egypt or the classical world, the metalwork of the Orient and the New World, the dazzling array of ceramics from so many cultures. How can one possibly narrow this down to a few examples?

'A GROUP OF ANTIQUARIES' BY THOMAS ROWLANDSON (1756–1827).

In making our choices, it was first decided to concentrate on movable objects; in other words, rock art, cave art and murals were largely omitted, as otherwise they would have had to constitute a sizeable proportion of the book. It was also determined largely to ignore finds from shipwrecks as these will be the focus of the next volume in the series. And in view of our sub-title, and our general theme, we have concentrated overwhelmingly on finds that have been discovered – though not necessarily by archaeologists, as it is well known that many of the greatest finds are made accidentally, often by peasants, quarrymen and the like. Many other discoveries in recent times have been made by the ever-growing army of metal-detector enthusiasts whose pastime, if carried out responsibly and with full regard for leaving the archaeological context undisturbed, is a valuable ally for archaeology.

To most people, the word 'treasure' probably conjures up images of pirate caves, buried chests and royal tombs. We have certainly included a few of the latter in this compilation, as well as buried hoards of various kinds. But as usual we have endeavoured to present a glimpse of the tremendous range of material that the archaeologist can recover, from letters on wood to jade masks, from bronze bells to Ice Age carvings. Some objects included here, such as the Rosetta Stone, are considered treasures for the incalculable role they have played in unlocking the secrets of the past.

For ultimately, while many treasures may appeal to us visually as being beautiful or striking, and while most may comprise fine materials or breath-taking craftsmanship, their most important quality and their most lasting value for archaeology surely lie in the information they can deliver about the lives of our ancestors. The array of treasures in this volume has yielded data on raw materials, tools, technology, craftsmanship and trade; on religion, ritual, status and hierarchy; on social life and physical appearance. All that glisters for archaeologists is not necessarily gold – indeed, even a coprolite (fossil faeces) can be considered priceless for the information it may reveal about diet and health!

Over the millennia, we have lost untold quantities of treasures from the activities of tomb robbers. Moreover, one of the most tragic losses of the recent past is the vast abundance of finely worked objects in precious metals that were melted down by the European conquerors of the New World – what must have been some of mankind's most fantastic achievements in metalworking were reduced to simple ingots, brutish lumps of metal. Such mindless greed and destruction, alas, continue to this day, as clandestine excavation and outright plundering of archaeological sites and graves provide a steady stream of 'treasures' to feed the ever-increasing hunger of the worldwide antiquities trade. Objects are torn from their context; anything that is not sellable is smashed or left to rot; and the result is huge quantities of 'ingots' – that is, attractive objects displayed in swank apartments by philistine 'art lovers' who know the price of everything but the value of nothing, and whose willingness to pay huge sums for such objects is the ultimate cause of the destruction.

So treasure may be coinage, or jewellery, or goldwork, or statuary – but the real treasure, the most valuable, is information. And that is what archaeology seeks to obtain from every object it encounters, from the most mundane to the most fantastic. A book of this size cannot hope to give more than a brief glimpse of the range of treasures in the archaeological record, but we hope that these examples selected from a wide variety of regions, cultures and periods will help to demonstrate the real and lasting wealth of the human past.

Paul G. Bahn

Treasures
of
Africa

Africa's Oldest Dated Rock Art

Southern Africa boasts one of the richest collections of Stone Age rock art in the world, including many thousands of paintings on the walls of rock shelters and caves in mountainous areas, as well as thousands of engravings on boulders on the interior plateau. Dating this abundant heritage has, however, proved challenging. A notable exception is a remarkable series of painted slabs unexpectedly found in the Apollo 11 Cave in southern Namibia.

In July 1969, archaeologist Erich Wendt was listening to broadcasts of the Apollo 11 moon landing on his radio while excavating in a cave in the remote, barren Huns mountains of southern Namibia, and decided to name the cave in honour of the mission that put the first people on the moon.

During this excavation season, and a subsequent one in 1972, he recovered seven small, portable, broken painted slabs from layers in the cave. Incredibly, one of the slabs found during the 1969 excavation fitted with one found during the 1972 excavation. The slabs depict a black, feline-looking animal with human-like rear legs, two examples of a white animal with black stripes, an outline of a rhino in black, the body of an antelope covered by a red line, and black lines with a red patch.

Wendt was able to obtain radiocarbon dates from charcoal found in the same layers as the slabs. The dates indicated that the layers and their contents accumulated between 28,000 and 19,000 years ago, a period that saw the end of the Middle Stone Age and the beginning of the Later Stone Age in southern Africa, and that is roughly the same age as some of the oldest known dated rock art in Europe. Southern African Stone Age rock art continued to be produced until the nineteenth century AD. The Apollo 11 dates indicate not only that this art is of considerable antiquity, but also

that it is one of the most outstanding achievements of humankind, being the longest lasting artistic tradition the world has seen.

At first, Europeans who were interested in southern African rock art thought it was simply a decorative and quaint record of daily life in the Stone Age. However, some researchers from the nineteenth century, and most since the 1970s, have argued that it is best understood as religious art. In particular, it has been claimed that some of the art depicts the experiences of shamans (medicine men and women), who were believed to be able to activate supernatural powers and perform tasks like curing sickness, bringing rain or attracting game, by going into a dream-like trance. Some features on the Apollo 11 slabs have been linked with such hallucinatory experiences. More recently, however, it has been suggested that paintings depicting figures with both human and animal features like that on the conjoined Apollo 11 slabs can also be understood in terms of mythology and beliefs about the spirits of the dead.

Above: CONJOINING SLABS FROM THE APOLLO 11 CAVE IN SOUTHERN NAMIBIA DEPICTING AN ANIMAL WITH HUMAN-LIKE REAR LEGS. SOME RESEARCHERS SUGGEST SUCH HALF-ANIMAL HALF-HUMAN IMAGES ARE RELATED TO THE TRANCE EXPERIENCES OF SHAMANS DURING CURING RITUALS.

Left: A DEPICTION OF A RHINOCEROS ON A SLAB EXCAVATED FROM THE APOLLO 11 CAVE IN SOUTHERN NAMIBIA.

The Hetepheres Treasures

Queen Hetepheres was at the heart of the Egyptian royal family when the Old Kingdom was at the height of its power and wealth. Her husband King Sneferu was the first king of the Fourth Dynasty and the most prodigious pyramid builder in Egyptian history, with two pyramids at the site of Dahshur, and possibly a third at Meidum, credited to him. Her son Khufu (also known as Cheops) was the builder of the single largest royal tomb ever erected in Egypt, the Great Pyramid at Giza.

But although these massive monuments are obvious evidence of the power and wealth of the Egyptian state embodied in the person of the king, the internal chambers of these and all other royal pyramids have long been emptied of their contents. We can only speculate on what burial equipment was provided for kings who had prepared for their afterlife on such a lavish scale.

Some idea of the quality of such royal burial equipment can be found in the contents of a small number of intact burials of royal women that were placed around kings' pyramids. From the Middle Kingdom a small number of burials of princesses are known from royal pyramid complexes; the tombs of the Princesses Khnumet and Ita near the pyramid of Amenemhat II at Dahshur and the tomb of Princess Sat-Hathor-Iunet from a shaft-tomb south of the pyramid of Senwosret II at Illahun are particularly known for the quality of the jewellery found within them. However, among the tombs of queens and princesses of the pyramid age, that of Queen Hetepheres is the most spectacular, and the most puzzling.

In 1925, the American archaeologist George Reisner was excavating to the south of the causeway of the pyramid of Khufu, close to the subsidiary pyramids that housed the burials of Khufu's royal women. Reisner's team discovered a vertical shaft 30 m deep, which led to a burial chamber containing an alabaster sarcophagus and a canopic box – a cubic alabaster box, whose interior was divided into four compartments, each containing a set of preserved internal organs removed during mummification. It is assumed that these organs belong to the queen; if so, they are the only parts of her body that remained within the tomb at the time of its discovery by Reisner because the sarcophagus was found mysteriously empty.

Nevertheless, the burial chamber also contained a range of breathtaking objects forming the queen's grave goods, which are now displayed in the Cairo Museum: exquisite toiletry and cosmetic items, a jewel-case and jewellery were among the objects one might have expected to find in the burial of a queen. More spectacular still was the furniture: a bed, two armchairs and the frame for a canopy, all wholly or partially cased in gold sheet. Similar gold casing was given to the queen's carrying-chair, which was fitted with exceptionally fine gold hieroglyphs listing the names and titles of Queen Hetepheres.

The most obvious missing object from the tomb is the body of the queen herself, and the jewellery that would have accompanied her wrapped mummy. The most apparent solution to this problem is that the queen's tomb was robbed shortly after burial, but the robbers could only make off with the most valuable objects, which

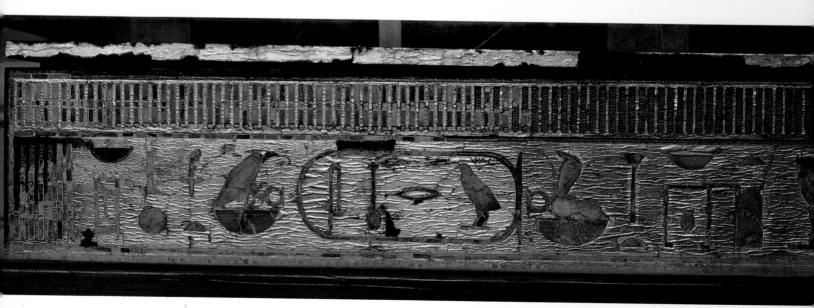

Left: THE BOX CONTAINING HETEPHERES' CURTAINS IS INLAID WITH THE NAMES AND TITLES OF HER HUSBAND, KING SNEFERU. *Above:* BEDROOM FURNITURE FIT FOR A QUEEN: THE GILDED BED, CHAIR AND CANOPY FROM THE TOMB OF HETEPHERES.

they knew would be close to the corpse, perhaps carrying off the mummified body or, more likely, ripping it apart in their search for loot. But was the tomb that Reisner discovered the original resting place of Hetepheres? The most commonly held theory regarding this burial assumes that Hetepheres was originally buried close to her husband Sneferu in a tomb near to his northern pyramid at Dahshur. This original tomb was the one that was robbed, either before or during the reign of her son Khufu; and once the robbery had been discovered, Khufu (who may not have been told about his mother's missing mummy) ordered a reburial close to his own pyramid. It is notable that this second tomb had no superstructure above the shaft, and evidence suggests that attempts were made to hide the entrance to the shaft under a layer of plaster and gravel. If this is the case, these attempts were indeed successful in concealing the whereabouts of the queen's burial, at least for four millennia.

The Tomb of Hemaka

The cemetery at Saqqara is one of the largest in Egypt, containing tombs of many rulers of the Old Kingdom and private tombs of that and later periods. Its importance is hardly surprising as Saqqara is the closest cemetery to Memphis, Egypt's capital during the Old Kingdom and probably the largest city during all periods of Egyptian history. In fact, the city of Memphis could be said to be intimately bound up with the beginnings of Egyptian history, as its foundation as the first capital for the unified country of Egypt around 3050 BC is one of the most significant events at the beginning of the First Dynasty, which ruled from around 3050 to 2700 BC.

However, although the effective government of the country took place in Memphis, it seems likely that the kings of Egypt were not, at first, buried close to their new capital (as they later would be, especially in pyramid tombs) but in the ancestral cemetery in the southern Egyptian town of Abydos. Yet, in a rare departure from the tradition of high-ranking officials being buried close to their king, the government ministers of the First Dynasty were buried on the edge of the plateau at Saqqara, overlooking Memphis, in enormous, rectangular, mudbrick tombs called mastabas.

These tombs were designed to contain vast amounts of provisions for the next life and objects that befitted the status of their noble occupants. Although the royal tombs at Abydos were badly robbed, the material from the great tombs at Saqqara give a clear picture of the wealth of the royal court of the First Dynasty.

The tombs were discovered by the British Egyptologist Walter Emery during his excavations at Saqqara in the period after 1935. The first to be found, numbered Mastaba 3035, was one of the most impressive measuring 57 m long by 26 m wide. The tomb had been originally located by Emery's predecessor, Firth, but it was Emery who decided to excavate what was thought to be the solid mudbrick superstructure, and in doing so discovered forty-five chambers containing the grave goods. Emery would come to regard this and later tombs as the true royal tombs of the First Dynasty, but his initial assumption, that they belonged to important non-royal individuals of the period, is now generally regarded as being correct.

The owner of Tomb 3035 was Hemaka, the highest official in Egypt during the reign of King Den, with the title of Seal-Bearer or Chancellor. Hemaka is referred to on inscriptions from his tomb, and that of the king himself at Abydos, as 'Ruling in the King's heart', an indication of his exalted status.

Different chambers in the superstructure of the mastaba contained different types of objects necessary for Hemaka's well-being in the next life. Magazine AA, for example, contained dozens of flint tools, some sealed in a large leather bag; Magazines C–E were effectively a wine cellar containing hundreds of large wine jars; while the bones of oxen were the sole contents of Magazines I, L and O. The general impression is of a high-ranking nobleman ensuring that his quality of life in the next world would be as luxurious as it was in this world.

Non-consumable luxury items were also found within the tomb, most remarkably in Magazine Z, which contained hunting equipment, the earliest roll of papyrus known, and a box containing a series of discs, averaging 10 cm in diameter but only 7–8 mm thick. The best of these are made of steatite elaborately inlaid with geometric patterns or, in one example, hunting dogs. Each disc has a central hole, and although their exact purpose is unknown it is possible that they were used in a game in which they were spun using a central wooden spindle.

Right: THIS, THE MOST SPLENDID OF THE DISCS FROM HEMAKA'S TOMB, SHOWS A HUNTING SCENE OF ALABASTER ANIMALS ON A BLACK STEATITE BACKGROUND.

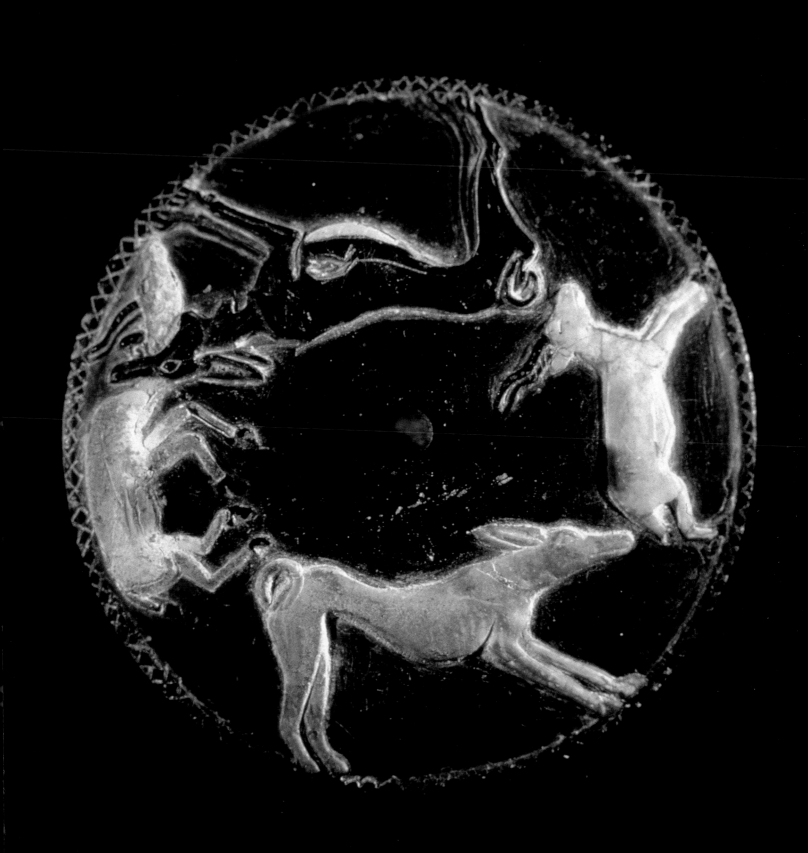

The 'Main Deposit' from Hierakonpolis

Throughout Egyptian history temples were places where kings made offerings to the gods. These might be day-to-day offerings of food and drink, or statues of the king himself, or special gifts to mark special events. Such benefactions would undoubtedly have filled the shrines of favoured deities with a range of ceremonial clutter that needed to be cleared out at regular intervals to make space for future favours. But the spring-cleaned artefacts could not be simply thrown away – they were, after all, the personal possessions of the gods – so they were buried in a series of sacred deposits within the bounds of the temple precinct. These deposits are known to Egyptologists as 'caches'.

Right: THIS GOLD HEAD OF THE FALCON-GOD HORUS SEEMS TO HAVE BEEN PART OF A COPPER-SHEATHED WOODEN STATUE.

The earliest of these royal caches is the most important and comes from the early temple in Hierakonpolis, a southern Egyptian city. Hierakonpolis may have been the capital of a kingdom that unified Egypt through military conquest around 3050 BC. In 1897–8 the English archaeologists Quibell and Green, protégés of the renowned British Egyptologist Flinders Petrie, excavated at Hierakonpolis and in doing so stumbled upon the single most significant discovery from the 'Unification period', around 3050 BC.

The rulers who felt the need to give solid offerings in the temple at Nekhen did so by donating objects typical of the time: simple utilitarian objects – the small slate palettes used for grinding cosmetics and the pear-shaped maceheads – were vastly enlarged to produce ceremonial gifts, with large surfaces bearing carved depictions of historical events, or at least the 'official' version of these events. Some time during the Old or Middle Kingdom a number of these very early artefacts were taken out of the shrine of the god Horus of Nekhen (Hierakonpolis) and buried in what is now known as the 'Main Deposit'.

From the Hierakonpolis Main Deposit we can see that the kings of the early dynastic period were keen on military conquest and the consolidation of authority over a wide area. On the 'Scorpion Macehead' (so-called because we do not know how to read the name of the king portrayed on it, whose name is written with the hieroglyphic sign of a scorpion) the king seems to inaugurate an

irrigation project by breaching a small dam with a
hoe, while his conquests include the olive-tree
growing area of the Libyan people.

But the most significant objects from the Main
Deposit name a ruler who can probably be
regarded as the first king of Egypt, King Narmer.
The Narmer Palette, a shield-shaped slate palette,
is carved on both sides; on one side the king,
accompanied by his sandal bearer, prepares to
administer the *coup de grâce* to a fallen enemy
(perhaps a chieftain from the Delta); on the
reverse, the upper register shows the king
inspecting the beheaded bodies of his enemies,
while the central panel shows the intertwining of
the necks of mythical beasts, perhaps symbolizing
the unification of the two lands, Lower and Upper
Egypt. The fact that Narmer wears the crown of
Upper Egypt on one side of the palette and that of
Lower Egypt on the other might also be taken as
evidence that he is at least claiming to be king of the
whole of Egypt.

The third piece of historical significance is the
'Narmer Wedding Macehead', on which the king
waits on a dais while a female figure is brought to
him on a carrying chair. This is perhaps a commemo-
ration of the wedding of the southern King Narmer and
a northern princess in order to consolidate the newly
unified country by creating a royal family drawn from both
parts of Egypt.

Right: THE SMALLER 'TWO-DOG' PALETTE
FROM HIERAKONPOLIS DEPICTS REAL AND
MYTHICAL CREATURES ATTACKING EACH
OTHER, PERHAPS A REFLECTION OF THE
DISRUPTION AT THE UNIFICATION OF
EGYPT.

The Statues of Menkaure

As we have seen (see Hetepheres, p.14), the internal chambers of the Egyptian royal pyramids of the Old and Middle Kingdoms were robbed in antiquity and stripped of their most valuable contents. Even the elaborate labyrinthine arrangements of Middle Kingdom pyramids such as that of Amenemhat III at Hawara (effectively the last of the great royal pyramids) failed to preserve their royal contents intact. This has not, however, prevented modern explorers from seeking further, hitherto undisturbed 'hidden' chambers within the pyramids. Nevertheless, the pyramids have yielded up 'treasure', of a kind.

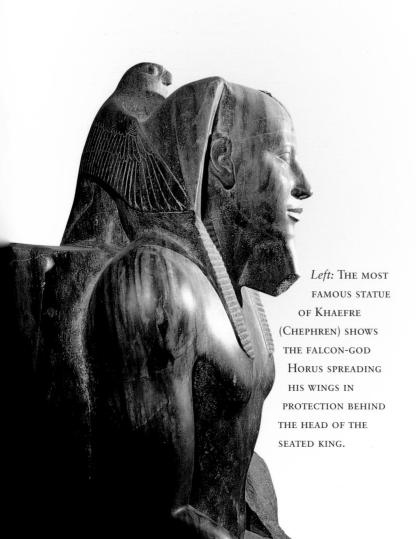

Left: THE MOST FAMOUS STATUE OF KHAEFRE (CHEPHREN) SHOWS THE FALCON-GOD HORUS SPREADING HIS WINGS IN PROTECTION BEHIND THE HEAD OF THE SEATED KING.

An Egyptian royal pyramid complex was made up of a series of connected elements, each with a vital part to play in the functioning of the whole. The pyramid itself is the largest and most obvious of these elements, acting as the royal tomb and possibly a representation of the king's connection with the sun-god Ra. In a 'standard plan' pyramid, on the eastern side was built a mortuary temple, whose function seems to have been to serve as a place where offerings were made to the Ka-spirit of the king, which remained within the pyramid. Leading eastwards away from the mortuary temple, a long causeway served to connect the upper parts of the pyramid complex, built on the high desert edge, to the lower parts of the complex, particularly the so-called valley building, which was placed close to the cultivated land of the Nile valley. The valley building acted as the place where the body of the king entered the pyramid complex during his funeral, and the causeway served as a means whereby the cortège could proceed up to the pyramid itself for burial of the royal remains.

In addition to these reasonably simple functions, the mortuary temple, causeway and valley building also served as places where the complex mythology of kingship could be celebrated, including representations of both the king and the land he ruled. Wall-reliefs with this subject matter are common in such buildings.

A different form of royal representation took the form of statues of the king housed within the pyramid complex. The single most spectacular example of this phenomenon comes from the valley building of the second pyramid at Giza, belonging to King Khaefre (Chephren). This building, of limestone cased with massive slabs of granite, is the best surviving example of a valley building from any known pyramid complex. It was excavated by the French archaeologist Auguste Mariette in 1853 and again in 1869, and under the alabaster floor he discovered a pit containing a larger than lifesize green diorite-gneiss statue of the king. Khaefre is shown seated on a throne, with the god Horus as a falcon spreading his wings protectively behind his head. It is possible that this may be one of twenty-three similar statues of the king that once stood within the valley building to represent the king in cult ceremonies performed within this part of the pyramid complex.

An even more important cache of royal sculpture was found by American Egyptologist George Reisner during his excavation of the third pyramid at Giza, belonging to Menkaure (Mycerinus), between 1905 and 1927. This pyramid, although the smallest of the three at Giza, showed considerable ambition in its use of granite to case the lower parts of the pyramid itself. It is likely that other parts of the complex were intended to receive a similar treatment, but the possibly premature death of Menkaure meant that the valley building only had its foundations built of stone, while the rest of the structure was completed in mud-brick, presumably by Menkaure's successor Shepseskaf combining ancestral piety with economy. Nevertheless, the building was occupied by priests acting for the cult of Menkaure for the remaining period of the Old Kingdom, and although the interior of the building seems to have become a kind of village as a result of these holy squatters, the basic fabric of the building was maintained and repaired.

These priests would, of course, have needed an object for cult ceremonies. Contenders for this role were found by Reisner in the valley building: firstly, four complete statues depicting the king standing between the goddess Hathor 'Lady of the Sycamore', recognizable by her headdress of a sun-disc between cow's horns, and a deity representing one of the nomes or regions of Egypt. These divine personifications could be either male or female, and it is likely that the originally intended full complement of these statues was forty-two, one for each of the nomes. A further particularly fine group statue from the valley building depicts Menkaure with his principal wife, Queen Khamerernebty II. The queen is shown in the same scale as the king, and with her arm around his waist in a gesture of support – the earliest known example of this type of statue.

These statues are masterpieces of sculpture, finely carved in greywacke (slate) with the modelling of the bodies of the male and female figures and the surface polish being particularly well rendered.

Left: KING MENKAURE IS THE CENTRAL, STRIDING FIGURE ON THIS TRIAD STATUE, FLANKED BY THE GODDESS HATHOR AND A GODDESS REPRESENTING THE SEVENTH UPPER EGYPTIAN NOME. *Following Page:* QUEEN KHAMERERNEBTY II IS DEPICTED AT THE SAME SCALE AS HER HUSBAND MENKAURE, AND PUTS HER ARM AROUND HIM IN A GESTURE OF SUPPORT.

The Tod Treasure

After the king himself, the temples were the wealthiest institutions of Ancient Egypt. This wealth could come as gifts from the king, perhaps some of the booty of a successful foreign campaign, or could be generated by the temple from productive assets like agricultural land.

In addition, in the second millennium BC an elaborate system of gift exchange and international commerce grew up around the eastern edges of the Mediterranean, stretching from the palaces of Minoan Crete in the west to the coastal cities of Syro-Palestine and the mighty pharaonic civilization of Egypt in the east.

For Ancient Egypt as for today, the most obvious and tangible way of holding wealth was in the form of precious metals, particularly gold and silver. Many temples of the New Kingdom show on their walls the contents of the temple treasuries, including extravagantly expensive vessels and ritual equipment. Not surprisingly, few of the contents of these treasuries have survived – the relative portability and reusability of gold and silver are part of their value. Similarly, numerous pictorial representations in Egypt attest to the above-mentioned gift exchanges, but all too often the goods exchanged have been long-since lost.

There are, however, a small number of exceptions, where temple treasure has been hidden, forgotten and only rediscovered by chance much later, or as part of an archaeological excavation. Perhaps the most remarkable of these is the so-called Tod treasure.

In 1933, a team from France's Louvre Museum began to excavate at the site of Tod, an ancient town once known as Djerty, on the east bank of the Nile 25 km to the south of Thebes. The main god worshipped here was the falcon-headed Monthu, who probably had a temple dedicated to him as early as the Old Kingdom, with later major building phases in the Middle Kingdom, the Eighteenth Dynasty and the Graeco-Roman period. In 1934, during excavations of the temple of Monthu, most of which dated to the Ptolemaic and Roman periods, massive limestone foundation blocks were found, together with the façade of an earlier temple of the Middle Kingdom. Inscriptions on the temple façade dated it to the reign of Senoswret I, the second ruler of the Twelfth Dynasty.

In February 1936, when they removed the foundation blocks, the excavators found four copper-bronze boxes in a side-room of the temple. They had been deliberately hidden for security in clean virgin sand under the temple floor. Two of them had lids inscribed with the cartouche of Amenemhet II (1929-1892 BC), the son of Senoswret I, and when opened, the boxes were found to be treasure chests full of gold, silver and lapis lazuli.

The two larger boxes contained jewellery and fragments of jewellery, precious materials such as carnelian and quartz, pieces of unworked lapis lazuli, and numerous beads, amulets and cylinder seals also of lapis lazuli - this material was probably the most valuable of all, being highly regarded by the Egyptians and probably imported from a region of Afghanistan.

The two smaller boxes contained precious metals, including ten ingots of gold totalling over 6.5 kg, and a whole range of silver objects in the form of ingots, chains and silver vessels. There was a silver lion, some pieces of jewellery, and a large number of plate metal vessels, 153 of silver and one of gold. Most striking of all are the silver 'jelly-mould' cups whose form and decoration show that they, too, are exotic foreign imports. In fact, other than the copper-bronze boxes, not a single item of the Tod treasure was of Egyptian manufacture. The date of the deposition of the treasure, its origins and how it came to be in Egypt have been hotly disputed but still remain something of a mystery.

Most discussion of the Tod treasure has focused on the plate metal. Stylistically, the actual forms of the vases and their embossed decoration of spirals and rosettes are thought to recall specific elements of Cretan craftsmanship. In fact, very little plate metal has been found on Crete other than a famous two-handled drinking cup found in a tomb at Gournia, and dating to the nineteenth century BC. Plate metal vases are more common in the East Mediterranean, and are thought by many archaeologists to be typical of the elegant dinner services of precious metals that would have furnished the tables of the Minoan palaces back in Crete. Either they arrived in the Near East as diplomatic gifts from the Minoan rulers, or possibly the rare and highly prized Minoan imports were copied in the east.

Other archaeologists have suggested that the vases were made in Anatolia (modern Turkey). From the latter part of the third millennium BC the Anatolian tradition of working in plate metal to make dinner services of gold and silver is well established at sites such as Troy and Alaca Höyük. This very diversity of parallels suggests that the Tod treasure is in fact an eclectic collection of vases that is impossible to tie down to a particular geographical region, and there is no specific evidence that it was made by Minoan craftsmen. Lead isotope analyses have been used to indicate the source of a number of the ingots and two of the vases,

Right: THE RICH DIVERSITY OF PRECIOUS OBJECTS THAT MADE UP THE TOD TEMPLE TREASURE.

although this procedure can only tell us where the silver was mined and not necessarily where it was subsequently worked. The ingots have a common source compatible with the Taurus mountains of southern Turkey, but the cups appear to come from a separate, as yet unidentified source.

The close association of the Tod treasure with the cartouche of Amenemhet II has resulted in the treasure being used to synchronize the Cretan Middle Bronze Age with the absolute dates of Egypt derived from her king lists. In fact, this deposit is very unsafe as a basis for historical synchronism, and not only because of the problems inherent in attributing the plate metal to Crete. Detailed studies of the temple foundations and a new reconstruction of the history of the site suggest that the paving under which the treasure was found actually dates to the New Kingdom, to the reign of Tuthmosis III (1479-1425 BC). Other New Kingdom caches have been found in similar locations in the temple, including one containing several bronze figurines. If the Tod treasure is contemporary with the copper-bronze boxes inscribed with the name of Amenemhet II, they had been preserved piously for some four centuries. On the other hand, the treasures might be much later in date, and were simply gathered together in the reign of Tuthmosis III and put in copper-bronze boxes from an earlier dedication at the temple.

Traditionally, the Tod treasure has been viewed as tribute paid by a Syrian ruler to the pharaoh, which he had collected together over a long time. The habit of rulers exchanging metal vessels is well recorded in ancient texts, and the weight and size of vases were closely related to the status of the recipient. More prosaically, much of the Tod treasure appears to have a purely commercial value. Many of the vases had been deliberately damaged, crushed and broken for recycling rather than being presented as finished objects, of value in their own right. On a number of the vases, written in ink, were the Egyptian words *nefer nefer* (meaning 'good'), indicating that they had been checked for quality on arrival. The lapis lazuli was also sent to Egypt as a raw commodity rather than as finished items. Rather than an impressive tribute of luxury objects sent to the pharaoh from a wealthy Syrian potentate, the Tod treasure is important evidence of early commercial interactions in the Near East.

In short, this treasure is of great importance to archaeologists, not so much for its monetary value, but as a rare example of the survival of imported goods from Middle Kingdom Egypt, hinting at the international trade networks that must have been in existence at that time. For the 'owners' of the treasure, however, it is clear that the Tod objects were kept and hidden not for the skill of the craftsmanship, nor for their usefulness, but for the value of the metal itself. The Tod treasure offers an important insight into the amount of such precious objects available even to small temples in Ancient Egypt.

The Tomb of Kha

The vast majority of Egyptian objects in the collections of many museums in the west, from the great national collections to small local museums, have their origin in the grave goods that were placed in their tombs by the Egyptians to provide for their afterlife. The natural preservative properties of the Egyptian desert cemeteries and the desire of the Egyptians to equip their tombs with as much as possible of what might be of use in the next life may give the impression that many unrobbed tombs have been found by archaeologists in Egypt.

In fact, although the excavation of cemeteries has provided a wealth of objects, a very small proportion comes from intact and undisturbed tombs of well-to-do individuals; the ancient cemeteries were as easily detected by ancient robbers as by modern archaeologists, and it is only the sheer quantity of archaeological material these cemeteries originally contained that has caused so much to remain.

One special group of private tombs on the west bank at Thebes is that at Deir el-Medina, the village that housed the workers on the royal tomb in the Valley of the Kings. Most of the tombs here are of the Nineteenth and Twentieth Dynasties, the most famous being that of Sennedjem, of the early Nineteenth Dynasty, whose tomb is rightly celebrated for its lively decorated chapel, but also for the contents of its burial chamber, which included the mummified bodies of Sennedjem and his family along with their funerary equipment, including food, furniture and simple surveying instruments, which may represent the working tools of the tomb owner.

A smaller group of tombs at Deir el-Medina date to the Eighteenth Dynasty, including that of the architect Kha and his wife Meryt. His tomb also has the conventional decorated offering chapel at an upper level, but is unusual in having a burial chamber that remained undisturbed until its discovery early this century as part of the work at Deir el-Medina by the Italian Egyptologist Ernesto Schiaparelli, who started to excavate there in 1905. The tomb of Kha – the contents of which now have pride of place in the Egyptian Museum in Turin – was his most significant discovery.

The tomb of Kha, like that of Sennedjem, is particularly interesting as a comparatively rare example in which we can see the full range of goods that a relatively prosperous Ancient Egyptian needed to have in his or her tomb for the afterlife. In the case of Kha, this not only meant the consumer durables of clothes, wigs and toilet equipment, but also, and of more particular note, a vast larder of foodstuffs including the herbs and spices required to give variety to an eternal diet.

Left: A BOXED SET OF ELABORATE GLASS AND STONE COSMETIC JARS, SOME EDGED WITH GOLD FOIL.

Left: A WOODEN
FIGURE OF KHA IS
THE MOST
STRIKING OBJECT
IN THIS GROUP,
STANDING ON A
CHAIR FROM HIS
TOMB.

The Amarna Letters

The archaeological site of el-Amarna represents the ruins of the ancient city of Akhetaten, founded by King Akhenaten of the Eighteenth Dynasty as a new capital of Egypt where he could worship his new pre-eminent god, the Aten, or 'sun's disk'. Built quickly, but inhabited for less than a generation, Amarna was abandoned soon after Akhenaten's death as Egypt returned to the status quo of its traditional gods and cities.

Above: RECTANGULAR CLAY TABLETS, NO BIGGER THAN THE PALM OF A HAND, WERE THE STANDARD FORM OF RECORD-KEEPING AND CORRESPONDENCE IN THE ANCIENT NEAR EAST.

As the capital of New Kingdom Egypt, Amarna was the place where the business of running an empire was conducted. This involved, among other things, the maintenance of relationships with vassals of the Egyptian empire and with other great powers of the Late Bronze Age. We know more about these relationships during the Amarna period than any other period in Egyptian history because of the discovery of a remarkable treasure at the site, whose importance is much greater than the more obviously spectacular discovery of the famous bust of Queen Nefertiti, Akhenaten's wife, from the workshop of the sculptor Tuthmose.

Some time around 1887 some local Egyptians digging at Amarna discovered a group of small clay tablets. When these were taken to dealers in illicit antiquities they were not viewed with enthusiasm; in fact anything up to a hundred and fifty of the tablets dug up in this way were thrown away as worthless.

However, when the importance of the tablets was recognized they were avidly acquired by museums – 382 are now preserved in Berlin, Cairo, London and Paris – and attempts to find more were launched, including British Egyptologist Flinders Petrie's 1891–2 expedition to Amarna, which found 22 fragments.

These tablets were the largest surviving archive of international diplomatic correspondence from the Late Bronze Age. At this time the lingua franca was the Akkadian language written using cuneiform script on clay tablets. The survival of the Amarna letters is partly due to this material – the more traditionally Egyptian papyrus does not survive so well. The 350 tablets that were letters to or, usually, from foreign rulers and vassal cities were all found in the same place, referred to as 'The Place of the Letters of Pharaoh' – effectively the area where foreign correspondence was filed. The letters cover the reigns of Akhenaten and Tutankhamen, and the latter part of the reign of Akhenaten's father, the great pharaoh Amenhotep III, the period from approximately 1355 to 1330 BC.

The Egyptian king refers to kings of equivalent authority as 'brother' – these include the rulers of Babylonia, Assyria, Cyprus and the Hittite empire. A major concern in these letters seems to be the exchange of gifts between rulers, with no embarrassment shown in demanding bigger and better presents from the richest of all, the king of Egypt; in one letter (EA 19) the king of Mitanni (North Syria) demands presents, saying, 'In my brother's country gold is as plentiful as dirt.' The enormous quantities of precious goods involved in this elite exchange make clear the amount of

luxury goods produced during the Late Bronze Age and now lost
to the archaeological record.

But the majority of the correspondence is with various local
rulers in Syro-Palestine who owed allegiance to the Egyptian
throne, and who were expected to quarter Egyptian troops and to
send tribute in the form of useful goods like raw glass and
beautiful girls. The nature of this king/vassal relationship is
reflected in the form of address used by the latter when writing to
Egypt, a good example being the following letter (EA319):

'To the king, my lord, my god, my sun, the sun from the sky.
This is a message from Shur-Ashar, the ruler of Akhtishana, who is
your servant, the dirt at your feet, the groom of your horses. I
prostrate myself at the feet of the king, my lord, my god, my sun,
the sun from the sky, seven times and seven times on the stomach
and on the back. I have listened carefully to the orders of the
commissioner of the king, my lord, very carefully. Who is the dog
that would not obey the orders of the king, his lord, the sun from
the sky, the son of the sun?'

The very model of a polite letter to the king of Egypt.

Above: A REGULAR
CORRESPONDENT TO
THE KING OF EGYPT
WAS RIB-ADDI, MAYOR
OF BYBLOS, SEEKING
MILITARY SUPPORT
AGAINST HIS ENEMIES.

Tutankhamen

The most spectacular example of archaeological treasure ever to be discovered is the tomb of Tutankhamen. The only intact royal burial to have been found in the Valley of the Kings, the sheer quantity and quality of its objects of outstanding craftsmanship using extraordinary amounts of precious materials make this tomb a discovery in a league of its own.

The Valley of the Kings began to be used as a royal necropolis early in the New Kingdom. Both the pyramidal form of royal tomb and the cemeteries close to the northern capital at Memphis had been abandoned, for security reasons and in order to perform the royal burials at the important religious centre of Thebes, where kings identified with the god Amen, patron deity of the Egyptian empire. But if the use of the desert valleys on the west bank of the Nile was intended to make the royal burials more hidden, and therefore more secure, than the pyramids of earlier periods, then the intention was only partly realized.

Tutankhamen himself had been born at the court of King Akhenaten, during a phase of the Eighteenth Dynasty of the New Kingdom known as the Amarna period. Although in many ways the Eighteenth Dynasty represented a political and artistic high-water mark of Egyptian history, the Amarna period itself was not a success; the attempts of Akhenaten to install the god Aten as supreme deity of Egypt and to rule from a new capital at Amarna were reversed under the short-lived king Tutankhamen, who came to the throne as a boy and died while not yet nineteen, in about 1323 BC. The ignominy with which the Amarna period was regarded by later kings also meant that the memory of Tutankhamen was slight, with comparatively few monuments to his name. Moreover, his premature death seems to have resulted in a hasty burial in a tomb that was not originally intended for a royal occupant.

Tutankhamen's tomb is very simple in plan, with a staircase and descending corridor leading to an antechamber from which led a small annexe in the south-west corner, and to the north the burial chamber, which itself had a side-room now called the treasury. The comparative smallness of the tomb may be judged by the combined length of the antechamber and burial chamber being just over 12 m long. The site of the tomb, if it had not already been forgotten, was hidden in the Twentieth Dynasty with the construction close by of the much larger tomb of King Ramesses VI.

Right:
TUTANKHAMEN POURS LIQUID INTO THE CUPPED HAND OF QUEEN ANKHESENAMEN, IN A SCENE FROM THE KING'S GOLD SHRINE.

Left: CARTER
DELICATELY CLEANS THE
INNERMOST GOLD
COFFIN OF
TUTANKHAMEN.

Right: THIS MASSIVE
COLLAR OF GOLD,
GLASS AND SEMI-
PRECIOUS STONES
REPRESENTS THE
VULTURE-GODDESS
NEKHBET.

By the early twentieth century the locations of the great
majority of tombs of the New Kingdom pharaohs were known and
appreciated as great underground vaults whose walls were usually
covered with brightly painted religious scenes. The contents of
these tombs were, for the most part, long gone; documents of the
period show that by the end of the New Kingdom, the organized
pillaging of royal tombs in the Valley of the Kings had become a
serious problem for the administration on the west bank.
Doubtless the speed of the robbery moved up several gears when
that administration itself collapsed.

The presence of Tutankhamen's tomb somewhere in the Valley
of the Kings had been suggested to archaeologists by the discovery
in 1907 of a pit containing a small number of objects, including
materials used in mummification, but including the name of the
king. British Egyptologist Howard Carter became convinced that
the tomb of Tutankhamen was in the Valley of the Kings, awaiting
discovery. He persuaded Lord Carnarvon to sponsor the quest for
the tomb, which, after five years, finally resulted in its discovery
on 4 November 1922.

The doorway to the tomb bore seals naming Tutankhamen as
its owner, but it was clear that the re-sealing of the tomb by
officials of the royal necropolis meant that it had been broken into
at some time. Carter and Carnarvon must have wondered how
much of the tomb's contents had been robbed. They need not have
worried. When Carter cut a viewing hole in the entrance to the
antechamber, he could see that the room was filled with furniture:
elaborate beds and couches, chests and dismantled chariots, and
the two life-size statues of the king that acted as guardians

Above: THIS ELABORATE PECTORAL CONTAINS
WITHIN IT A COMPLEX SERIES OF PROTECTIVE
AMULETS.

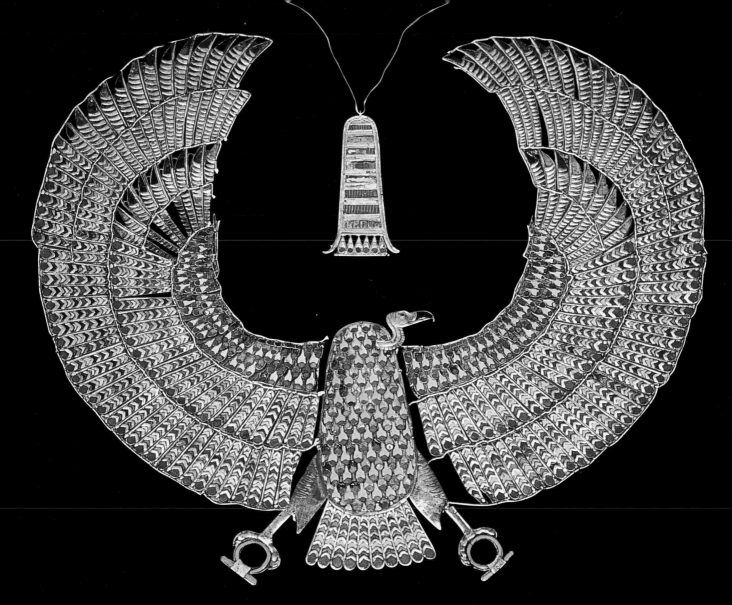

flanking the entrance to the burial chamber itself. Carnarvon did not live to see the opening of the innermost parts of the tomb, dying of an infected mosquito bite in April 1923.

Once opened, the door to the burial chamber seemed to reveal a wall of gold. This was the outermost of four gilded shrines, nesting within one another and surrounding the quartzite sarcophagus. Inside the sarcophagus, again neatly fitting within each other like Russian dolls, were three golden mummiform coffins, the innermost 1.82 m tall, of solid gold and weighing 110.4 kg. The famous gold mask of Tutankhamen is just the largest and most obvious of a wealth of jewellery and amulets on and within the king's mummy wrappings.

The other two rooms in the tomb, the annexe and the treasury, were also filled with objects of the highest artistic quality: thrones, inlaid chests, figures of gods, the king's canopic chest (where the internal organs removed during mummification were placed), weapons, models, musical instruments and a wine cellar.

The quantity of precious objects found within the tomb makes it easy for us to forget that they come from a comparatively tiny tomb and a hastily prepared burial. It is tempting to 'scale up' the treasure from Tutankhamen's tomb and imagine the wealth of riches that may once have filled much larger tombs of longer reigning and better known kings also buried in the Valley, such as Amenhotep III or Ramesses II. However, even if other kings did have a larger set of burial equipment than Tutankhamen, it is unlikely that they would surpass in quality the best of Tutankhamen's grave goods. The period in which Tutankhamen lived, the end of the Eighteenth Dynasty, is widely regarded as a golden age of arts and crafts in Ancient Egypt; the abilities of craftsmen in a wide range of precious and semi-precious materials were complemented by unparalleled access to these materials either within Egypt's empire or beyond as far as equatorial Africa, the Near East as far as Afghanistan and, through Minoan Crete, Europe.

Carter worked on the clearance of the tomb and the conservation of its objects until 1932. Such is the quantity and the enormous interest of the material from this tomb that the task of recording and publishing all of its contents remains to be completed even today.

Tanis

*The largest number of relatively undisturbed royal burials of
Ancient Egyptian kings comes not from the Old Kingdom
pyramid sites near Memphis, nor the New Kingdom
necropolis at the Valley of the Kings, but from what is now
a village in the Eastern Delta called San el-Hagar, a name
derived from the ancient 'Tanis'.*

The collapse of a central royal authority that could lay
serious claim to rule all of the Egyptian empire at the end
of the New Kingdom did not leave any shortage of
families claiming to represent an effective royal line. One of the
most important of these local dynasties was based in the Eastern
Delta at Tanis, a town that seems to have become important
towards the end of the New Kingdom, replacing Ramesses II's
new capital of Pi-Ramesses as the most significant city in the
Eastern Delta.

After the death of Ramesses XI in 1069 BC the effective
partitioning of Egypt into separate political entities became more
obvious with no nominal ruler of the whole country. The most
important power blocs were the priesthood of the god Amen,
which ruled most of southern Egypt from Thebes, and the so-
called Twenty-first Dynasty (possibly blood relatives of the
Twentieth Dynasty), which ruled at Tanis. The fifth king of the
Tanite Twenty-first Dynasty was Osorkon I, whose strange, un-
Egyptian name reveals his Libyan origins. The Libyan ethnic
element (probably the descendants of Libyan prisoners of war who
had been settled in the Delta during the Nineteenth and Twentieth
Dynasties) was even more noticeable in the Twenty-second
Dynasty, which followed the Twenty-first Dynasty in ruling from
Tanis, from around 945 to 712 BC.

During Dynasties Twenty-one and Twenty-two Tanis as a
'royal' capital had aspirations to emulate the great city of Thebes,
and a great temple enclosure for the god Amen was constructed,
partly from the 'borrowing' of statues, obelisks and masonry from
Pi-Ramesses. But one thing that was essential to a royal capital
was, of course, a royal necropolis. The form of tomb used by the
Tanite kings was very different from the pyramid form of the Old
Kingdom, and indeed the underground tombs of the New
Kingdom, hidden in the desert. As a large sand-island in the
middle of the annually flooding Delta, Tanis provided few
opportunities for the siting of the royal tomb, and the robbing of
the royal Theban tombs during the New Kingdom must have
provided a further incentive for security. The burials of the Tanite
kings were placed in the most secure and pious place possible,
within the enclosure of the Amen temple. These tombs were small,
modest in appearance and unobtrusive enough to be lost and
forgotten until the twentieth century.

In 1929, the French archaeologist Pierre Montet began what
was to be a long series of excavations at Tanis. Up to 1939 he
concentrated on the temple area at the site, and in that year
extended his excavations southwards towards the enclosure wall of
the sacred area. In doing so he began to clear a group of mudbrick
buildings, which were found to have been built over a stone
pavement that had been broken and revealed a deep hole leading
to a series of underground chambers lined with limestone. The
excavation of these chambers showed that they had been
reorganized more than once in ancient times, because of their use
as a tomb for multiple royal burials. Among the Tanite royalty to
have been buried here was Osorkon II.

Immediately to the north of this group-tomb Montet
discovered another stone pavement, this time undisturbed and,
presumably, still concealing and sealing the royal burial below.
This tomb was opened early in 1940. The principal burials here
seem to have been King Psusennes and his wife Mutnodjmet,
although the queen's sarcophagus and burial chamber were
usurped by a later king, Amenemope. The tomb of Psusennes is
perhaps the most magnificent at Tanis; small in size, it was just
large enough to contain the pink granite sarcophagus of the king
and, at its feet, the king's canopic jars (containers for the internal
organs removed during mummification) and other vessels of gold
and silver. The sarcophagus contained a mummiform coffin of
black granite and, within that, the body of Psusennes encased in a
silver coffin and wearing a gold mask similar to that found on the
body of Tutankhamen (see p. 30).

In the anteroom leading to the burial chambers of Psusennes
and Amenemope, Montet found the silver falcon-headed coffin of
King Shoshenq II, while a side-room contained the richly equipped
burial of General Wendjebaendjed. Other single vaults close to the
multiple tombs contained the robbed burial of King Shoshenq III
and the unused tomb prepared for Amenemope.

The Tanite kings seem to have had a taste for antiquities, as
the funerary equipment of Shoshenq II included a bracelet whose
main feature was an Akkadian seal cut over a thousand years
before, while General Wendjebaendjed owned a ring with a lapis
lazuli seal inscribed for the long-dead Ramesses IX. Among the
most remarkable objects found in Psusennes' burial was a ritual
brazier made during the reign of Ramesses II.

In short, the Tanis royal burials have yielded up a wealth of
exquisite grave goods that, in their quality and quantity, are
surpassed only by the contents of the tomb of Tutankhamen.

Left: THE
FUNERARY MASK
OF KING
PSUSENNES, GOLD
INLAID WITH
LAPIS LAZULI AND
BLACK AND WHITE
GLASS.

The Rosetta Stone

Below: CHAMPOLLION
RECEIVED MANY
HONOURS FOR HIS
CONTRIBUTION TO THE
DECIPHERMENT OF
EGYPTIAN
HIEROGLYPHS,
INCLUDING THIS
STATUE AT THE
COLLÈGE DE
FRANCE.

Treasure comes in many forms. To Egyptologists the single most precious discovery was made completely by accident, was not immediately spectacular in form, and its importance was not at first recognized. Yet the Rosetta Stone, discovered during the brief Napoleonic occupation of Egypt, provided the main key to the decipherment of the hieroglyphic script and the understanding of the written records of Ancient Egypt.

In 1799, a working party led by a certain Lieutenant Bouchard was constructing a fort at the important port of Rashid (also called Rosetta) on Egypt's Mediterranean coast. They stumbled upon a slab of basalt, just over a metre high and inscribed with a text that was in three versions: Egyptian hieroglyphic, Egyptian cursive demotic and Greek. This trilingual text consists of a decree issued by an assembly of priests at Memphis, recording the benefits bestowed upon Egypt by the king and marking the anniversary of his coronation, and dated to 27 March 196 BC. It is hardly momentous in terms of its contents, but the recognition by European scholars that the known Greek version must be identical to the unknown Egyptian versions provided the key to decipherment.

The stone soon found its way into the possession of the British – as part of the 'spoils of war' after their ejection of the Napoleonic forces – and more particularly to the British Museum. However, most of the important work of decipherment was carried out by the French Egyptologist Jean-François Champollion, who was able to assign phonetic values to the hieroglyphic signs, starting with the royal name 'Ptolemy', and then actually translating words using his knowledge of Coptic, the ancestor of the Ancient Egyptian language.

Although other texts proved useful for translating purposes, and many other inscriptions have provided more fascinating insights into Ancient Egyptian history and culture, it is trite but true to say that the Rosetta Stone is the keystone of Egyptology.

Right: THE ROSETTA STONE WITH ITS TRILINGUAL
INSCRIPTION.

Nigerian Sculpture

Right: TERRACOTTA HEAD FROM IFE, NIGERIA,
ELEVENTH – FIFTEENTH CENTURY AD.
Below: TERRACOTTA SCULPTURED HEAD FROM
NOK, NIGERIA.

Nigeria's extraordinarily rich heritage of artistic treasures, especially finely crafted pottery, wood and metal sculptures, some of which date from the first millennium BC, was unknown outside Africa until a hundred years ago, when artworks first from Benin and later Ife, Igbo-Ukwu and Nok, the oldest known pottery sculpture tradition in sub-Saharan Africa, fell under the international art spotlight. Sadly, the art pieces usually provide only a tantalizing, and frequently the sole, glimpse of bygone cultures, as most were collected without documentation that could inform us about the historical and social circumstances of which they were part.

TERRACOTTAS FROM TIN MINES

In 1928, Colonel Dent Young, co-owner of a tin mine near the village of Nok on the slopes of the Jos plateau in central Nigeria, recovered a 100-mm-high terracotta sculpture of a human head (originally thought to represent a monkey) from tin-bearing gravels, and presented it to the museum of the Department of Mines in Jos. Some fifteen years later, a second, larger terracotta head 220 mm high, which had been found in similar gravels at Jemaa, 65 km east of Nok, and used as a scarecrow in a yam plot, was taken to Jos. There the finds attracted the interest of a young, Cambridge-trained archaeologist, Bernard Fagg, who visited the tin workings and, after his subsequent appointment to the newly formed Nigeria Antiquities Service, arranged the rescue and description of the ever-increasing amount of 'Nok Culture' material being uncovered by miners and others.

Around two hundred Nok terracotta sculptures are now known. The artisans used clay tempered with materials like quartz, mica and granite, probably pre-heated it, and then fired it in an open fire. Radiocarbon dates associated with the sculptures indicate an age in the latter half of the first millennium BC and first few centuries AD. A few of the sculptures are small, solid clay figurines of humans or animals that were, or are still, attached to pots. Others are small enough to have been worn as pendants, but most are hollow fragments typically of heads or free-standing human figurines that ranged in size from 100 mm to an estimated almost life-size height of 1.2 m, with the head enlarged out of proportion to the body.

A particular characteristic is the treatment of the eyes, which are usually triangular or in the shape of a segment of a circle, with a circular hole that extends into the hollow interior for the pupil. The faces are clearly Negroid. Elaborate hairstyles, including topknots and various styles of buns, were favoured; beards and moustaches are also represented. Attention seems to have been given to reproducing physical idiosyncrasies, sicknesses and deformities. Indeed, in the absence of skeletal remains, much of what is known about the makers of the Nok figurines is derived from the sculptures themselves. Some are adorned with necklaces, pendants, bracelets, bangles and anklets, and appear to be wearing waistbands and pubic aprons. Others sit on stools. In one example, a man carries a hafted axe.

Excavations by Fagg's archaeologist daughter Angela at Samun Dukiya in the Nok Valley in 1969 uncovered fragments of sculptures together with quantities of broken pots, grinding and pounding stones, stone beads, lip plugs and fragments of iron, including hooks, bracelets, knives, as well as arrow- and spearheads. Excavations by Fagg at Taruga, some 100 km south-west of Nok, produced terracottas at an iron smelting site. This indicated that iron was not only used, but also smelted by the manufacturers of the artworks. It was once thought that Nok represented the earliest known evidence for ironworking in sub-Saharan Africa, but it is now known that such evidence is only part of a series of such West African sites dating to the last millennium BC.

Some of the terracottas seem to be linked to a residence, others to a smelting furnace, and still others to a possible shrine. However, as most were recovered from disturbed contexts or in circumstances without detailed archaeological investigations, the function of these strange and intriguing sculptures remains conjectural.

A NERVE-WRACKING EXPERIENCE AT IGBO-UKWU

West Africa saw the emergence of many complex societies, states and kingdoms during the second millennium AD. However, little was known about their forerunners of the late first millennium AD, until the 1938 discovery of a cache of remarkable bronze and copper artefacts and Thurstan Shaw's subsequent 1959–60 excavation of the burial chamber of a high-ranking person at Igbo-Ukwu on the edge of the forest in south-east Nigeria. These finds dated to between the eighth and eleventh centuries AD, and showed that, by the end of the first millennium, there was an indigenous West African process of increasing social stratification that concentrated wealth in the hands of a few individuals who had religious authority and, in all likelihood, also political power.

The individual buried at Igbo-Ukwu was seated on a stool in the corner of a roofed burial chamber lined with wooden planks and matting, dressed in ceremonial attire that included large numbers of beads, a beaded headdress, copper crown, copper chest-plate and wristlets of blue beads set in copper wire, and holding a fan holder and fly-whisk. The remains of at least five attendants were found above the roof, and other finds include over a hundred thousand glass and carnelian beads, some of which originated in India and indicate far-flung trading links, a stylized leopard skull with a copper supporting rod, ivory tusks and a mass of other ivory, bone, copper, bronze and iron pieces. Igbo-Ukwu provides the earliest sub-Saharan African evidence for the use of copper alloys in art. The bronze objects, which were cast by the lost wax method (by replacing wax inside a clay model with molten bronze), are of a leaded bronze apparently made from locally available materials, and attest to the existence of highly accomplished local craft specialists, who created an idiosyncratic intricate and elaborate style.

Shaw quickly realized that he was 'into something unique and important', and he wrote of 'The anxiety to see that no mistakes were being made in the recording and labelling; only one camera, and that sticking; fourteen miles to go at the end of every day's digging to get water…attempt in the night after the first bronze was discovered to steal it from under my bed; dysentery most of the time…' Thanks to Shaw's efforts to ensure that 'we didn't lose any of the finds, and I do not think any important evidence went unobserved or unrecorded', the Igbo-Ukwu treasures document a late first-millennium AD West African social revolution that was to result in the rise of states in the subsequent millennium.

IFE

By the eleventh to fifteenth centuries AD, Ife in south-west Nigeria was a substantial urban trading settlement with courtyards paved by setting pieces of pottery on edge, a royal palace, shrines and a glass-making industry.

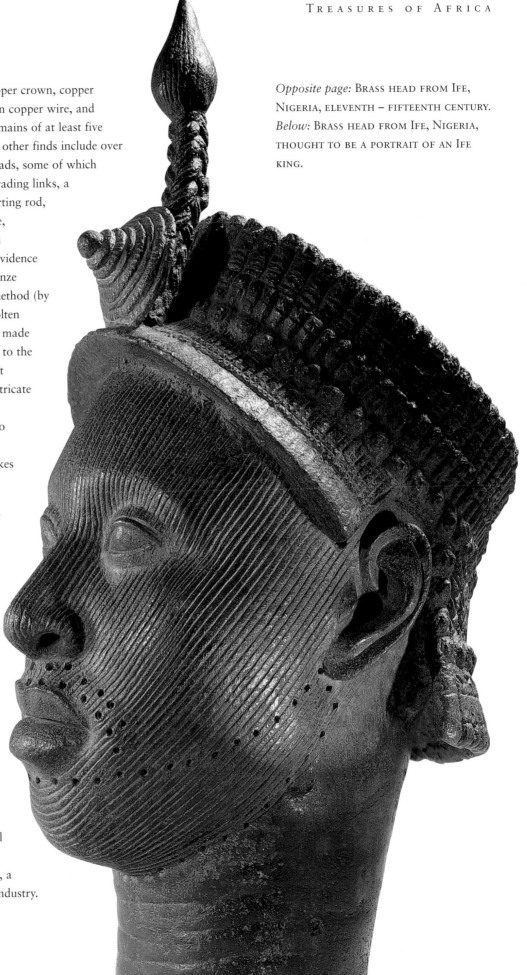

Opposite page: BRASS HEAD FROM IFE, NIGERIA, ELEVENTH – FIFTEENTH CENTURY. *Below:* BRASS HEAD FROM IFE, NIGERIA, THOUGHT TO BE A PORTRAIT OF AN IFE KING.

Although only traces of its sun-dried mud buildings have survived, it has yielded treasures in the form of a remarkable series of naturalistic figures, mostly in terracotta and some in 'bronze' (actually brass) of trans-Saharan origin. The successful firing of life-size terracotta figures in an open fire reveals the technical skill of the Ife sculptors, who may have been women, like Yoruba potters of the region today.

The sculptures are thought to have been created for religious reasons as they seem to have been kept in shrines or on altars in homes. Art historians consider that the Ife style may have originated indirectly from the earlier Nok Culture.

BENIN BRASS

The first sub-Saharan African art to make an impact in Europe comprised a large quantity of brass castings and ivory carvings from the southern Nigerian city of Benin, which was seized when its king was exiled and much of it destroyed by the British Punitive Expedition of 1897. The consequent flooding of museum and art markets all over the world meant that, with rare exceptions, more interest was shown in Nigerian art per se than in documenting the societies and processes of which the art was part. The early twentieth-century assumption that Nigerian urbanism and craft specialization could be explained purely as a result of the importation of ideas from across the Sahara has only recently yielded to evidence of indigenous West African development.

Archaeological excavations have shown that there were earthworks at Benin from the end of the first millennium AD, and that there was a town there from at least the thirteenth century. This town later became notorious for human sacrifices, as well as for a brass-casting tradition of standing figures and human heads, mostly made from imported metal, and also for plaques apparently depicting ritual events, between the fifteenth and nineteenth centuries. Early European visitors were greatly impressed by the organization and architecture of Benin City, especially the palace towers, which were decorated with huge brass pythons that snaked down columns to large heads with open jaws.

The brassworking was produced for the obas (rulers), who originally had strong links with Ife, and it is thought that their style was derived from the Ife tradition. Brass casting was revived in Benin in the early twentieth century and still flourishes today.

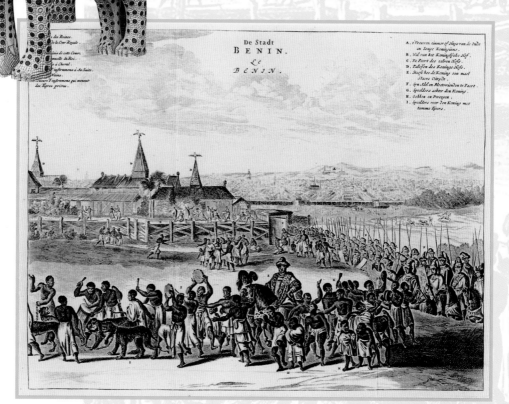

Above: A PAIR OF IVORY AND COPPER LEOPARDS PLACED ON EITHER SIDE OF THE BENIN OBA'S THRONE ON STATE OCCASIONS. *Right:* BENIN CITY IN 1686. *Opposite page:* EARLY SEVENTEENTH-CENTURY BRASS PLAQUE DEPICTING AN OBA (RULER) OF BENIN WITH HIS PAGES AND GUARDS. SUCH PLAQUES DECORATED THE OBA'S PALACE.

The Lydenburg Heads

Seven hollow ceramic heads from the seventh century AD, found at Lydenburg in the Mpumalanga Province of eastern South Africa by Dr K. L. von Bezing while a teenager, are among the oldest surviving examples of Iron Age art in southern Africa. They are thought to have been used in rituals such as initiation ceremonies, after which they appear to have been deliberately smashed and the sherds discarded in deep pits. The presence of similar fragments at other southern African Early Iron Age sites suggests that such heads were widely used at the time.

Pieces of the heads were first noticed by Dr von Bezing in about 1956 or 1957, when he walked across the site as a ten-year-old schoolboy. Some years later, between 1962 and 1964, having developed an interest in archaeology, he collected pieces from the site. Shortly thereafter, he enrolled at the University of Cape Town to study medicine and mentioned his discovery to a student at a meeting of the students' Archaeological Field Club. The student reported the matter to her lecturer, R. R. Inskeep, and a series of systematic investigations of the site, the heads and other ceramics from the site has since been undertaken by researchers.

The Lydenburg site provided one of the first early radiocarbon dates for Iron Age settlement in southern Africa, and the ceramics have proved important in interpretations of the expansion of Iron Age agriculturalists into the subcontinent. Unfortunately, erosion has caused extensive damage to the site and it has not been possible to identify structures apart from the bases of pits containing mainly pottery and animal bones. However, fragments of wall plaster indicate that structures were originally present, iron slag attests to the occurrence of metalworking, and domestic animal bones show that sheep and goats were important, although hunting of wild animals also took place.

The ceramic fragments found by von Bezing have been pieced together and found to comprise two large heads and five smaller ones, all of which have a remarkable degree of similarity. Excluding animals or 'topknots' on top, from base to crown they range in height from 200 mm to 380 mm, with a rim diameter at the neck opening ranging from 108 mm to 225 mm.

Above: TWO OF THE SEVEN ENIGMATIC CERAMIC HEADS FROM LYDENBURG IN SOUTH AFRICA.

They resemble elongated pots turned upside down so that the 'rim' of the pot forms the neck of the head. Above the neck is an incised or moulded groove followed by two or three diagonally incised rings encircling the neck with a herringbone or cross-hatching pattern. Each of the smaller heads has a small hole on each side of the neck on the lowest ring of hatching. Various sections of the heads are covered with incised cross-hatching, ridges or applied clay, as well as small studs of applied clay, set in clusters.

The lips are formed by the application of two crescent-shaped clay plates, and in some of the smaller heads teeth are represented by strips of clay placed between the lips, always showing a gap between the two front teeth. An exception is a head with exaggerated lips forming a snout-like projection. The eyes are represented by the application of elliptical-shaped pieces of clay slit across with a piece added to form eyebrows, while ears were moulded to the side of the head.

The two larger heads are topped by an animal attached to the head by moulding on the legs and tail. The animals have thick legs and a flat, almost featureless face without eyes, but otherwise lack distinguishing features. The five smaller heads have a shaped column of clay as a topknot.

The heads are generally reddish in colour, with patches of grey or black formed by the firing process. All have traces of a cream-coloured paint and of specularite. This is a crystalline form of haematite that is steel-grey or iron-black in colour with a silvery sparkle; it is soft and greasy to the touch, and found in restricted localities in southern Africa. Historical records indicate that it was highly prized as a cosmetic among indigenous peoples of the region. When new, with fresh paint and glittering specularite, the heads must have been spectacular objects.

The holes in the sides of the smaller heads suggest that they might have been attached to something, such as a frame worn over a person's head, a post or a part of a building, though it does not seem likely that they were dancing headdresses, as they would not have survived vigorous movement. The two larger heads lack holes for possible attachment, but are large enough to have been worn over the head like a helmet or mask. The animals on top of the two larger heads and also their more elaborate decoration suggest a purpose somewhat different from the other five, which are nevertheless stylistically similar.

Of course, the heads are silent about their function, but it seems likely that they could have been part of the equipment used in a ritual or ceremonial event. Accounts of puberty initiation rites from Tanzania record figurines being thrown into a pool of water after the ceremony, and it has been suggested that the Lydenburg heads may represent the remains of objects used for a similar purpose.

Gold from Mapungubwe

Above: A RHINOCEROS FIGURINE, BOWL AND
SCEPTRE COVERED IN GOLD FOIL FROM AN
ELITE THIRTEENTH-CENTURY AD GRAVEYARD ON
TOP OF MAPUNGUBWE HILL.

Mapungubwe ('the Hill of the Jackals') is a flat-topped sandstone outcrop that rises suddenly from the surrounding valley in the Northern Province of South Africa, near the confluence of the Limpopo and Shashi Rivers, where South Africa, Botswana and Zimbabwe meet. During its occupation between about AD 1220 and 1270, it was probably the largest urban settlement in southern Africa at that time, and saw the development of a highly stratified society with ruling chiefs enjoying great wealth and status. It also saw the emergence of features that were to characterize the subsequent development of the Great Zimbabwe tradition (see p.48). A remarkable collection of gold objects, including rhinoceros models, was found in an elite graveyard on the hilltop.

Mapungubwe was the capital of a southern African Shona state that controlled trade, at first in ivory and later in gold with city states on the East African coast, in exchange for items like ceramics, glass beads and cotton and silk cloth. In addition to these objects, large numbers of bone and ivory artefacts as well as clay animal figurines have been found there.

The earliest evidence of the trade is from the nearby site of Schroda, about 6 km north-west of Mapungubwe, which was occupied by between three hundred and five hundred people for a short period in the ninth century. Schroda was abandoned in about 1000, when the region and the trade seem to have been taken over by the ancestors of present-day Shona-speaking people, whose largest and most important settlement at that time became K2, about a kilometre south-west of Mapungubwe, occupied by some two thousand people. K2, so named by an early excavator, Captain Guy Gardner, because its huge, 6-m-high midden of ashy material reminded him of the koms or tells of North Africa, is also sometimes called Bambandyanalo, although this name actually refers only to a hill that forms the eastern boundary of the site. In about 1220, K2 was abruptly abandoned at the same time as the capital moved to Mapungubwe.

In the tenth century, most Iron Age settlements in southern Africa were laid out according to what is termed the Central Cattle Pattern. This comprised a central area containing male-oriented features such as the cattle byre, grain storage pits, elite burials and a men's court. Surrounding this was an outer arc of houses and grain bins associated with women, arranged in a pattern according to seniority, with the 'great house' located upslope behind the byre and men's court. This settlement pattern is evident at both Schroda and K2, but when the capital moved to Mapungubwe, the leader and his family moved not only upslope, but uphill, settling on the hilltop and leaving the common folk to build and rebuild their houses in the valley below over the ensuing decades.

Mapungubwe was the first place in southern African history where leaders became physically separated from their followers. This affirmed a class distinction that led to the creation of a highly stratified society of some three thousand to five thousand people, based on the unequal distribution of wealth, and hence political power, generated by trade with the East African coast, in which the origins of the Great Zimbabwe tradition can be traced. It has been suggested that gold objects found in graves on the summit of Mapungubwe Hill are a tangible expression of this new order.

DISCOVERY

Mysterious tales of a buried fortune led E. S. J. van Graan to ascend Mapungubwe Hill where, on 29 December 1932, he and his party found a treasure trove of gold objects associated with a burial. The find was reported to the University of Pretoria, whereupon the site came under the protection of the South African government and the university, and has been the subject of archaeological investigation ever since.

GOLD OBJECTS

Gold objects were found in three out of the twenty-three graves in an elite graveyard on the summit of Mapungubwe Hill. One grave was probably that of a woman, who had been buried in a sitting position facing west, with over twelve thousand gold beads and at least a hundred gold bangles around her ankles. Another grave was of a middle-aged man, also buried in a sitting position facing west, who wore a necklace of gold beads and cowrie shells, and who was buried with objects covered in gold foil, one of which resembles a crocodile head. The third gold-associated burial, also

Above: THE REMAINS OF A DOUBLE-WALLED HUT FROM THE COMMONERS' AREA ON THE SOUTHERN TERRACE AT MAPUNGUBWE.

male, contained a wooden headrest, a bowl, a sceptre shaped like a knobkierrie (fighting club) and a rhinoceros figurine 142 mm long, all covered with gold foil. At least two more such rhinos (or possibly other animals) are also associated with the graveyard.

The gold objects were not in good condition when found, but it was possible to establish that they comprised thin sheets of beaten gold hammered on to wooden, or possibly mastic, cores with tiny gold tacks. The gold is exceptionally pure (91.2–93.8 per cent assay for the sheets and 100 per cent for the beads). Chemical analysis indicates that it originated from a variety of sources in the region.

THE RHINOCEROS FIGURINE

This remarkable piece of craftsmanship depicts a powerfully built stocky animal on thick short legs. Its tail consists of a solid thin cylinder with a slightly thickened tip, the ears are made of thicker curved plates attached to the head by a small tack positioned deep inside the plates, while another small tack is used for the surviving eye, and the horn is a cone of gold plate. Interestingly, there does not seem to be a place for the second horn found on African black or white rhino.

It has been suggested that the black rhino could have been a symbol of leadership, because its solitary life and dangerous nature reflect attributes traditionally ascribed to Shona leaders. Whatever its significance, the rhino and the other gold objects indicate that the individuals buried with them on the summit of Mapungubwe Hill were of high status, perhaps kings.

Birds from Great Zimbabwe

Great Zimbabwe is a dramatic, ruined Late Iron Age settlement in the southern African country of Zimbabwe, which took its name from this famous archaeological site on achieving independence from Great Britain in 1980. At its height in the fourteenth century AD, it was the capital of a vast Shona empire that stretched from the Zambezi River to northern South Africa and from eastern Botswana to western Mozambique, and was home to some eighteen thousand people. Perhaps the most remarkable objects found there are eight unique posts carved with birds, one of which is depicted on the flag of modern Zimbabwe.

The site of Great Zimbabwe was first occupied between about AD 500 and 900 by Early Iron Age farmers who did not build in stone. Shona-speaking people arrived thereafter and began building in stone from between about 1270 and 1290, until the political importance of the town declined by about 1420–50. Part of the site was reoccupied in the late fifteenth and early sixteenth centuries. The site provided water, sweet grass for cattle, fertile soil for crops and, importantly, gold. In time, the rulers accumulated great wealth and prestige by controlling a trade network, which saw the export of gold, ivory and iron to trading towns on the East African coast in exchange for the importation of glazed ceramics, glass beads and silk and cotton cloth.

Unlike most other Iron Age societies in southern Africa, social organization at Great Zimbabwe was based on a clear distinction between a ruling class and commoners. This social hierarchy was reflected in the spatial layout of the town.

Atop the large, bare, granite hill that dominates the site, Zimbabwe Hill, are stone-walled enclosures collectively termed the Hill Ruin or Complex (or Acropolis), where the king, members of his family and important officials lived, and where places of religious and ritual importance were located.

In the valley below, a central area included a complex for the royal wives, grain bins and the Great Enclosure (also known as the Elliptical Building). This is the largest and most impressive structure at Great Zimbabwe: the outer wall is thought to contain 900,000 stone blocks. A portion standing 11 m high is decorated by a double chevron design that extends over 85 m. It is thought to have been used as a premarital initiation school for young men and women. Commoners lived in the surrounding town.

The site was abandoned, probably for social and environmental reasons, and by the time Portuguese explorers arrived in south-east Africa in the sixteenth century, the Shona capital had moved to other centres.

Great Zimbabwe was made known to the western world in 1872 by a German geologist, Carl Mauch, whose romantic account of the overgrown ruins and interpretation that they were built by the Queen of Sheba spawned exotic interpretations that continue to dog the site today, despite decades of scientific investigations that have unequivocally established the medieval date and local African origin of the site. Zimbabweans today regard the site as a symbol of past achievements and freedom from colonial rule. Probably no other archaeological site in the world has excited such passion, patriotism and political fervour.

At many entrances in the Great Zimbabwe ruins are slots designed to hold posts of stone or wood, which were carved with animals, birds or designs. Among the posts that have survived are

Above: STONE WALLING FROM GREAT ZIMBABWE.

seven grey-green soapstone examples carved with birds found in the palace area of the Hill Ruin, and an eighth, which is depicted on the flag of modern Zimbabwe, found in the valley area. Soapstone outcrops are common in the region and the nearest is about 25 km from Great Zimbabwe.

Each bird is about 300 mm high and rests on top of a pillar a metre or more high. Of the seven birds from the Hill Ruin, three have wings wrapped around a vertical body, and a short tail, while four have wings folded back over a sloping body with bent

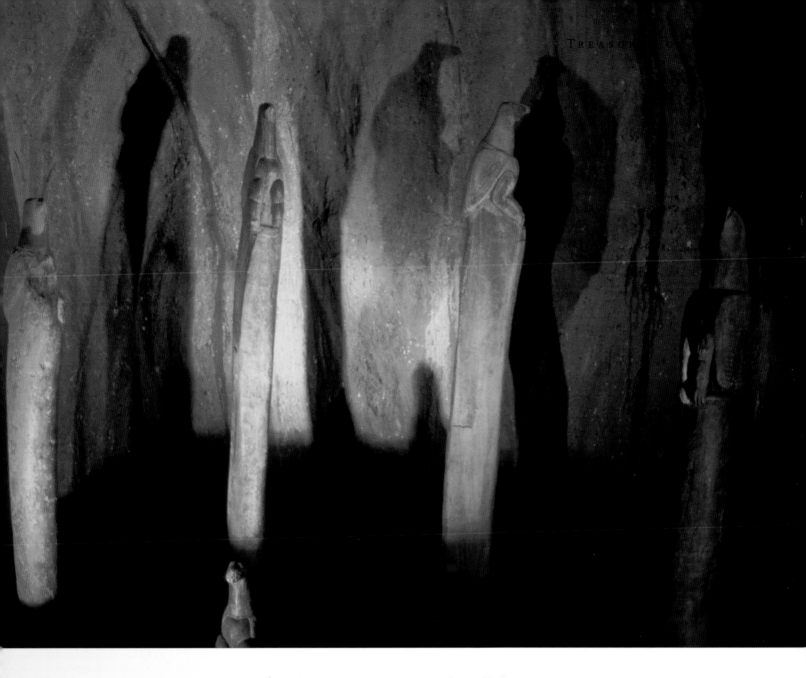

Above: SOAPSTONE BIRDS FOUND AT GREAT ZIMBABWE.

legs. It is not possible to identify the birds beyond saying that they look raptor-like; indeed, they combine human and bird features, as most have toes instead of talons, human limbs and one has lips.

The precise original location of the birds from the Hill Ruin is not known, but it is possible that they stood in a religious centre. The eighth bird, from the valley area, was found lying upside down against a symbolic grain bin in a small enclosure, and could have been placed originally either on the grain bin, or on a low platform in front of it, or on a shelf on the back wall of the enclosure. It is thought that the enclosure was a sanctuary, close to the area where royal wives gave birth.

Nothing like these birds has ever been found anywhere else, although posts like those on which the birds perch are commonly found at Zimbabwe Tradition sites.

In Shona symbolism, birds are considered to carry messages from ancestors and 'the great one of the sky'. Ancestor spirits are thought to be free to fly like birds. Those of an ordinary person are considered to look after his individual needs, but those of former kings are thought to be concerned with problems affecting the whole society, such as plagues, disease, famine and drought, and to be able to intercede with God on behalf of the nation. The carved birds can, therefore, be interpreted as symbols of the role of royal ancestors.

After being housed in the South African Museum in Cape Town for decades, the birds have recently been repatriated to Zimbabwe and can now be seen in the museum at the Great Zimbabwe site.

The Royal Graves of Thulamela

Fifteenth and sixteenth-century AD *royal graves from the walled town of Thulamela (a Venda word meaning 'the place of giving birth') in South Africa's Kruger National Park have recently yielded the first golden grave goods to be recovered from a southern African archaeological site using modern archaeological recording techniques. Thulamela is also breaking new ground in the way southern African archaeologists work: for the first time, scientists, officials of the National Parks Board and represen-tatives of neighbouring communities have formed a committee directing the rebuilding of collapsed walling and the development of the site as an environmental educational centre and museum.*

Above: AN EARLY SIXTEENTH-CENTURY AD FEMALE SKELETON FROM THULAMELA. *Left:* ANATOMIST COEN NIENABER EXAMINES THE SKELETON.

Thulamela was built at the edge of a plateau overlooking the Levuvhu River near Pafuri in the northern Kruger National Park, close to the meeting point of the borders of South Africa, Zimbabwe and Mozambique. Archaeologists first visited the site in 1984, initial excavations were undertaken in 1990, and there has been ongoing investigation of the site since 1993.

Material recovered from the lowest levels of the excavation indicate that Thulamela was already occupied by the middle of the thirteenth century. During the subsequent phase the first stone structures were erected by the middle of the fifteenth century, which coincided with the flowering of Great Zimbabwe (see p.48) just over 200 km to the north. Ceramics indicate that there was contact with Great Zimbabwe at this time, while gold beads and gold droplets suggest that Thulamela was becoming more affluent during this period.

The final phase of occupation is linked with ceramics similar to those of the Khami period of the seventeenth century in Zimbabwe. It is thought that royal people of great wealth lived at Thulamela during this time. The stone-walled royal palace was situated on Thulamela Hill, aloof from the thatched dwellings of some one and a half thousand commoners. The finds from this period include large quantities of ceramics, beads, ivory, gold, iron tools, spindle whorls and needles. There is also evidence for skilled goldworking.

It is hoped that continuing study of Thulamela will establish why the site was abandoned in the late seventeenth century. People from neighbouring communities, who are assisting with the reconstruction of the site and its development as an educational centre and museum, may be descendants of Thulamela's people.

GLINTS OF GOLD

While uncovering the clay floor of a senior wife's house in an area known as Enclosure 13 during July 1996, archaeologist Sidney Miller came upon a depression in the floor, below which he spied human bones and glints of gold. Continuing excavations led to the discovery the following month of a female skeleton with gold grave goods. The almost perfectly preserved skeleton was lying in a north–south flexed position with her head at the north turned to face east. Her hands had been placed under her left cheek. Among

Above: GOLD BRACELETS, IRON AND GOLD BANGLES AND OSTRICH EGGSHELL BEADS FOUND WITH AN EARLY FIFTEENTH-CENTURY GRAVE AT THULAMELA.

the local Venda people, holding hands together under the left cheek when greeting is considered a gesture of respect, known as *losha*. Accordingly, locals who watched the four-day excavation by members of the University of Pretoria's Department of Anatomy named the skeleton 'Queen Losha'. She is thought to have been a senior wife of the king.

She was between forty-five and sixty years old, unusually tall (about 1.73 m) and in good health at the time of her death in the early sixteenth century. She wore two gold bracelets. One was of solid gold made from flattened gold wire twisted around some sort of core, probably grass, to form spirals that were then loosely twisted around each other. The other was apparently a double bracelet made from at least two hundred and ninety-one tiny gold beads, roughly 2 mm in diameter.

THE LEOPARD KING

Clues from 'Queen Losha's' grave suggested to Sidney Miller where he might find a king's grave. He demarcated a rectangle nearby, dug down and found the grave in September 1996. Miller refers to the king as 'Ingwe', meaning 'leopard', because on the day the grave was found, a leopard was waiting for the team as they returned to their vehicle.

The 'leopard king' was buried underneath the floor of his house. He was aged between forty-five and sixty when he died in the early fifteenth century. The skeleton was disarticulated and it seems it was placed in the grave some time after his death, after the flesh had rotted away. The long bones were lying in a north–south direction with the other bones placed at the southern end. The skull was placed on top of these, with grave goods in front of the skull. It is possible that his body was left to decompose in his house before the bones were buried under the floor. It is known that the custom of some Venda people is to wrap the body of an important person in cowhide and leave it in his house until it has fallen apart.

The grave goods included several rolls of iron wire, some of which has rusted away, and which were clamped with small pieces of gold. There were seven complete and many broken spirals of gold wire, sixty large gold beads and a handful of ostrich eggshell beads.

Excavations in the area around the king's burial have produced interesting artefacts, including a pair of iron gongs. These are similar to cow bells and can be used as bells on cattle or as musical instruments. Gongs originated in West Africa and are known to have been a status symbol in southern Africa; the Thulamela gongs suggest possible trade links with West Africa. Other artefacts include sturdy iron harpoons and spears, which may have been used to hunt hippopotamus, a carved ivory amulet, glass beads from India, copper and iron bracelets, and a piece of Ming Dynasty porcelain from China.

After detailed records were made and samples were removed for radiocarbon dating and DNA testing, the Thulamela royal couple were reburied according to local custom.

GOLD BRACELETS FOUND WITH AN EARLY SIXTEENTH-CENTURY FEMALE BURIAL AT THULAMELA.

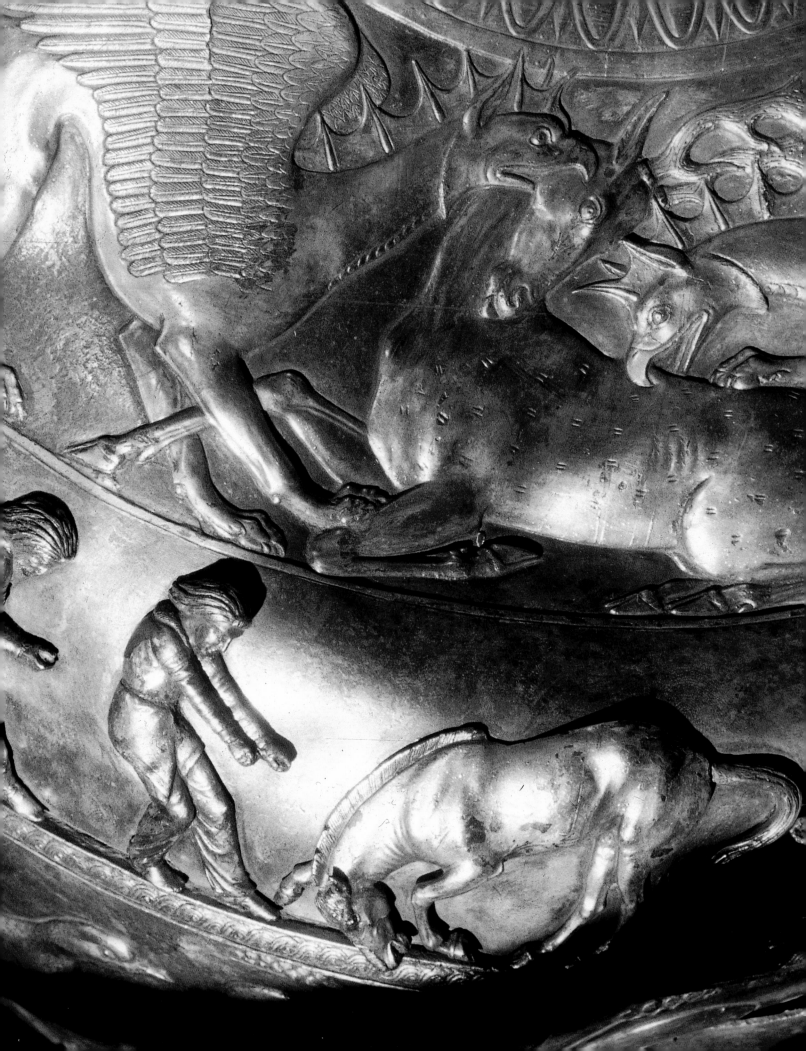

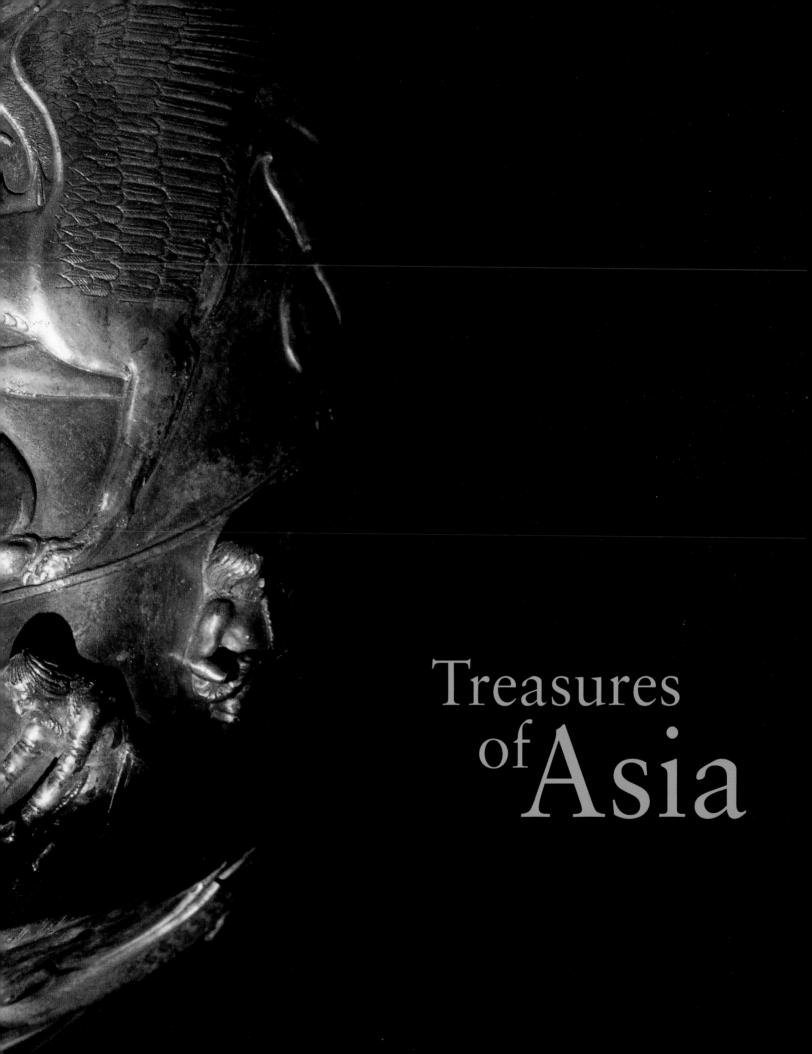

Treasures
of Asia

'Ain Ghazal

The objects used in rituals and cults around the world ordinarily have a special, symbolic value. When they are worn out or obsolete, and need to be replaced, the old cult objects often keep their high value and cannot be thrown away like normal refuse. A common way around this disposal problem is to bury cult objects in special pits, often near the place of their use. This practice has a long history in the Near East, where it can be traced back to neolithic society and the first farming villages.

The recent excavation at 'Ain Ghazal, near Amman in Jordan, has uncovered one of the great early neolithic towns of world prehistory. Occupied for two millennia (*c.* 7200–5000 BC), the town sprawled across 12 ha, and held perhaps two and a half thousand people. The inhabitants of the early town, during the Pre-Pottery Neolithic B, or PPNB, period (pottery appeared only later, after *c.* 5800 BC), lived in stone houses with painted plastered floors, feeding themselves from the fruits of their fields and flocks. A remarkable aspect of the PPNB Culture appears in its burial customs, in which defleshed bodies were often interred, without their skulls, in common graves (a practice often called secondary or fractional burial), while the crania were often plastered to model the features of the dead individuals. These practices seem connected to an ancestor cult. Another facet of this cult may be the plaster figures that also appear at this time.

The excavations at 'Ain Ghazal have uncovered two caches of several dozen figures that date to *c.* 7200–6500 BC. So fragile were the plaster figures that the excavators removed them as a block, and then 'excavated' them carefully in the laboratory. Both caches contain two different kinds of figures made of lime plaster modelled over a core of reeds and twigs. The statues, standing 80–90 cm high, present short legs, broad and flat torsos, elongated

Left: A NEARLY COMPLETE PRE-POTTERY NEOLITHIC B FIGURE FROM 'AIN GHAZAL, THE EYES OUTLINED WITH BLACK. THIS FIGURE IS UNUSUAL IN ITS REPRESENTATION OF SEXUAL CHARACTERISTICS.

Right: DETAIL OF THE HEAD OF AN 'AIN GHAZAL FIGURE, WITH BANDS OF PAINT ON ITS FOREHEAD.

necks and large, flat faces. Features are painted, the eyes outlined with bitumen (sometimes emphasized with a green or blue-green eyeliner); paint, mostly red, often appears as stripes on the forehead, cheeks, torso or legs, perhaps as an indication of clothing, ritual scarring or tattooing. The statues usually lack clear indication of their sex, although several appear to be female. The second kind of figure are busts, only 35–45 cm high, with only the face and head – similar to those of the statues – shown in detail. Analogous figures have been found, in a much more fragmentary state, at other sites of the same period in the region, notably at Jericho.

So far, the information about them is inadequate to understand their original use. The 'Ain Ghazal statues are not buried in a ritual location, but rather within the ruins of abandoned houses. Nevertheless, the figures were deliberately and carefully placed in layers, within large, deep pits that had been dug

for this purpose; this action denotes respectful disposal of important objects. Moreover, the figures appear to have been damaged before burial, indicating some period of use before their ritual interment. The variability of the figures, evident in the details like facial features and painted stripes, suggests efforts to represent individuals; the representation of six-toed feet on one statue reinforces this impression. Although the supposition cannot be proven, the figures are probably connected to an ancestor cult, perhaps used in conjunction with the plastered portrait skulls and the collective secondary burials. These practices can be understood as the ritual of kin groups that served to declare their ancestral claim to a portion of land within the newly developing agricultural world of settled communities.

The Uruk 'Sammelfund'

The German excavations at Warka (also called Uruk), a Sumerian city in southern Iraq, have been one of the most important archaeological projects of the past century in the Near East. Working since the early years of the twentieth century, the Germans have uncovered important remains of various periods from prehistory down to the end of Mesopotamian civilization, some five thousand years later. Perhaps the most significant of the German results pertain to the fourth millennium, a period that archaeologists have named 'Uruk' after this same site. These thousand years saw the rise of Mesopotamian civilization from less complicated antecedents, complete with massive religious architecture, the invention of writing and the institutions of bureaucracy that have characterized state government ever since. The same area remained sacred space, and even a thousand years later the king Ur-Nammu erected a ziggurat (stepped tower) near the buried remains of the earlier temples.

The German effort concentrated on religious precincts. One of these was the area of the temple of the goddess Inanna, called the Eanna, where in the fourth millennium the Sumerians built a complex of large temples and other buildings upon platforms. Much of our evidence for early writing comes from this excavation.

In the winter of 1933–4 the German team explored the ruined architecture buried beneath the south-west corner of the ziggurat. The ziggurat in fact covered a succession of buildings – the scrappy remains of the youngest level dated to the early third millennium and covered a somewhat better preserved building whose architectural details place it at the end of the fourth millennium. Two rooms of this building contained a dense collection of art objects, ornaments and other items, the so-called Sammelfund. Erosion in this portion of the site had already revealed similar objects, implying that the collection had once been larger.

Several pieces stand out as exemplary pieces of Sumerian art. The most impressive of these masterpieces is a vase, made of gypsum and standing nearly a metre high. The vase is decorated with scenes carved in low relief, arranged in four registers stacked

Left: AMONG THE STONE VESSELS OF THE
SAMMELFUND ARE BOWLS DECORATED WITH
ANIMALS CARVED IN RELIEF, A STYLE TYPICAL OF
URUK PERIOD MESOPOTAMIA.
Below: THE URUK SAMMELFUND SITE.

one above another. The lowest register is a narrow band of
alternating grain stalks and date palms, and the next equally
narrow register shows cattle alternating with sheep all walking to
the right. These two scenes represent the earth's bounty, and the
lower rungs of the world order. The third and fourth registers are
wider, separated from one another and from the lower registers by
wide blank spaces. The third scene is a procession of nude men
walking to the left, each carrying a large basket, bowl or spouted
jar filled with different materials. Although not explicit, these men
are probably adorants carrying offerings for presentation to the
god evident in the uppermost register. Here we see the culmination
of the entire vase, centred on a figure facing left and dressed in a
long robe and flanked by two curved objects that have come to be
called 'hut symbols', the sign of the goddess Inanna. Before the
goddess stands a naked man proffering a full basket, while other
dressed figures follow this first adorant. Behind the goddess are
represented gifts that she has already accepted, among them
statues of worshippers, sheep and cattle, vessels full of the earth's
riches, and several tall vases of the same shape as the actual
Sammelfund vase. These scenes have been linked to Sumerian
myths like the marriage of Inanna (goddess
of the storehouse) to Dumuzi (god of the
date palm), or to rituals like the New Year's
festival. Except for the life-sized head of a
stone statue, also found at Warka, this
piece remains unrivalled in the body of
early Sumerian artwork.

Spouted vessels of stone or metal
provided additional opportunity for artistic
expression. One spouted jar, made of limey
sandstone, has arranged around its sides
alternating figures of lions and bulls carved
in high relief, their heads turned outward,
while two standing lions in the round flank
the spout. Other spouted jars of stone are
decorated with bands and rosettes of white,
blue, green, black and red coloured inlay
set in bitumen. The Sammelfund included a
large number of inlay pieces once used to
create rosettes, flowers and other
decorations on such vessels. These pieces

are of various materials, including mother-of-pearl, bituminous
limestone, red limestone and lapis lazuli. Another frequent find are
animals – sheep, kneeling cows, lions, birds and fish carved in shell
or stone. Most of these pieces are pierced, as though once attached
to more substantial works of art; indeed, one sheep has a silver pin
still preserved.

Metal is not a common substance in the Sammelfund, though
several vessels do appear, among them a silver pot with a long
spout and a gold spout from another vessel. Other metalwork is
largely restricted to sheets of gold and silver once attached to
wooden frames by copper nails. The collection also contains
thousands of beads of various shapes; some made of local
materials such as limestone and seashell, and many more are made
of more exotic stones like lapis lazuli, amazonite, amethyst,
carnelian and rock crystal. The Warka stonecutters also used
exotic semi-precious stones to make cylinder seals, whose fine
work marks an apogee of craftsmanship in this characteristically
Mesopotamian art.

The Sammelfund seems to have been a collection of temple
furnishings – the trappings and ritual equipment of a temple
perhaps stored during a periodic renovation. The building in which
the collection was stored can be dated to the end of the fourth
millennium, during the period archaeologists call the 'Jemdet
Nasr'. Some of the objects in the collection belong to this period.
But most of the Sammelfund seems more properly to belong to the
Uruk period itself, several centuries earlier, when the
Mesopotamian tradition crystallized into its historically
recognizable form.

The Mishmar Treasure

The rugged limestone hills of the Judaean desert, along the western shore of the Dead Sea, are deeply incised by twisting erosion channels, or nahals *in Hebrew. The numerous caves of the region have hosted human occupation back to the palaeolithic period; more recently, they have sheltered shepherds, and even given refuge in times of war. The arid climate helps preserve the contents of these caves, which sometimes include objects of great importance, like the Dead Sea Scrolls (see p. 108).*

In 1960, Israeli archaeologists mounted a systematic effort to investigate all the caves, and uncovered evidence of use from the time of the Roman occupation and the Bar Kokhba revolt, nearly two thousand years ago. Earlier occupation seemed sparse until the Chalcolithic period (Copper Age; *c.* 4500–3500 BC), when most of the caves seem to have been used. Pessah Bar-Adon made one of the most exciting discoveries when he found an unprecedentedly rich hoard of metals and other objects (dated shortly before 3500 BC) in the Nahal Mishmar.

Initially called 'Scouts Cave', and later dubbed 'Cave of the Treasure', the Nahal Mishmar Cave contained remains from the Roman period stratified above Chalcolithic deposits. In addition to the more ordinary pottery, stone and bone tools, the Chalcolithic levels contained more unusual items like a disc of ivory, beads of semi-precious stone and a copper awl. The excellent preservation of organic materials also permitted the archaeologists to recover basketry, a straw sieve, leather sandals, textiles of linen and wool (dyed red, yellow, black and green) and remains of a wooden loom. Several burials also appeared. But the most amazing discovery was a hoard of 429 objects that had been wrapped in reed matting and thrust into a crevice in the rock, at the bottom of a pit in the dirt at one side of the cave, and then covered over with a large stone and buried. This treasure included 416 pieces of metalwork, the total weight of which (about 140 kg) marks an impressive accumulation for the time; a few items of ivory and stone accompanied the metallic wealth.

The most elaborate of the metal objects are five cylindrical, concave bands (7–11 cm high, 15–18 cm across) decorated with geometric designs on their outer surfaces. Several of these objects, which the excavator called 'crowns', are mounted with figures of animals like birds and caprid (goat family) heads, horns and other

simple elements. More numerous are the 'standards', shafts (8–35 cm long) with bulbous, pear-shaped (piriform), globular or discoidal ends, and elaborated with other decorative elements like caprid heads, human faces, 'bosses' and horizontal or spiral ribs. The shafts, often decorated with geometric motifs or knobs, are usually hollow and a few still enclose wood, showing that these objects were mounted on poles. Another group of objects, the 'finials', were like the standards without the shaft (only 6–14 cm long). A few items, called 'sceptres', present solid, longer shafts (43–77 cm in total length), but are otherwise similar to the standards. The 'maceheads' are the most common type of object in the treasure. These items, made occasionally in haematite or limestone as well as metal, are highly polished spheres, piriforms or discs (3–6 cm in diameter), pierced through the centre with a shaft-hole. While most of the maceheads are solid around the shaft-hole, a few are hollow with thin walls and look more like ornamental elements. A few examples still contain traces of wood within the shaft-hole. Several maceheads bear caprids, heavy knobs and other projections; a plaque with a shaft through its centre

Above: THE METALWORK IN THE MISHMAR TREASURE INCLUDED 'CROWNS' (TOP), 'MACEHEADS' (CENTRE), AND 'STANDARDS' (BELOW).
Left: AN ALLOYED COPPER 'STANDARD' DECORATED WITH HEADS OF WILD GOATS, FROM NAHAL MISHMAR.

is ornamented with a bird's head and wings, along with geometric decoration. Small jars and horns also appear in the hoard. All these objects have no obvious use, and may be identified as ritual in nature. Some items have a utilitarian form, including axes, other blades and a hammer. A few enigmatic ivory objects complete the hoard, among them are sections of hippopotamus tusk drilled with rows of holes, and a box made from a hollowed section of elephant tusk.

The intricate, beautiful objects of the Mishmar hoard attest to a highly developed artistic sensibility in the Chalcolithic culture of Palestine. Beyond that, the hoard has yielded important information about the high, sophisticated standards of early metalworking in the Near East. Native copper had already long been used to make small objects like beads. In these cases, the metal was simply hammered into shape. By the Chalcolithic period, the metalworkers had made important technological

advances, like smelting ores to extract copper, and adding other metals to create new alloys; the most common additive was arsenic, which acted to harden the copper into a bronze-like material. Craftsmen handling metal became more confident, and many objects were cast in moulds as well as hammered into shape. Analysis of the Mishmar artefacts reveals a surprising sophistication, even by these new standards. The ordinary tools were made of pure copper, simply cast in open or two-piece moulds. The ritual objects, on the other hand, were technologically much more exotic. These were cast using a lost wax technique, each piece cast in a unique mould that included all the decorative elements. The evidence suggests that each mould centred on a ceramic core around which the object was modelled in every detail using wax or resin; an outer ceramic shell then completed the mould. The molten metal poured into this complex mould then melted and replaced the wax, making a metal copy of the object. Once the mould was broken apart, any casting defects could be repaired by hammering or even recasting, and the outer surface polished to a high gloss. While a few ritual objects were cast in pure copper most were made of unusual alloys. The most common alloy combined high proportions of antimony and arsenic with copper, and in a few cases the alloy joined nickel and arsenic with the copper. These alloys allowed the creation of a less viscous metal in the liquid state, more suited to casting complicated shapes.

The Mishmar objects may have come from two separate metalworking shops, one perhaps relying on ores brought from far away. If so, the hoard attests to a flourishing trade in metals over great distances, and the ability of certain people to amass considerable wealth. Many archaeologists suggest that the hoard was the ritual paraphernalia of a regional cult centre, like the one found at 'En Gedi just to the north. Although this supposition can never be demonstrated, the Mishmar hoard does contain many objects without obvious practical use, of types found occasionally in contemporary sites of Palestine.

The 'Royal' Tomb at Maikop

Above: A zoomorphic metal ornament.

At Maikop (sometimes also spelled Maykop), on the Belaya River in the Kuban region of Russia, north of the Caucasus mountains and east of the Black Sea, a large burial tumulus (kurgan in Russian) was opened in 1897 by the Russian archaeologist N. I. Veselovskii. The 'Maikop Kurgan' was enormous: nearly 11 m high and about 200 m in circumference. It contained two graves, a rather impoverished one lying on the prehistoric ground surface under the mound, and a spectacularly rich one in a sunken chamber.

The rich burial contained a wooden mortuary structure 5.5 x 3.75 m and 1.5 m deep, with a stone-lined floor and roofed over with two layers of timber. The structure was divided into three chambers by interior partitions. There was a northern and a southern half, with the northern half divided into an eastern and a western part. Each chamber contained a single skeleton. In the two smaller chambers were the skeletons of females, while the larger chamber in the southern half contained a male. The skeletons were lightly flexed and accompanied by red ochre.

The finds in the Maikop mortuary chamber, particularly those associated with the male burial, are extraordinary. Four silver posts about a metre long with cast golden and silver finials in the shape of three-dimensional bulls supported a canopy with 135 figures of bulls and lions as frontal ornaments. Associated with the man's skeleton were a gold diadem with rosettes; carnelian, turquoise, and gold beads and earrings; six rings of gold and silver; and seventeen vessels of gold, silver and stone. One of the bowls was decorated with engraved figures of mountains, streams and animals (lions, bulls, leopards, goats and birds), seemingly following each other in a procession. Another vessel also had

animal motifs for decoration. Nearby were tools and weapons of copper and bronze, flint arrowheads and a number of ceramic vessels.

The various artefacts in the tumulus are interpreted as emblems of the royalty or divinity of the man in the southern chamber, while the women in each of the northern chambers are presumed to have been his wives. It is safe to assume that the individual in the Maikop burial was a person of very high status, and he is typically referred to as a 'chieftain'. The quality of the metalwork found in the burial may also reflect the existence of specialists, perhaps under the patronage of the elite group to which this chief belonged. What was the source of his prestige and wealth? How large was the state that he ruled?

The large number of metal artefacts in the tomb points toward metallurgy and metalworking as possible sources of wealth. Maikop bronze is of a high-quality arsenical type whose copper came from sources across the Caucasus or even further south. It does not appear that there are copper deposits with this composition in the Maikop region, nor is there evidence that the Maikop people practised mining or metallurgy. Bronze from Transcaucasian copper is also found in significant quantities in the steppe region north of the Black Sea. Between Transcaucasia and the steppes lay Maikop and related sites. Quite possibly, these communities profited by their geographical location, which enabled them to obtain bronze from Transcaucasia and trade it to groups further to the north.

The cultural affinities of the Maikop finds are still the subject of heated debate a century after their discovery. Since the tumulus was excavated before the advent of radiocarbon dating, archaeologists have tried to date it through parallels with other finds from the Caucasus and beyond. The remarkable metalwork in the tomb pointed first to a dating in the Early Bronze Age, and the artefacts have parallels with materials from Early Dynastic III contexts in northern Mesopotamia and from Alaca Höyük in Anatolia see p. 80). Such analogies would make it probable that the Maikop grave dates between 2500 and 2200 BC. Recently, however, arguments have been advanced for an earlier dating, contemporaneous with the Copper Age Cultures of the Black Sea region in the late fourth millennium BC.

Some important information about the dating of Maikop has been provided recently by burials excavated at Krasnogvardeisk in the northern Caucasus. In a mound about 3.5 m high, seven burials with Maikop Culture pottery were found, one of which appears to have been that of an important individual. Although metalwork was lacking, a cylinder seal made from jet was found near the skull. The seal was engraved with a representation of a deer and a figure interpreted as a Tree of Life. Cylinder seals appear in Mesopotamia late in the fourth millennium BC, which leads the excavator of the Krasnogvardeisk grave to suggest a dating early in the third millennium BC. This would place the analogous material from Maikop somewhat earlier than previously believed, but still within the early centuries of the Bronze Age in the Caucasus.

Over the last century, other rich burial mounds have been found at Novosvobodnaya (a lavish burial of a man and a child, with most of the grave goods around the body of the child),

Nalchik (a collective tomb with 120 burials) and Stavropol, all in the Kuban region. At Staromyshastovskaya, a hoard with finds similar to those at Maikop, including 2500 gold and silver beads, is believed to be the remains of a destroyed burial mound. In addition, there are many ordinary burials, often in stone cists, which have much more modest finds. These graves, along with a number of settlements such as the large site at Meshoko, make up what is known as the Maikop Culture of the Early Bronze Age in the Kuban region. The settlements are distinguished by stone defensive walls that enclose up to ten houses. The habitation sites, however, have few metal finds and little evidence of metalworking; their pottery is plain and unimpressive. These seemingly impoverished settlements contrast sharply with the spectacular burial sites.

Above: AN EXAMPLE OF THE REMARKABLY REALISTIC METALWORK OF THE CAUCASUS REGION IN THE THIRD MILLENNIUM BC.

Tell Asmar

The excavation during the 1930s at Tell Asmar, in southern Mesopotamia, uncovered a good example of the special disposal of worn-out or obsolete cult objects, which could not simply be discarded in the usual way.

Set on hallowed ground within cities, Mesopotamian temples were often rebuilt many times over the course of several millennia. At Tell Asmar, the temple of the god Abu (also called Ninurta or Imdugud, a deity of rainfall and the plough) was rebuilt many times during the third millennium BC, undergoing changes in size, floor plan and interior details. Its excavators gave the name Square Temple to one manifestation of the Abu temple, dated to the period archaeologists call the Early Dynastic II (*c.* 2750–2600 BC). At this time, the temple contained three shrine rooms, each fitted with an altar and set around a central courtyard. The temple also held other facilities, like the 'priest's room' with an oven and storage jars, and an ablution room lined with an asphalt seal. The temple was renovated several times, each occasion marked by a new floor laid down on the older ones.

Above: THE FINAL THREE VOTIVE STATUES IN THE CACHE FROM THE SQUARE TEMPLE (TELL ASMAR).

Right: AN ARRAY OF EARLY DYNASTIC VOTIVE STATUES, WITH THEIR CHARACTERISTIC WIDE-EYED GAZE AND CLASPED HANDS.

While peeling off these superimposed floors in one of the shrine rooms, the excavators came upon a pit next to the altar. This pit, dug 60 cm deep from the third floor, held a cache of a dozen statues, carefully stacked on top of each other. Made of soft rock like gypsum and limestone, the statues are standing figures with one hand holding a cup in front of the chest, and huge, staring eyes of shell, black limestone or lapis lazuli set in asphalt. The male figures have long, square-cut beards and long, flowing hair, also coloured black with asphalt, and sport flounced skirts with their torsos left naked. The several female figures have their hair tied up in a large bun, and wear simple dresses that leave one shoulder bare. Each rests on its own circular base.

Although their arrangement in the Square Temple remains a mystery, statues of this type were probably arranged on low benches along the walls of shrine rooms or similarly displayed within the temple. While the largest figure (72 cm high) may represent the god Abu, the remainder (30–60 cm high) are individual worshippers standing in constant prayer to the god, pleading for intercession and benevolence on behalf of the person who dedicated the figure. The figures had been gathered together and carefully interred before the shrine was remodelled, perhaps to make room for new dedications even while assuring continued supplication for the original dedicators. Similar statues were discarded in the courtyard of a later version of the Abu temple, and also appear at other temples in Tell Asmar and other cities of Mesopotamia.

The Gold of Troy

Heinrich Schliemann, the legendary city of Troy and magnificent hoards of gold are inextricably linked in the popular imagination. Unlike many of his contemporaries the German businessman believed the Trojan War of Greek epic was a historical event, and he went to Turkey to try to find the city of Priam. Persuaded by his friend, the archaeologist Frank Calvert, to excavate at the site of Hisarlik in north-west Turkey, Schliemann indeed found the remains of a flourishing pre-classical civilization, which he attributed to the heroic age of Greece, and a large city, which he identified as the site of ancient Troy.

Schliemann's first major series of campaigns was between 1870 and 1873. He found nine superimposed cities, the latest dating to the Roman period, and identified the second city with King Priam's Troy. It is in fact an important Early Bronze Age settlement dating to the second half of the third millennium BC, many centuries earlier than the events described by Homer in the *Iliad*.

Late in May 1873, Schliemann made one of the most spectacular and famous of archaeological discoveries – a fabulous hoard of gold and other metal objects. He was excavating inside a huge double gateway in the second city, in an area he had identified as Priam's palace. Here, in a thick layer of burned ruins from the destruction of the second city of Troy, he noticed a large copper object and gold in a narrow space between two walls. The treasure was found in a rectangular mass, as though packed in a wooden box. According to his own romanticized account, Schliemann, helped by his Greek wife Sophia, cut out the treasure and packed it away in Sophia's shawl: but in fact his wife was not even in Troy at this time, and the discrepancy in Schliemann's account has caused many scholars to question the veracity of the hoard. He concealed the treasures from the Turkish authorities and spirited them away to Athens, where he deposited them in a bank. Furious at the theft, the Turkish officials instituted legal proceedings against Schliemann, resulting in a hefty fine. Although he paid the fine and in total some 50,000 francs to become the legal owner of the treasures, Schliemann was unable to return to Troy for several years to resume his excavations.

This was only the first of some nineteen hoards that he uncovered at Troy, comprising in total more than ten thousand objects of metal and semi-precious stone. Schliemann's treasures

Above: HEINRICH SCHLIEMANN'S WIFE, SOPHIA, WEARING SOME OF THE ELABORATE GOLD JEWELLERY, 'PRIAM'S TREASURE', WHICH WAS UNCOVERED AT TROY.
Left: PHOTOGRAPH TAKEN BY SCHLIEMANN IN 1875 OF SOME OF THE GOLD EARRINGS, DIADEMS AND BEADS FROM 'PRIAM'S TREASURE'.
Right: ELABORATE GOLD EARRING FROM ONE OF THE EARLY BRONZE AGE TREASURE HOARDS FOUND BY SCHLIEMANN AT TROY.

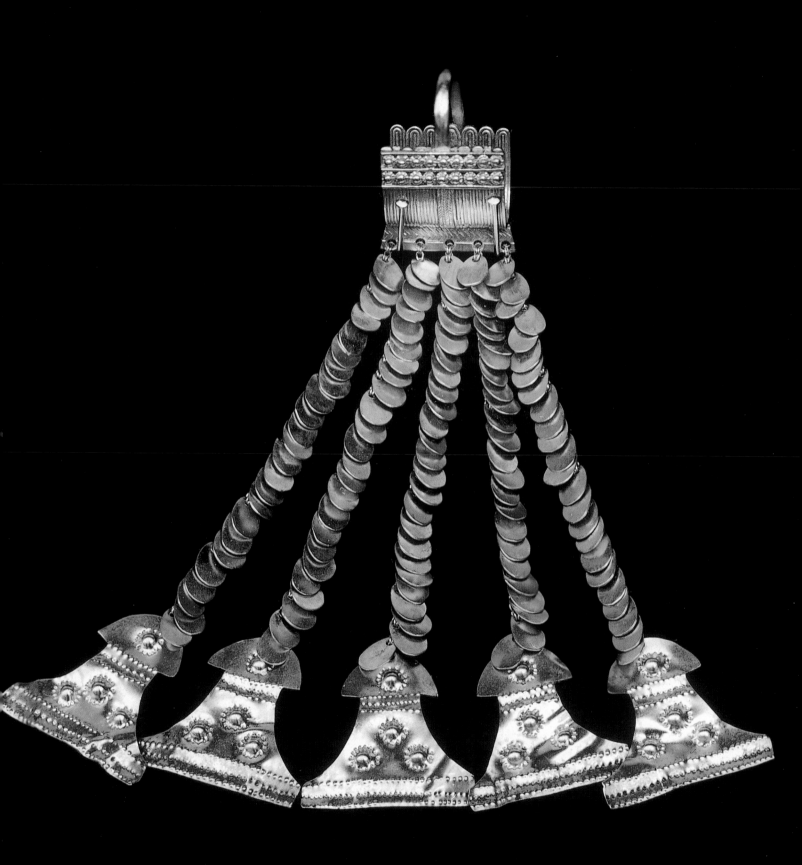

Left: 'PRIAM'S
TREASURE', JEWELLERY
AND PLATE METAL,
PHOTOGRAPHED BY
SCHLIEMANN IN 1875.
Right: GOLDEN TWIN-
HANDLED CUP, OR SO-
CALLED SAUCEBOAT,
FROM TROY.

are an important collection of jewellery, plate metal vases, weapons, anthropomorphic figurines and rock crystal 'lenses' dating to the middle to late third millennium BC. Gold, in particular, was deposited in enormous quantities, suggesting that Troy was a thriving and prosperous trading emporium during the Early Bronze Age. Certainly, the city was an important goldworking centre, and highly skilled craftsmen produced exquisite objects for the local rulers who had accumulated vast wealth through their control of the trade of mineral resources. These goldsmiths used sheet metal decorated with embossed motifs, as well as the more advanced techniques of filigree and granulation (fine wires and small beads of gold soldered on to a gold background).

The most famous pieces of jewellery are undoubtedly the two diadems worn by Sophia Schliemann, made of numerous fine gold chains with schematic, idol-shaped pendants of sheet gold. Originally, the diadems were mounted on a headdress made of cloth or leather, and framed the face. There were also two types of earring (crescent-shaped and 'basket'-shaped), numerous gold hair ornaments, torcs (neckrings) of plain or twisted gold wire, pins including one elaborate example with a rectangular gold head decorated in filigree spirals and topped by miniature gold vases, thousands of beads of gold, silver, bronze and carnelian from necklaces, and occasional bracelets made of hammered gold wire. The plate metal vases include anthropomorphic flasks of silver (containers for precious perfumed oils), the famous gold sauceboat, and several gold and silver cups.

In addition to the beautiful gold objects in many of the hoards, Schliemann also found an impressive set of weapons in his excavations of 1890. Principal among them are four ceremonial hammer-axes, three made of green stone and the fourth of a blue stone recently identified as lazurite, which probably came from Afghanistan. The lazurite hammer-axe had been used and was 'killed', or ceremonially broken, before being deposited in the hoard, perhaps to divest it of special powers or symbolic

significance. The other hammer-axes, however, show no signs of use and were even deposited unfinished. The stone hoard also contained six rock crystal pommels, probably maceheads, and numerous rock crystal 'lenses'. The macehead is a typical emblem of power in the Early Bronze Age civilizations of the East Mediterranean, such as in the wealthy cemetery of Alaca Höyük in central Turkey (see p. 80), or more notably the maceheads used by the early pharaonic rulers of Egypt. The function of the lenses is less clear. It has been suggested that they were gaming pieces from an early board game. Alternatively, they might have been used by the jewellers of Troy in their intricate goldwork. Other notable objects from the Trojan hoards include metal figurines – one of bronze and one of lead – and remarkably an iron pommel, probably a macehead. The widespread use of iron in the East Mediterranean only dates to the first millennium BC, although occasional ceremonial, high status weapons are found sporadically before then.

Schliemann believed the treasures had been hidden for safekeeping just before the sack of Troy of Greek legend, but instead it appears that many of the objects had simply been gathered together for recycling. Many pieces of jewellery were unfinished and others had been broken. In addition there were several notched 'ingots' of gold, possibly preliminary preparation for the manufacture of gold beads. Likewise, the lenses bear the hallmarks of the equipment of a master goldworker. Hence, rather than the victims of an ancient war, it is more probable that many of the treasures were simply the repositories of ancient craftsmen.

The treasures were, however, casualties of the turbulent events of the twentieth century. In 1881, Schliemann had donated his collection to the city of Berlin in return for honorary citizenship. At the outbreak of the Second World War in 1939 they were packed away, but in the final days of the war they disappeared. In 1993, the Russian government admitted possession of the treasures, which have now been authenticated by an international team of experts, and are on display in Moscow's Pushkin Museum.

Royal Treasures at Ur

The city of Ur, in the deep south of Mesopotamia, remains one of the best studied Sumerian cities of the third millennium BC, the period when the Mesopotamian civilization first flourished. Excavations by the British archaeologist Sir Leonard Woolley, during the 1920s, uncovered the Royal Cemetery, where members of Ur's ruling elite were buried along with an incredible array of precious and finely crafted objects, and vivid indications of human sacrifice.

Around 2600 BC the residents of Ur created near the city's sacred precinct a cemetery that remained in use for about six centuries. Leonard Woolley excavated some two and a half thousand graves in this cemetery. Most of these were the simple interments of common folk, the body wrapped in matting and placed in a hole along with a clay pot or two, if that much. Other graves contained an abundance of expensive, even exotic, materials, including copper objects sometimes inlaid with silver or gold, jewellery made from precious metals and lapis lazuli, and jars carved from alabaster or soapstone. Amid this modest display of genteel wealth, a few graves, a tight cluster of scarcely more than a dozen, stood apart. These tombs were underground chambers with vaulted roofs, made of brick and stone, and entered along a sloped ramp or through a pit. Although some had been robbed of their contents during antiquity, others retained their original,

Left: A LYRE FROM UR (RECONSTRUCTED), THE SOUNDING BOX ORNAMENTED WITH A BULL'S HEAD AND INLAY WORK.

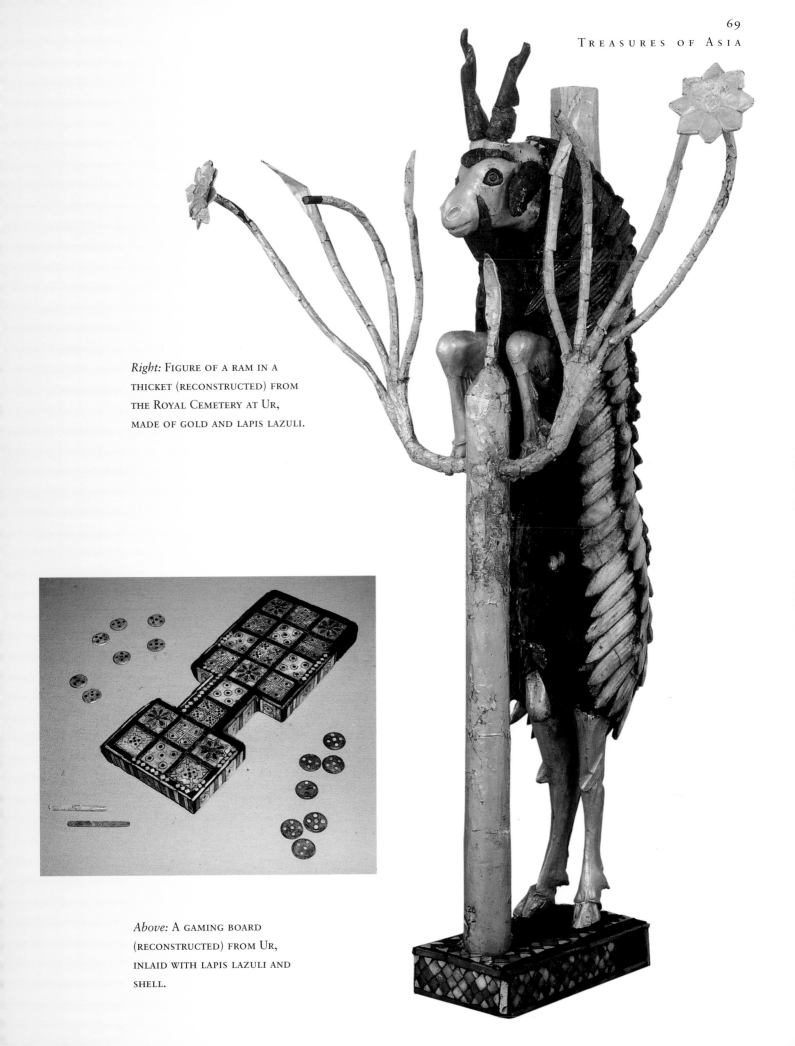

Right: FIGURE OF A RAM IN A
THICKET (RECONSTRUCTED) FROM
THE ROYAL CEMETERY AT UR,
MADE OF GOLD AND LAPIS LAZULI.

Above: A GAMING BOARD
(RECONSTRUCTED) FROM UR,
INLAID WITH LAPIS LAZULI AND
SHELL.

Above: EVEN THE MANY RETAINERS WHO ACCOMPANIED THE ROYAL FIGURE IN DEATH WORE
ELABORATE JEWELLERY OF GOLD, SILVER, LAPIS LAZULI AND CARNELIAN.
Right: DETAIL FROM THE STANDARD OF UR, SHOWING THE CELEBRATORY RITUAL SCENE
(PERHAPS AFTER THE MILITARY ACTION DEPICTED ON THE REVERSE SIDE OF THE PANEL).

fantastically luxurious contents, the riches for the afterlife. Cuneiform inscriptions on some objects identify several of the deceased as the kings Meskalamdug and Akalamdug, and the queen Pu-abi; although some uncertainty still remains about their identity, these people are today widely regarded as members of a royal dynasty that ruled Ur around 2600–2500 BC. These sixteen tombs formed the heart of the Royal Cemetery of Ur.

The wealth in these tombs is unparalleled in Mesopotamian archaeology, and provides some of the most celebrated pieces of Sumerian art. The so-called Standard of Ur presents scenes, inlaid with nacre and lapis lazuli, of victorious warfare and ritual celebration on each side of a wooden panel. Lyres, three-dimensional figures of a ram caught in a thicket and gaming boards were also created in wood and ornamented with geometric designs and figured scenes executed with inlaid mother-of-pearl, carnelian and lapis lazuli. The helmet of Meskalamdug, made of electrum (a mixture of gold and silver), expresses a mastery of the smith's craft just as much as the tangible wealth of Ur's kings. Myriad other objects, like metal weapons, gold and silver jewellery and vessels, ostrich eggs inlaid with asphalt, cylinder seals of semi-precious stones and cosmetic containers merely punctuated the message of riches and power.

Equally spectacular was the evidence in the royal burials of the ceremonies that were performed with the interments – including human sacrifice. The remains of wagons and oxen and the skeletons of many court attendants accompanied the dead royalty into the afterlife. Woolley described the macabre scene of one grave with these words: 'The burial of the kings was accompanied by human sacrifice on a lavish scale, the bottom of the grave pit being crowded with the bodies of men and women who seemed to have been brought down here and butchered where they stood. In one grave the soldiers of the guard, wearing copper helmets and carrying spears, lie at the foot of the steep ramp that led down into the grave; against the end of the tomb chamber are nine ladies of the court with elaborate golden head-dresses; in front of the entrance are drawn up two heavy four-wheeled carts with three bullocks harnessed to each other, and the driver's bones lie in the carts and grooms are by the heads of the animals.'

The contents of the royal tomb display a remarkable power over people and riches – the power to take subordinates into death, the power to bury forever an incredible wealth. The latter was all the more significant because Mesopotamia lacks most raw materials, including metals and stones. The mortuary goods at Ur were made largely from imported materials, some brought from great distances like the lapis lazuli that travelled 2400 km overland from north-east Afghanistan, and the copper that moved 1450 km miles by sea from Oman. Once it was brought to their workshops, Ur's artisans then transformed this raw wealth into objects of great beauty, all to be buried with the dead.

The Luristan Bronzes

Above: A BRONZE CHEEK PIECE (OF A HORSE BIT) IN THE SHAPE OF A HUMAN-HEADED GRIFFIN, IRON AGE LURISTAN.

During the 1920s an extraordinary number of bronze objects, many decorated in a highly original style, began to appear on the antiquities markets of Europe and North America. By the early 1930s, several scholars working in Iran had traced the bronzes back to Luristan, the rugged country of the central Zagros mountains that form the western boundary of the Iranian plateau. At that time, and indeed for many decades afterwards, Luristan was not a congenial place for archaeological research, being the homeland of animal herders suspicious of outsiders and state officials. Despite the risks, several scholars soon determined that in fact the bronzes came from tombs that the local tribesmen were busy looting.

Below: DETAIL OF ANIMAL HEADS DECORATING THE TOP OF A BRONZE 'SCEPTRE' FROM LURISTAN.

One intrepid traveller, Freya Stark, was a participant observer of the treasure hunt, as she reported in a 1932 issue of the *Geographical Journal*: 'The system of treasure hunting is now thoroughly elaborated and has evidently come from much practice. Men go out with stout skewers about a yard long which they dig into the ground at intervals: if they hit a flat surface about 2 feet underground, they try again close by in suitable places, and if the surface appears to continue in the shape of a presumed grave, they gather hopefully to dig.'

Such enterprises continued to supply antiquities markets with these Luristan bronzes, but for a long time prevented any clear understanding of them. The archaeologists and art historians who studied the bronzes disagreed about several critical issues, such as what counts as a Luristan bronze, what are their dates, and what was the ultimate inspiration for their style. Several archaeological expeditions went in search of these bronzes. As early as 1934 an American team began several years of surveys and excavation that produced good results, including an Iron Age (early first millennium) sanctuary stuffed with metal objects; unfortunately, the Americans did not fully publish their findings for another sixty years. Not until the Belgian archaeologist Louis van den Berghe began exploring the cemeteries of Luristan in the 1960s and 1970s did the history and context of these bronzes become clearer.

The archaeological work demonstrates that the bronzes looted from cemeteries and sanctuaries of ancient Luristan span a considerable length of time, from the Early Bronze Age down to the end of the Iron Age (*c.* 2600-500 BC). Moreover, some cemeteries were a thousand years older than that, establishing that the basic ideas of burial in Luristan preceded the deposits of metals in graves. The lengthy history of Luristan bronzes confirmed the arguments of some scholars that the shapes of certain bronzes indicate an Early Bronze Age date, and others a Late Bronze Age or Iron Age date for their production. At the same time, the archaeo-logical and art historical evidence showed that most of the Luristan bronzes are very similar to metalwork of surrounding regions, whereas some forms are distinctive of Luristan itself. Moreover, the widespread forms belong to the Bronze Age while the more special pieces come from Iron Age times. In other words, the metalworking tradition of Luristan for a long time was indistinguishable from that of other parts of the Near East, but developed an individual style near the beginning of the Iron Age.

This distinctive Luristan style began to appear soon after 1200 BC, and achieved full expression during the ninth, eighth and seventh centuries BC. The style centres on imaginative and elaborate depictions of animals, taking in new directions the sensibility of Elamite art to the south and some traditional motifs of Mesopotamia to the west. The style appears on a relatively narrow range of objects. Socketed axes often have three or four long spikes that project from the socket opposite the blade, which itself is so elongated and strongly curved as to be non-functional. The points of the spike often transform into animal heads or entire animals, and the axe blade sometimes issues from a lion's mouth. A related form is a shaft-hole axe with a crescent blade, where the three-dimensional figure of a lion, bull or other animal sits opposite the blade. Animals fahioned in the round are the centrepiece of two other typical objects. Bronze handles for whetstones often end with the head of an ibex with elongated neck and exaggerated horns, and sometimes a second animal stands on its back. Bronzes of another group are often identified as 'standards', or simply finials. These are small objects (generally less than 15 cm tall) composed of pairs of animals,

Left: A BRONZE HARNESS RING
ORNAMENTED WITH ANIMAL FIGURES, PART
OF THE IRON AGE HORSE GEAR FROM
LURISTAN.

Below: BRONZE FINIAL DECORATED WITH
HIGHLY STYLIZED ANIMALS, FROM
LURISTAN.

usually ibexes, on their hind legs facing each other. The animals
are often attenuated, forming graceful curves and arches with their
horns, necks and legs. In some finials, a highly stylized tree
separates the two animals; in others a human figure, itself often
attenuated and highly decorated, grasps both animals in a re-
creation of that traditional Mesopotamian theme of the
master (or mistress) of beasts.

Horse gear makes up another distinctive aspect
of the Luristan bronzes. The cheek pieces of bits
often took the form of animals – horses, wild
sheep, bulls and lions as well as legendary animals
like winged ibex and sphinx – and even more
complex images like the master of beasts.
Animal figures in the round could grace harness
rings and other trappings. Similar figures,
including the master of beasts and animals
upright on each side of a tree, also appear as
the heads of some hair or clothing
pins. The heads of other pins take the shape of a
relatively large flat disc, ornamented with
geometric designs on animals created by
hammering (repoussé) or grooving (chased). The
same techniques were used to decorate metal cases
for quivers, decorative plaques for belts, vessels and
other objects fashioned from sheet metal, but these
objects were not particularly distinctive of Iron Age
Luristan. Similarly, the abundant weapons from Luristan
take forms that also occur in other regions. Many daggers
are distinctive in their manufacture – bronze (and
occasionally silver) handles cast on to iron blades. Pins and
bracelets often present the same use of two metals, the decorative
element being of cast bronze.

Van den Berghe's cemetery excavations help put this wealth of
bronzework in some context. The cemeteries at the height of this
artistic production are usually made up of individual burials placed
within a pit or stone cist and covered with stone slabs, the tomb
roof that Freya Stark's tribesmen sought with their probes. The
dead were nearly all adult (the few children that were found

accompanied an adult), with roughly the same
numbers of men and women. The grave goods placed
with the dead were highly varied – numerous tombs contained
nothing and others were extremely rich, while the majority
included roughly half a dozen objects. Interestingly, more men than
women were buried with a rich assortment of offerings, a probable
insight into differences of social standing. In the aggregate, roughly
half the grave goods were simple pottery vessels, the other half
were objects of bronze and iron, and occasionally gold or silver. By
this time, iron had come to be used for ordinary tools, weapons
and other objects. Bronze, on the other hand, was used to make
the decorated artefacts that indicated social standing and wealth
among the partly settled communities of nomadic herders in the
mountains of Luristan.

Bronze Age
Treasures of Bactria

Bactria, the Central Asian land near the Amu Darya (or Oxus River) in northern Afghanistan, played a role in Near Eastern affairs of antiquity and formed part of empires from the time of the Persians and Alexander the Great. Bactria's connections with the Near East go back long before the first millennium BC. *Treasures of metalwork bear witness to the impact of western artistic ideas on Bactrian artisans during the Bronze Age.*

I n 1841, a Russian diplomat reported the discovery of treasure at Astrabad, in north-east Persia. The diplomat sketched the objects and ascertained the circumstances of their discovery, reporting these details for an English publication; the objects themselves disappeared. When the Sumerian Culture of Mesopotamia was discovered half a century later, art historians soon noticed certain strong resemblances between features of the Astrabad objects and typically Sumerian motifs, and suggested a strong connection across the Iranian plateau. But in the absence of additional discoveries, the connection could not be further described. So matters rested until the 1960s, when a hoard of gold and silver vessels was found in north-east Afghanistan, perhaps by farmers digging into the mound of Khosh Tapa. Like several metal vessels in the Astrabad collection, the Khosh Tapa vessels presented some distinctly Sumerian features. But by now, prehistoric cultures of neighbouring regions were better known, and characteristics of Central Asian and Iranian art could also be detected.

Within two decades, an explosion of new information became available, especially from Bactria. Here, illegal looting of graves flooded the antiquities market with certain characteristic objects, including other metal vessels with engraved scenes, numerous plain vessels in metal or stone, seated figures in stone, weapons, mirrors with figured handles, pins with ornamented heads and metal

Left: STATUETTE OF BEARDED MAN WITH SCARRED FACE AND AN IRON HEADBAND, MADE OF SOAPSTONE AND LIMESTONE, FROM THE BACTRIAN AREA.
Right above: ONE FACE OF A DOUBLE-SIDED DISC (PERHAPS A STAMP SEAL), GOLD LEAF OVER SOAPSTONE, SHOWING A LION AND SNAKE (BULL ON THE REVERSE SIDE), FROM THE BACTRIAN AREA.
Right below: BRONZE COSMETIC JAR IN THE SHAPE OF A BACTRIAN CAMEL, WITH BIRD-HEADED APPLICATION STICK.

Left: SILVER POT WITH ORNAMENTED LID FROM A BRONZE AGE BACTRIAN GRAVE.
Below: BACTRIAN STATUETTE OF A SEATED WOMAN WEARING A FLOUNCED DRESS AND A ROUND CAP, MADE OF SOAPSTONE AND LIMESTONE.

geometric stamp seals. Similar objects turned up as far away as western Iran and north-west Pakistan. By the 1980s, archaeologists had come to realize that these kinds of objects reflected a Central Asian, Bactrian culture that produced an aesthetic synthesis, on its own terms, of artistic ideas from the older civilizations of Mesopotamia, western Iran and the Indus Valley. Although none of the brilliant finds could be dated – almost all the finest objects came from undocumented digging – various indications suggested that the art belonged to the final centuries of the third and first few centuries of the second millennium BC.

The Bactrian civilization had its main roots in the Central Asian world of towns along the mountain piedmont in Turkmenistan, just south of the Kara Kum desert. Until the last years of the third millennium BC Bactria itself seemingly lacked settled occupations; around 2200–2000 BC towns began to appear in the area, and the Bronze Age civilization of Bactria quickly came into being. Although taking inspiration from its neighbours, the Bactrian civilization created a brilliant new art style, elements of which spread through much of Afghanistan, Iran and into Pakistan. The metal vessels – of gold, silver and copper – of the kind found in the Astrabad and Khosh Tapa hoards exemplify the spirit of this art. The metal vessels often parallel typical Bactrian pottery in their forms, among them pedestalled cups, goblets, chalices with a bevelled rim, bottles, jars and plates. While many vessels are undecorated, others bear often elaborate incised or embossed designs. A common decoration is the stepped

triangles and lozenges that recall woven designs on tapestries, ancient motifs of Central Asia that go back to the fourth millennium. Other vessels bear various animals – boars, snakes, birds and bulls – in isolation or combinations, often depicted amid foliage. Many bulls reveal a similarity with the style typical of the Indus Valley civilization. Others are shown in a very peculiar fashion, the body in profile and the horned head turned full face, with a long, curly beard and human-like features. This style was particularly current in Mesopotamia during the third millennium. A few vessels depict human figures, often wearing flounced skirts that leave the torso bare, reminiscent of the Mesopotamian style. These figures are sometimes grouped into scenes. On one vessel, men – individually or in pairs – ride ox-drawn carts or chariots, with other figures (including several naked men) placed around. Another scene depicts agricultural activities, including a yoke of oxen pulling a plough, urged on by an ox-drover and guided by the ploughman; a third figure behind the team holds a box from which he is broadcasting seed.

These vessels are by no means the only characteristic artefact of the Bronze Age Central Asian arts, nor the most common or widespread. The metal stamp seals, with elaborate geometric or figurative themes, are as distinctive as any style of the ancient Near East. The stone statues, made in steatite and limestone, show seated men and women, again wearing the flounced skirt; this style of sculpture occurs in large numbers in certain Iranian cemeteries, and even appears on cylinder seals carved at Susa, on Mesopotamia's borders. Other, smaller objects, like stone bottles, and many kinds of metalwork have also been discovered across a wide section of West Asia. The elegant metal vessels, however, are central to the Bactrian phenomenon, the seamless incorporation of foreign influences into a basic Central Asian pattern, thus creating a brilliant new civilization.

Alaca Höyük

The central Anatolian plateau, a landscape of dramatic hills and narrow river valleys, was home to the Hittites, a people prominent in Near Eastern history during the second millennium BC. Hittite antecedents remain cloudy. Early Bronze Age towns dot this landscape, but the Hittites often built upon the remains of these third-millennium settlements, making it more difficult to uncover the earlier remains. Alaca Höyük is one such place with important Hittite remains on top of an Early Bronze Age settlement.

Located some 50 km from Bogazköy, and about 160 km east of Ankara, the modern capital of Turkey, Alaca Höyük was fairly small (the mound covered a mere 7 ha) but nevertheless an important town. The Turkish archaeologists Hamit Kosay and Remzi Arik began excavating the town in 1935, and work has continued here up to the present day. Within the mound, 14 m in height, this work has identified four broad periods of occupation that stretch almost continuously from the beginning of the Early Bronze Age (perhaps around 3500 BC) into Ottoman times. The second of these periods is the Hittite town of the second millennium BC, the settlement that has been the main focus of the archaeological work at Alaca Höyük. Like other Hittite centres, this place contained large temples and other public buildings,

protected by a city wall and rampart, and entered through a formal gate flanked by large figures of sphinxes.

The Early Bronze Age settlement below the Hittite town, the earliest two periods, was much less substantial. The houses of mudbrick walls set on stone footings underwent several phases of renovation or rebuilding, and give no hint of any particular sophistication or wealth of the town's residents. But in fact the second period of the Early Bronze Age, which the excavators called Alaca III, contains the royal tombs.

Kosay and Arik found these thirteen graves during the first years of their excavations, during the 1930s. The tombs are similar in their design and contents. The basic structure is a rectangular pit of variable dimensions, the smallest a mere 2 x 1.7 m in area and the largest a more substantial 9 x 5.2 m. Clay lined the floor of the pits, except in two tombs whose floors were paved with stone slabs. Stones lined the pit walls to a height of 0.5 or 0.75 m, where a timber roof capped with clay stretched across the grave chamber. Each chamber contained a single interment, except for one that contained three skeletons. The body was laid at one end of the chamber, positioned on its side in a flexed position. The rich grave goods surrounded the body, while the remaining space within the chamber was largely devoid of preserved artefacts. After the body had been placed within the chamber, and the roof had sealed the chamber, a mortuary feast took place upon the clay roof cap, a ceremony that left behind the carefully arranged skulls and paired forelimbs of as many as ten cattle (or sometimes sheep or goats); the other parts of the animals are missing. Several tombs also contained complete skeletons of dogs. This ceremony complete, the rest of the tomb shaft was then filled with dirt, and its location probably marked with a ring of stones.

Right: A GOLDEN CROWN OF OPEN LATTICE WORK, NEARLY 20 CM ACROSS, FROM ALACA HÖYÜK. *Background:* A DIAMOND SHAPED 'STANDARD' FILLED WITH A GRILL OF SWASTIKAS, FROM ALACA HÖYÜK.

Above: AN ELEGANTLY FORMED GOLDEN
PITCHER FROM ALACA HÖYÜK.

The tombs have been designated as royal because of their
wealth in metals. Metal vessels are common: plates and deep bowls
of copper or bronze; cups with loop handles and footed goblets of
silver and gold; pitchers of copper, silver and gold, embellished
with elaborate geometric decorations; jars of gold or silver
decorated with knobs (in one instance jadeite knobs affixed with
golden nails). Weapons are also prominent. Many of these, like
bronze spear blades, are relatively mundane, while others are
extraordinary – an ornamental gilt macehead, a dagger made of
silver, and a pair of daggers fashioned from meteoric iron with
gold leaf on the handles. More ordinary copper tools, like awls,
chisels and flat axes, likewise appear. Jewellery in silver, gold and
copper also figure among the grave goods, among them some
classic Early Bronze Age forms like pins with double-spiral heads,
as well as other pin forms, bracelets, necklaces of gold discs,
figure-eight brooches and sheet gold cut-out figures.

A number of complex objects are grouped together under the
rubric 'standards' with a presumed ritual and symbolic function.

The standards take several different forms. A common form is a
circle or semicircle of metal, generally some 20–30 cm across, that
frames a grill or more complex pattern of metal openwork. Smaller
circles of open grillwork are often attached at intervals to the arc
of the frame, or dangled loosely from cross-pieces of the standard's
grillwork. These standards are equipped with a double-pronged
tang, and sometimes a pair of horns project laterally from the base
of the tang. Presumably, the entire standard once fitted into a
wooden mount of some kind. The standards of this kind have been
called 'sun-discs'. Another type of standard is similar in general
shape to the semicircular sun-discs, complete with horns and
double tang, although tending to be somewhat larger (40–55 cm
across). But instead of geometric openwork, statuettes of animals –
large horned stags and bulls – fill the frame. These statuettes are
detailed figures, sometimes decorated with silver concentric circles
and zigzags. These same statuettes also appear as individual
figures, fitted with tenons for attachment to larger pieces.

Analysis of the metalwork reveals the sophistication of the
Alaca smiths. These artisans used different techniques, both casting
objects in open moulds and using the lost wax technique. They
also show an interest in a wide variety of metals. The daggers of
meteoric iron are among the oldest known iron artefacts, a
material that must be counted as a scarce and precious commodity
during the Early Bronze Age. Examination of about forty copper
pieces shows that roughly one-third are relatively pure copper,
about half are copper deliberately alloyed with tin to make true
bronze, and the remainder are arsenical copper. The latter
combination of copper and arsenic was the more usual alloy
during the Early Bronze Age, and the addition of arsenic lent
copper greater hardness in much the same manner as bronze.
The abundance of tin alloy marks a significant departure from
these more 'normal' practices, and may reflect the exploitation
of Anatolian tin sources that recent investigations have begun
to document.

The dates of the Alaca royal tombs remain uncertain, with
different scholars offering widely varying dates within the third
millennium. Although not definite, the best guess would put the
tombs in the range of 2500–2200 BC, give or take a century or so.
But solving the chronological problem does not help to sort out
the basic puzzle – what are such rich tombs, with their sophisticated metalwork, doing in an otherwise undistinguished
settlement? Some scholars suggest that these are the graves of
partly nomadic rulers of Pontic tribes whose home was nearer the
Black Sea. Others argue that local dynasts were buried in the
tombs, and point out that we still do not understand very much of
the settlement and society at Alaca Höyük and elsewhere in north
central Anatolia during the Early Bronze Age. Perhaps future work
at the site will resolve these questions.

The Gold from Tell el-Ajjul

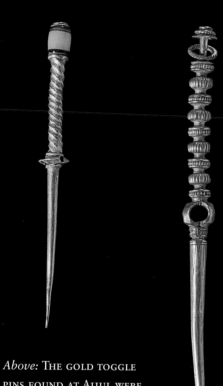

Above: THE GOLD TOGGLE PINS FOUND AT AJJUL WERE USED TO FASTEN CLOTHES. *Below:* A PAIR OF ELABORATE GOLD EARRINGS AND A SWIVEL SIGNET RING FROM THE HOARDS OF GOLD FOUND AT AJJUL.

Tell el-Ajjul, the 'mound of the little ox', lies on the northern banks of the Wadi Azza, some 6 km south-west of the modern Palestinian city of Gaza. During the 1930s, a team of British archaeologists, led by the renowned Egyptologist Sir William Matthews Flinders Petrie, conducted a series of excavations at the site. Petrie identified the site with the ancient city of Gaza, and suggested that it was the seat of the Egyptian governor in southern Palestine during the period of the Egyptian New Kingdom empire.

Conditions were hard in the field. The Gaza region was politically unstable, and the site was malarial because of its proximity to the waters of the Wadi Azza. In addition, Petrie was unable to cope with the complexities of the archaeology of this particular tell site. In spite of the problems he faced, however, Petrie's finds from Ajjul rank among the most spectacular and wealthy from any Bronze Age city in southern Palestine. In particular, during the 1933 season, numerous pieces of gold jewellery were found on the tell. Indeed, never before had so much gold been recovered from any Palestinian site. Petrie attributed this to his practice of rewarding his workmen with the exact value of the weight of the metal, calculated by taking the price of gold from the most recent edition of *The Times* at the base camp.

In total, five large hoards of gold were found in the town buildings and so-called palace on the southern and northern areas of the mound. In addition, several minor groups of gold objects were recovered on the mound itself and in tombs from cemeteries surrounding the tell. The largest and richest hoards contained many outstanding pieces of gold, but very few objects in other materials. The jewellery from Ajjul was made of both sheet gold and solid gold, either by casting or hammering and impressing. Some twenty-six main types have been identified among the jewellery from Ajjul. The principal groups of ornaments are earrings, pendants, beads, circlets, bracelets and toggle-pins. The majority of the earrings are plain hoops cast from solid gold. In some instances these are decorated with a cluster of tiny gold beads, made by the granulation technique, hanging from the loop. Also common are loop earrings made from sheet gold and twisted. Another typical kind of earring from the Ajjul hoards is crescent-shaped, created from two embossed sheets of gold attached together by a wire and decorated on both sides with tiny beads of gold

THE GOLD ORNAMENTS FROM AJJUL
INCLUDED LARGE CRESCENT-SHAPED
EARRINGS AND A VARIETY OF PENDANTS.

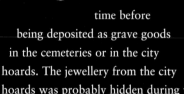

soldered on to the surface in arrangements of triangles or circles. More unusual are the falcon earrings, a single sheet of embossed gold cut in a crescent shape, with a falcon's head rising between the two ends and decorated with small granulated beads of gold. A pair of sheet-gold cruciform earrings, decorated with granulation and tiny cloisons (cells defined by gold wire) and filled with blue glass, were found in one of the tombs.

The hoards are particularly striking for the collection of complex pendants in a variety of forms. Most impressive are the so-called Astarte pendants, comprising piriform (pear-shaped) sheets of gold decorated with a nude female figure in low relief. The face and hair or wig are very Egyptianized, reminiscent of the Egyptian goddess Hathor. Frequently, the figure holds a goat or a lotus flower in each hand. These figures are thought to represent Astarte, the ancient Near Eastern goddess of fertility. In addition there are a small number of sheet-gold pendants cut out in the shape of female figures. More typical are crescent-shaped pendants of solid gold, star-shaped pendants, discs decorated with repoussé stars, and sheet-gold pendants depicting a variety of plant motifs. Particularly unusual are four pendants cast from solid gold in the shape of a fly.

Other jewellery includes a necklace made of five long narrow tubes of sheet gold and two triangular pendants decorated in repoussé, and a number of headdresses of sheet gold decorated with four-leaf rosettes decorated in repoussé. There are a number of bracelets cast from solid silver or gold, which appear for the most part to be cut off as scrap metal for recasting. Clothes were fastened by toggle-pins cast from solid gold, silver or bronze. Occasional Egyptian scarabs, set in swivel rings of gold and silver, were found in three of the hoards.

This fine collection of jewellery, largely made of gold, was fashioned locally and appears to have been used for a considerable time before being deposited as grave goods in the cemeteries or in the city hoards. The jewellery from the city hoards was probably hidden during the unsettled political conditions of the second millennium BC, possibly at the time of the expulsion of the Hyksos (Asiatic rulers) from Egypt. Hoarding of precious metals was repeated throughout the ancient world during times of trouble, as, for example, at Troy (see p. 64). Much of the jewellery also appears to have been scrap metal, which would have been melted down to make new jewellery. This recycling of metal is a common feature of ancient societies, and reflects the rarity of the metals being used. Often these hidden treasures are the only information that archaeologists have about the ornamentation worn by ancient peoples.

The Ajjul hoards are a window on to the past and illustrate the wealth of one of the major towns of Palestine at the beginning of the second millennium BC. The aristocracy of Ajjul wore elaborate gold and silver jewellery. They fastened their clothes with impressive solid gold or silver pins, and wore opulent gold necklaces with pendants of the major Canaanite fertility goddess Astarte. Much of the jewellery displays a strong Egyptian influence, although it appears for the most part to have been manufactured locally. The wealth of the inhabitants of Ajjul was no doubt derived from the town's location at the end of the land route between Egypt and Asia, known as the Way of Horus.

The Burial Pits at Sanxingdui

Right: OVERALL MORE
THAN 2.5 M TALL AND
WEIGHING 180 KG, THIS
REMARKABLE STANDING
FIGURE PERHAPS HELD
AN ELEPHANT TUSK IN
ITS HUGE GRIP. FOUR
ELEPHANT HEADS
SUPPORT THE BASE.

The discovery in 1986 of sacrificial pits filled with extraordinary objects of bronze, jade and gold catapulted the site of Sanxingdui, in Sichuan Province, south-west China, to archaeological fame. These finds provided for the first time a detailed picture of an early bronze-using culture outside the Central Plains of China.

In an area of some 17 sq km on the banks of the Yazi and Mamu Rivers, the ancient city of Sanxingdui lies about 40 km to the north of the provincial capital, Chengdu. Although the site has been known since 1929, systematic archaeological investigation has only been undertaken since 1984. This work has so far identified a series of high earth mounds around the site as city walls made of stamped earth, the remains of many buildings including a large multi-roomed structure over 200 sq m in area, and industrial workshops and kilns. It is the presence of large numbers of spectacular jade, bronze and gold objects that has led Chinese archaeologists to consider Sanxingdui not only as a thriving and populous city dating to the second millennium BC, but also possibly as some kind of centre of pilgrimage.

A number of pits filled with apparently sacrificial deposits have been discovered at various locations around Sanxingdui, concentrated along the main north–south axis of the town. The first two pits to be excavated, following their discovery by workers at a brickyard, contained about three hundred objects of gold, bronze, jade, stone and pottery. One of these pits is rectangular, about 4.7 m long, 3.5 m wide and 1.6 m deep, with clearly defined sides. The floor of the pit was covered with ritual jade sceptres, bronze vessels, heads and masks, some of which are decorated with gold leaf. Above this the pit was filled with layers of compacted earth, the middle one containing many burnt animal bones, suggesting the remains of a large-scale sacrifice. A second pit, dated a little later than the first, some 30 m to the south-east, had at its base jade discs and blades, small zoomorphic masks, bronze figurines and seashells. Above this layer was a series of large bronze objects including a larger-than-life standing figure, heads, masks, ritual vessels and a model tree, some 4 m high when reconstructed, in whose branches perched a flock of splendid birds. The uppermost layer contained over sixty elephant tusks. Other pits with equally remarkable contents have been recorded in other parts of Sichuan Province.

Traces of beam slots for structures built over some of the pits have been recognized in some places, possibly halls in which the ritual sacrifices took place. These ritual practices, with the resulting burned animal bones and smashed bronzes, are quite distinct from those carried out in association with the royal funerals of the Shang state in northern China with which they were contemporary. The Shang ritual items are mainly magnificent bronze vessels and there are no counterparts of the tall standing figure or the heads. In addition, the Shang rituals focused overwhelmingly on funerary ceremonies and ancestor worship, while those at Sanxingdui appear more concerned with liaising between the natural and spirit worlds.

Archaeologists have so far recovered over fifty life-size bronze human heads, but the standing figure remains unique. Being 2.62 m tall and weighing 180 kg, it may have represented a god, an ancestor figure or priest, possibly leading the rituals. Dressed in a representation of a long, finely embroidered robe, the figure has huge hands quite out of proportion with the rest of its slender

Left: ONE OF TWO BRONZE HEADS WITH A MASK OF FINE GOLD LEAF. THE LINE AROUND THE FOREHEAD SUGGESTS THE FIGURE IS WEARING A CAP. IT IS NOTABLY DIFFERENT FROM THE OTHER FIFTY-TWO HEADS FOUND IN THE TREASURE PITS AT SANXINGDUI.

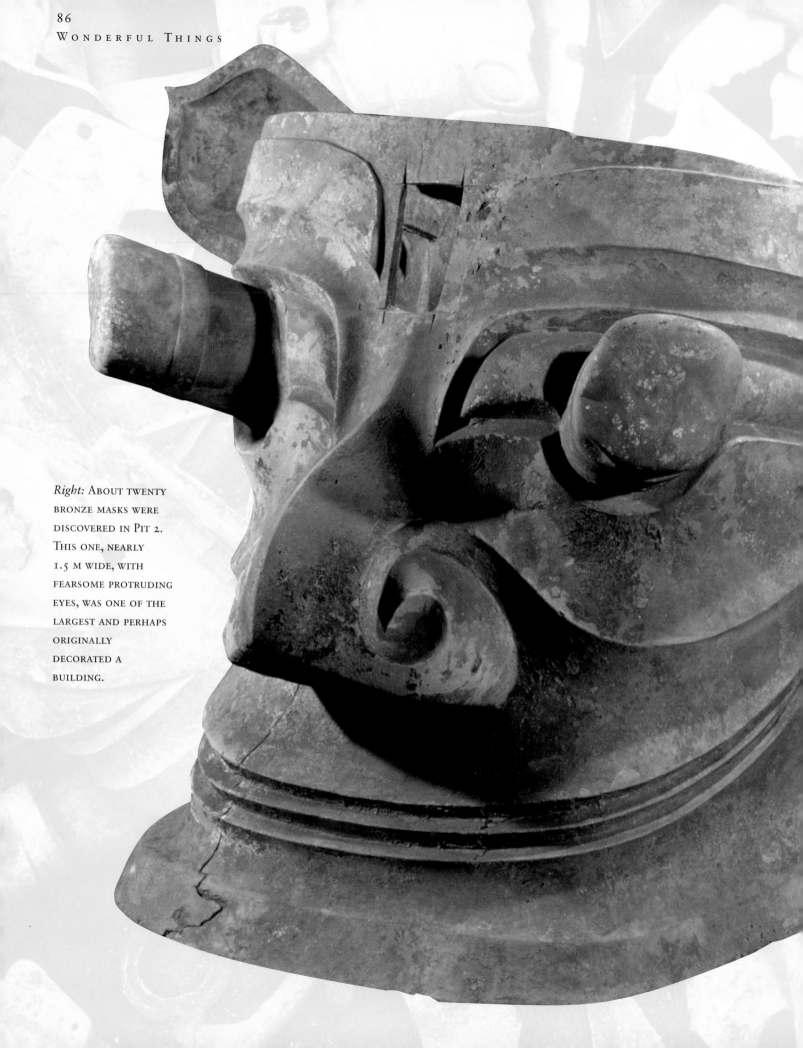

Right: ABOUT TWENTY
BRONZE MASKS WERE
DISCOVERED IN PIT 2.
THIS ONE, NEARLY
1.5 M WIDE, WITH
FEARSOME PROTRUDING
EYES, WAS ONE OF THE
LARGEST AND PERHAPS
ORIGINALLY
DECORATED A
BUILDING.

body. It is possible that they held a curved elephant's tusk, and the whole figure stands on a square base supported by four elephant heads. It had been deliberately broken before being placed in the sacrificial pit. The large bronze heads may originally have been attached to bodies made of more perishable and perhaps less highly valued materials, possibly clay, traces of which are found inside the rather long necks of some specimens. They exhibit a variety of hairstyles, possibly indicative of the presence of different peoples, or of different classes within Sanxingdui society. Some appear to be wearing headdresses. Of the forty-one bronze heads from the second pit two had gold-leaf masks. The heads have large eyes, heavy eyebrows, broad noses and wide, thin-lipped mouths. Their large, protruding ears are pierced as if for earrings. Most of the heads were deliberately damaged or burned prior to being placed in the pits, and some of them bore traces of paint – blackened hair and reddened lips.

In addition to the heads and the statue, many bronze masks were found in the pits. The biggest of three large masks is 1.34 m wide. These masks are grotesque in comparison with the bronze heads. They have bizarre bulging eyes, and many have elaborately decorated projections standing up and out from their noses and foreheads. These fantastic visages may represent a deity whose identity we have yet to discover. The bulging eyes of the masks have led some scholars to suggest that they represent Cancong, the mythical first ruler of the state of Shu, who was described in early historical documents describing Sichuan as having remarkable protruding eyes. The sacrificial pits also contained several smaller animal masks, and a bird's head, over 40 cm high, with a fearsome hooked beak. Birds and elephants appear to have played an especially important role in the cosmology of Sanxingdui. There were also bronze vessels with forms much more reminiscent of the Shang state to the north-east.

The discoveries at Sanxingdui are both fascinating and sobering. They remind archaeologists that there are still many unsolved mysteries awaiting them in the Chinese earth. At the same time they stimulate us to explore the diversity of cultures that made up early Chinese civilization.

The Megiddo Ivories

In the mid-1920s, John D. Rockefeller financed an American excavation with the aim of completely excavating, from top to bottom, the mound of Megiddo, the principal town of the Jezreel Valley in what today is northern Israel. But not even the Rockefeller money could withstand the Great Depression, and the Americans had removed only the top four levels when the general belt-tightening of the time forced them to reduce their efforts to extensive deep soundings in several locations. One of these soundings was on the north side of the mound, where, for many centuries during the Bronze and Iron Ages, stood the main town gate, palaces and other fine buildings of Megiddo's elites.

In about 1400 BC, during the Late Bronze Age, the town's ruling family built themselves a large new palace immediately west of the gate (in the level identified as Megiddo VIII). The well-built edifice centred on a large courtyard that gave access to suites of rooms on three sides. At least one back room served as a kind of treasury, where the excavators discovered a hoard of precious objects made of gold and other expensive materials by master craftsmen of neighbouring civilizations in Egypt and Syria. This palace underwent several rebuildings and some modification in plan over the following several centuries. As part of the palace

in its final form, the builders added to its west side a suite of three rooms, sunk into the ground as a kind of cellar with a single stairway to gain entrance. Here the excavators found a second hoard, this time nearly four hundred pieces of carved ivory, during the spring of 1937.

The Americans came upon this hoard as a mass of objects upon the floor of the first room of the suite, with many other pieces broken in antiquity and scattered across the room. Other riches, like gold pomegranate beads, carnelian beads and alabaster jars (some painted with black and red designs), appeared with the ivories. Many ivories were in poor condition, requiring consolidation with celluloid, sometimes reinforced with tissue paper. But on the whole, the Megiddo ivories seem to have been in a better state than those discovered by a British team at Samaria, the capital of biblical Israel, where 'the most perfect…were found…embedded in a mass of sticky yellowish clay which was evidently composed of disintegrated mud bricks…The ivories in this lump were in a fragile state and as soft as cheese when they were first brought up: after the first ivories were found we removed the earth in sections and let it dry off before attempting to extricate the plaques.'

Although some of the carved ivories are fragments, often small and undistinguished, others are intact and offer glorious testimony to the skills of ivory carvers in the Late Bronze Age. Many of the objects, beautifully ornamented, graced the daily lives of the Megiddo elite families – hair combs with animals beautifully carved into their handles; ducks, human figures or heads, and other decorative devices that once ornamented spoons and cosmetic containers; elaborately carved plaques that served as furniture decoration, gaming boards and pieces, and such like.

A few pieces are even more noteworthy as masterpieces of Canaanite or foreign ivory carving. One of these is a square box made from a single piece of ivory, with lions and griffins carved in very high relief standing along its sides. In style these animal figures belong to a Syrian tradition, but they express forms more at home in Anatolia in the then-recently collapsed Hittite empire. Another piece is entirely Hittite in character, a panel or box lid on which is carved in low relief an extremely complex ritual scene. At the centre of the scene, two figures surmounted by winged solar discs face one another, while their attending retinues surround them. All these figures stand upon the upraised hands of kneeling bull-headed men and other weird beings, who in turn rest upon the upraised hands of a third and then fourth tier of mythological figures, the entire pyramid standing on the backs of lions. Several scholars suggest that this Hittite piece depicts the meeting of two great kings or sun gods, and may even represent the meeting of the Hittite and Egyptian worlds, a collision that dominated the international politics of Syria and Palestine for much of the Late Bronze Age.

The Egyptian side of this confrontation is itself expressed in a number of the Megiddo ivories. Several elongated plaques, fitted with tenons or mortises at the ends for attachment to furniture, depict scenes of chariot warfare, leading away dejected prisoners of war, presenting the spoils of victory to the ruler, and feasting in the subsequent celebration. These scenes carved in low relief contain typical New Kingdom Egyptian images, but as rendered by a local Canaanite artist. Several other ivories bear Egyptian hieroglyphics, including a pen case that belonged to an envoy of the Egyptian pharaoh Ramses III (1184–1152 BC). Whichever way this piece came into the hands of Megiddo's ruling family, it not only confirms the connections with Egypt, but also provides a rough date (around 1150 BC) for the destruction of the palace and the end of the Bronze Age political order at Megiddo.

The end of the Bronze Age world did not bring with it the demise of ivory carving. Indeed, if anything, the artistic apogée of the craft can be found in the products of Phoenician and Syrian artisans during the ninth and eighth centuries BC. Most of these Iron Age ivories have been found in storerooms of palaces in Syria and, in great quantities, Assyria. The previously mentioned ivory hoard from Samaria also came from a treasury within Ahab's palace, the 'ivory house' (1 Kings 22.39) that raised disdain and envy in the hearts of Judaeans to the south. The Iron Age schools of ivory carving specialized in fancily decorated insets for furniture, using various techniques (plaques, openwork, in the round), and sometimes further ornamented with gold leaf and coloured glass insets (cloisonné work).

Left: GRIFFEN CARVED ON AN IVORY PLAQUE FROM MEGIDDO.
Background: EGYPTIAN-INSPIRED SPHINX, PART OF IVORY FURNITURE ORNAMENTATION.
Below: DECORATED IVORY HAIR COMB.

The Splendours of Prehistoric Japanese Pottery

In 1877, archaeological excavations were undertaken at the shell mounds of Omori, between present-day Yokohama and Tokyo, by the American scholar Edward S. Morse. Because of the prevalent decorative technique, that of the impressions of twisted plant fibres pressed into the surface of the vessels, Morse named the pottery he discovered among the shellfish 'cord-marked', translated into Japanese as Jomon. Subsequent investigations of thousands of Jomon period (c. 10000–c. 300 BC) sites have shown that the prehistoric potters of the Japanese archipelago created some of the finest early ceramic treasures the world has seen.

Nearly a century after Morse, the first radiocarbon dates associated with this Jomon pottery provoked a furore in Japanese archaeological circles. Pottery from the Natsushima shell midden overlooking Tokyo Bay suggested that the site was being occupied in 7000 BC. These results rocked the world of Jomon studies, which had hitherto considered the Jomon period to be no more than three thousand years long. Many scholars rejected the newfangled techniques, as had some of their European counterparts when faced with dates that did not fit well-established chronological frameworks based on the cross-dating of types of artefacts. But in 1968 dates from the excavations at Fukui Cave, on the westernmost tip of the southern island of Kyushu, were to prove even more startling. Fragments of thin pottery associated with tiny stone tools were dated to around twelve thousand seven hundred years ago, making it the oldest scientifically dated pottery in the world.

These dates have since been confirmed at other sites, and a full picture of the development of an extraordinary and diverse series of pottery traditions within the Japanese archipelago has emerged through the meticulous study of sherds from excavations throughout the island chain. Some seventy major pottery styles are now recognized, possibly relating to different groups of Jomon peoples, each with a distinct sense of identity, perhaps speaking their own dialects and with their own cultures.

The earliest pottery vessels were cooking pots, and their appearance accompanied a revolution in the diet of the early inhabitants of the Japanese islands. Previously, cooking had been done on hot stones, suitable mainly for cooking steaks. Pottery opened up a whole new culinary world of boiling and steaming, methods well suited to the preparation of vegetable foods, soups and shellfish. As time went on, a whole range of pottery forms developed as increasing attention was paid to the contexts in which food was prepared, served and consumed.

The inhabitants of Japan during the Jomon period were not farmers, but derived their subsistence needs from the natural environment within which they lived. So rich were the pickings to be had from the temperate forests that dominated the landscape, and so abundant the harvests of fish and shellfish from the lakes, rivers and seas, that Jomon people were able to store some of the foodstuffs they collected in the productive seasons for use in winter. In such circumstances pottery storage vessels were invaluable. Storage and the availability of things to eat in the natural larder for most of the year allowed people to live in one place all year round and settled villages appeared, clusters of houses in forest clearings. Some of these settlements were occupied, even if not continuously, for many years. At the huge site of Sannai Maruyama, on the northern tip of Honshu overlooking the Tsugaru Straits and the northern island of Hokkaido, archaeologists have recently discovered the remains of perhaps a thousand houses. On the same site a 'pottery mound' has been discovered, a place where pottery was thrown away, or perhaps carefully deposited after its assigned lifespan. The many layers of pottery within the mound show that pots were being dumped here over a whole millennium.

For a thousand years, between about 2500 and 1500 BC, the potters of central Japan produced some of their most extraordinary and striking works. These deep-bodied vessels, some nearly half a metre tall, were decorated with bold incised lines and, most distinctively, fantastic protruding rim sculptures. These forms were created by applying clay strips to the rims of the vessel. The shapes evoke cockscombs, bejewelled crowns and fire licking the rims of the pots, from which the style derives its name – Flame-style pottery. Many of these vessels have been found along the Japan Sea coast and adjoining inland areas of central Japan. Originally thought by archaeologists to have had ritual functions, the soot with which some are encrusted suggests that these vessels, too, were used for cooking, although cooking and feasting may well also have had a religious significance to the Jomon peoples.

During the course of the later first millennium BC a new style of life appeared in the Japanese archipelago, associated with rice agriculture. These early farmers made different styles of pottery, much less flamboyant than their Jomon predecessors, whose creative designs lingered only in eastern Honshu and Hokkaido, where a gathering and hunting way of life continued the longest.

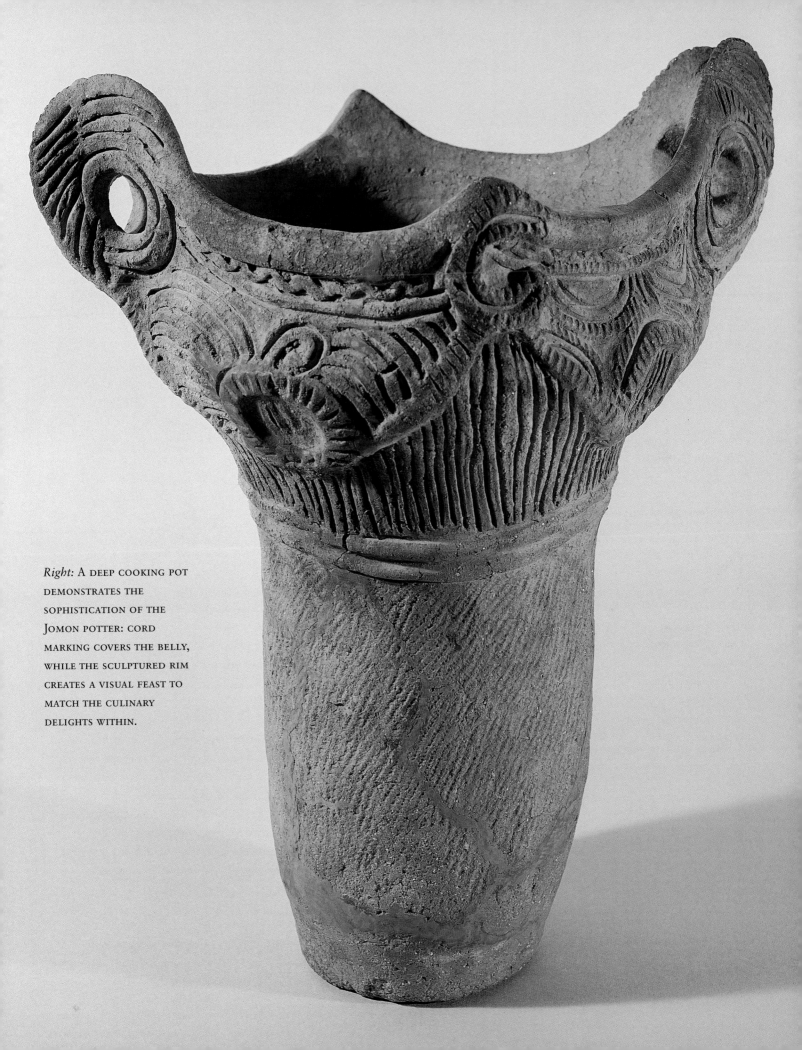

Right: A DEEP COOKING POT
DEMONSTRATES THE
SOPHISTICATION OF THE
JOMON POTTER: CORD
MARKING COVERS THE BELLY,
WHILE THE SCULPTURED RIM
CREATES A VISUAL FEAST TO
MATCH THE CULINARY
DELIGHTS WITHIN.

Scythian Treasures of the Steppes

North of the Black Sea, the steppes of Ukraine and southern Russia were inhabited by horse-riding nomads during the first millennium BC. Known to us through the works of Greek writers like Herodotus, the Scythians also left their mark on the archaeological record in the form of remarkable tombs dug into the firm loess soil and covered over with burial mounds. These tombs have yielded astonishing collections of gold and silver artefacts, along with the horse furnishings, weapons and wagons of a nomadic life.

Left: BRONZE BREASTPLATE EMBOSSED
WITH HEAD OF MEDUSA FROM THE
ELIZAVETINSKAYA TOMB, SIXTH – FOURTH
CENTURY BC.

Scythian tombs typically consist of a deep central shaft, 10–15 m deep, dug into the loess subsoil. At the base of the shaft, a tunnel leads off into a hollowed-out, cavern-like chamber, in which the main burial was placed. Frequently, the chambers were reinforced with massive timbers. Additional alcoves are sometimes found branching off from the main chamber. The grave shaft would then have been filled with earth and rocks, and the burial mound, which could reach a height of 20 m, was heaped up over the top of the shaft by scraping up the black topsoil for some distance around. Additional burials were sometimes added by digging adjacent shafts and either tunnelling into the original burial chamber or hollowing out another.

Unfortunately, the visibility of the burial mounds on the landscape and the ease with which the central burial shaft could be recognized and cleaned out mean that they were the object of looting in ancient times. From about the eighteenth century onwards, 'excavations' were carried out in order to recover the marvellous gold objects in these tombs, although if tsars like Peter the Great had not taken a personal interest in these finds, the Hermitage Museum in St Petersburg might not have the outstanding collection of Scythian artefacts that it does. Modern excavations are often frustrated by the discovery that looters had entered the burial chamber first. Occasionally, however, a tomb is found intact by today's archaeologists.

The most spectacular Scythian finds are gold and silver ornaments and vessels. These are often decorated with representations of animals or of humans engaged in battle, milking or other scenes typical of daily life. Wild animals fighting and warriors in battle are two prominent themes. Yet frequently there are more placid motifs. For example, a silver bowl excavated in the Gaymanova tomb was decorated with a gold-plated frieze of realistic human figures. In one scene, two elderly warriors are engaged in relaxed conversation. They are wearing typical Scythian tunics of fur-trimmed leather. A gold pectoral from the Tolstaya tomb has a variety of motifs, including a child milking a sheep and two men making a garment from a hide.

Although the first evidence of the Scythians in the Caucasus mountains occurs in the eighth century BC, and they had even dominated much of the Near East for twenty-eight years in the seventh century BC, the fourth century BC was truly the 'golden age' of Scythia in the region north of the Black Sea. The landscape along the Dnieper River was dominated by the graves of their elite. From this base, they penetrated into eastern Europe towards the Danube. Yet in 339 BC, Philip II of Macedonia invaded Scythia, and the death in battle of King Ateas led to the collapse of Scythian power. Nevertheless, their rule continued over the region for another century or more. Recent discoveries have shed light on these late Scythians.

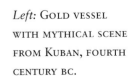

Left: GOLD VESSEL
WITH MYTHICAL SCENE
FROM KUBAN, FOURTH
CENTURY BC.

Below: DETAIL OF A TORC
WITH FIGURES OF HORSEMEN
AS FINIALS.

In 1996, a team of Polish and Ukrainian archaeologists excavated a remarkable late-Scythian tomb at Ryzhanovka, south of Kiev. For the first time in many years, an unlooted tomb of a Scythian chief could be excavated using modern techniques. The layout of the tomb resembles that of a two-room house, with one chamber analogous to a kitchen, with a mock hearth containing bronze kettles, while the other is more like a bedroom, in which the chief's body was placed. The two 'rooms' were separated by a curtain. The kettles on the hearth contained horse and lamb bones, apparently the remains of boiled meat. In the burial chamber, the chief's body was lying on a wooden platform. Around his neck was a gold torc (neckring) with lion-head finials. Nearby were thirty-four gold medallions and over a hundred appliqués that had been the decorations of a headdress, and two silver cups. In fact, two silver cups, decorated by griffins attacking a bull and a deer, were found in a tightly sealed bronze bucket. Outside the entrance to the burial chamber was the body of the chief's retainer, who was probably killed at the time of burial in order to guard the chief in death, and the skeleton of the retainer's horse.

The domestic quality of the Ryzhanovka tomb is intriguing, for it suggests that the late Scythians in the third century BC had adopted a more settled way of life. The mock hearth is considered by the excavators to be particularly indicative of such a transition. Whether or not that was the case, such finds will continue to shed additional light on these fascinating people.

Below: GOLD PECTORAL WITH SCENES OF SCYTHIANS MILKING SHEEP AND MAKING A SHIRT OF ANIMAL SKIN.

Musical Treasures from Ancient China

The 7,000 objects from the tomb of Marquis Yi, of the state of Zeng at Leigudun in China's Hubei Province, include a large number of musical instruments, foremost among which are a complete carillon of sixty-four bronze bells and a set of thirty-two stone and jade chimes, all remarkably preserved in their original positions. These treasures of musical history bring a new dimension to our appreciation of the culture of the Warring States in China (475–221 BC).

The bronze bells hang in three rows from a sturdy, bronze-covered, wooden, L-shaped frame, and were arranged into eight groups according to pitch and size. The carillon has a range of five octaves and each bell is inscribed with the note it plays when struck. The scale for the set is similar to the diatonic in C major. These *bian bells* were the successors to bells from the Shang Dynasty (*c.* 1700–*c.* 1100 BC). An extra bell hung in a very prominent place on the carillon. This was a *fu* bell that had been presented to the marquis by Prince Hui Yang of the state of Chu in 433 BC. The sixty-five bells weigh a total of nearly 3 tonnes and the largest is some 1.5 m high. Unlike previous bells, which were cast in single moulds, the *bian bells* were made using moulds in many different sections. Much of the decoration was added after

the casting was complete. Such bells represent an extremely high level of technological achievement by the Zeng bronzesmiths. These craftspeople were adept at using the lost wax technique (replacing wax inside a clay model with molten bronze) as well as casting using moulds. The stunning results of their expertise include a bronze wine vessel and tray with fine openwork decoration.

Along with the bronzes, Marquis Yi was buried with a set of string and wind instruments, including a sheng pipe, made of eighteen bamboo pipes each with a vibrating reed within, a ten-string zither and a five-stringed instrument. There was also a drum on a remarkable bronze base made out of the intertwined bodies of sixteen large dragons. Beautiful lacquer objects included food containers, some in the form of animals such as stags and ducks. A lacquered chest was decorated with a map of the constellations, with the Big Dipper at the centre. A gold bowl complete with its lid and a ladle with openwork decoration is the largest known gold object from China in the period before 221 BC.

The tomb was discovered in 1978. Some 220 sq m in area and 13 m deep, the tomb comprised of four wooden chambers containing the coffins of the interred, grave goods, including the splendid musical instruments, and in a small rear chamber, weapons and chariot parts. The Marquis was accompanied by all he would need to continue both his courtly and his private life in the world to come.

Historical documents tell us little about the state of Zeng or about Marquis Yi. He lived at a time of political and social upheaval, with China in the grip of endemic warfare between a multitude of small states. The prime position given to the bell presented by the prince of Chu may indicate that Zeng held Chu in some respect. We know that when the marquis died aged about forty-five he was accompanied to his tomb by twenty-one girls aged between fifteen and twenty-one. None of their skeletons bore signs of injury and it is probable that they committed suicide, or perhaps were poisoned. In this the marquis followed in the footsteps of the earliest rulers of China, whose deaths were marked by many human sacrifices. Whatever the marquis's beliefs about the afterlife, his bells and other musical instruments are a bequest whose value cannot be underestimated.

Left: THE CARILLON OF SIXTY-FOUR BRONZE BELLS, BURIED ALONG WITH THE JADE AND STONE CHIMES, ENSURED THAT THE MARQUIS YI WAS ACCOMPANIED IN THE AFTERLIFE BY THE MUSIC THAT HE LOVED.

The Golden Hoard of Tillya Tepe

Afghanistan has long been an archaeological terra incognita, *and large stretches of the country remain so today. Yet, thanks to Russian scholars working during the 1960s and 1970s, northern Afghanistan, or southern Bactria, can be counted among one of the better studied parts of the country. The research of Viktor I. Sarianidi in particular revealed the Bronze Age and Early Iron Age cultures of this region. Almost incidentally to this main focus of his research in Afghanistan, Sarianidi stumbled upon the golden hoard of Tillya Tepe.*

Tillya Tepe is a relatively small, low mound in the Shibarghan oasis, on the left bank of the Amu Darya (or Oxus River), in southern Bactria. Sarianidi first dug there in 1969 and returned in 1971 and 1977, looking for Bronze Age and Early Iron Age settlements. These efforts uncovered a regularly planned rectangular structure with corner towers set upon a high platform. This edifice, which Sarianidi chose to identify as a temple, dates to late in the Bronze Age. After its inhabitants left, the building collapsed and formed the 3-m-high mound of Tillya Tepe. During the early centuries of the first millennium AD, the mound again hosted human activity, this time as the place where a wealthy, perhaps princely, family buried its dead.

Sarianidi had come across no trace of these late burials until his fourth and final season, in the winter of 1978–9. In that final season before Afghanistan's descent into its war with the Soviet Union, Sarianidi found six graves dug into the ruins of the older building. These six burials yielded around twenty thousand artefacts, many of them gold and silver. This wealth forced Sarianidi to dig as quickly and as comprehensively as possible, because he knew that the local treasure hunters, once alerted to the riches of Tillya Tepe, would thoroughly and quickly loot the site. Moreover, the rich grave goods required very careful security and accounting with the Afghan antiquities officials – Sarianidi relates an anecdote of frantic overnight searches for a misplaced object. Despite these obstacles, the Soviet team managed to complete successfully its last season of excavation.

Below: HINGED GOLDEN PLAQUES WITH DEPICTIONS OF ARMED FIGURES, FROM THE TILLYA TEPE CEMETERY.

Above: AN ELABORATELY MADE GOLDEN DIADEM
FROM THE TILLYA TEPE CEMETERY.

The Tillya burials were basic wooden coffins held together with iron clamps and nails. After the body had been placed within it, a shroud on which silver and gold discs had been sewn was wrapped around the coffin. The coffin was then placed at the bottom of simple shafts and roofed over with wooden planks, the rest of the shaft then being filled with soil. Each coffin held the remains of a single person dressed in multiple layers of sumptuous ceremonial garb, heavy with precious metal plaques and pearls attached with golden thread. Elaborately figured diadems, necklaces, rings, earrings, bracelets, hairpins and other gold jewellery, busy with filigree and turquoise inlay, adorned the bodies; one individual even wore golden shoes. Other personal effects were fairly limited – cosmetics, ivory cosmetic containers and other toiletry equipment for women, swords and daggers with scabbards detailed in gold and ivory, arrows and other armaments for men.

Beyond the sheer volume of gold and other precious materials in these graves, the Tillya Tepe burials help reveal the cultural history of Central Asia. Bactria already enjoyed a measure of interaction with Mesopotamia and India during the Bronze Age. The Achaemenid Persians incorporated Central Asia within their empire during the sixth century BC, an empire that Alexander the Great inherited when he routed the great king in a succession of victories. Alexander's generals divided this empire after his death in 323 BC, and Bactria was the seat of a petty Greek dynasty during the third century. This regional political history introduced to Central Asia and northern India numerous elements of Hellenistic art that combined with indigenous forms. The result was the rise of innovative local traditions, like the Gandhara sculpture of north India that combined Buddhist imagery and Hellenistic sensibilities. This cultural background was the context in which the Kushan Dynasty arose from nomadic beginnings to control a vast portion of Central Asia and the northern marches of India.

The worked gold of the Tillya burials, created several centuries after this initial inspiration of Hellenistic art in the east, reveals perhaps an even broader confluence of art traditions. The Hellenistic aspect itself can be found in some characteristic motifs that appear on the goldwork, like cupids riding dolphins, the goddess Aphrodite and scenes from the Dionysos myths (in addition, some objects like intaglio rings and coins are purely Mediterranean). Other motifs, like the hero struggling with beasts, and the mistress of animals, belong to older traditions of the ancient Near East. The Kushan artisans combined these images with animal themes borrowed from the Scythian steppe tradition, and also added colouring from northern India and eastern Central Asia. Although short-lived, the Kushan artistic synthesis possesses a rough vitality – a density of detail and almost capricious use of inlay that overwhelms the eye – that fits its frontier setting, and separates it from its individual cultural sources.

Bronze Bells of Yayoi

Though originally inspired by continental prototypes, the bronze bells of ancient Japan underwent their own unique development. Like the bronze weapons that were also originally imported from China and Korea, they gradually became more and more exaggerated in form as their function changed from practical objects to ritual symbols. As one Japanese archaeologist has put it, the bells changed from 'bells to listen to' to 'bells to look at'.

Bronze bells dating from the Yayoi period (*c.* 400 BC–AD 300) are known as *dotaku*. The Yayoi was the period when full-scale rice farming was first introduced into the Japanese islands. As well as rice, a variety of other objects, techniques and ideas arrived from the Asian mainland. Bronze and iron implements began to be used in Japan at this time, iron arriving slightly before bronze.

Yayoi *dotaku* probably derive from a type of small bronze bell known from the Korean peninsula. These bells have also been found in Kyushu, but most Japanese archaeologists believe that *dotaku* proper were originally produced in the Kinai region around Nara and Kyoto and were never in fact made in Kyushu. Thus the precise beginnings of *dotaku* production remain something of a mystery.

There are around five hundred bronze bells known from the Yayoi period. Most of these were found buried on isolated hillsides well away from Yayoi villages. The lack of associated artefacts makes it very hard for archaeologists to understand the function that the bells served in Yayoi society, though some clues are provided by the context of the bell burial, pictures cast on the bells and incised drawings on Yayoi pottery. The sites where *dotaku* are buried are usually undisturbed and appear to represent the final resting place of the bells. This would seem to rule out an earlier theory that the bells were temporarily buried as part of an annual ritual cycle. However, whether the bells were simply abandoned or buried as some sort of votive offering is unclear.

An important piece of evidence relating to the use of the bells is provided by a drawing inscribed on a Middle Yayoi pottery jar from Inayoshi in Tottori Prefecture on the Japan Sea coast. The drawing contains several features of Yayoi ritual activity, and includes two oval objects suspended from what is probably a tree. Based on historical accounts of a similar custom in ancient Korea, it has been argued that the objects represent *dotaku* that were hung from a tree as part of a community agricultural festival. This interpretation builds on the theory first put forward in the 1950s that since bells are rarely discovered in houses or graves, they were owned and used by whole communities rather than individuals. As social stratification became more pronounced over the course of the Yayoi period, it is possible that *dotaku* dropped out of use as new rituals that bolstered the power of regional chieftains became more widespread.

The earliest Korean-style bronze bells found in Japan are only 10–20 cm high. Over time, however, the *dotaku* became larger and larger, eventually reaching some 135 cm in height and weighing over 45 kg. The earliest have thick, practical handles by which the bell could have been suspended and then struck to produce a musical note, but in later examples the handle becomes thin and covered with ornate attachments. The later bells were designed to be looked at rather than used as musical instruments.

Yayoi bronze bells are found widely distributed across central Japan though they are most common in the Kinai region. *Dotaku* proper have not yet been discovered in Kyushu. The bells were first cast in stone moulds, and later in clay moulds. Several examples of the stone moulds have been excavated from archaeological sites. Some bells are known to have been cast in the same mould, making it possible to trace complex patterns of regional interaction in Yayoi Japan.

Because they are usually buried on remote hillsides, it seems safe to say that finds of *dotaku* are set to increase in the near future. In recent years Japanese corporations have begun large-scale development of previously untouched upland areas, and as a result there have been several notable discoveries of bells. The most spectacular came in October 1996 when thirty-nine bells were found at Kamo Iwakura in Shimane Prefecture. This cache is the most from any site anywhere in the country, and shows that we still have much to learn about the bronze treasures of ancient Japan. A number of the bronze bells are decorated with relief panels showing a limited range of motifs, many of which had particular significance for the Yayoi paddy rice farmers. These include boats and fishermen, rice storehouses, people pounding rice, water birds, dragonflies, hunters with dogs pursuing wild boar, and an animal of special importance, deer. In one scene, three figures appear to be involved in a fight, or in an attempt to prevent one.

Right: THIS
BRONZE BELL
FROM KAGAWA
PREFECTURE HAS
SIX SCENES ON
EACH FACE, WITH
MOTIFS
IMPORTANT IN
THE LIVES OF
EARLY JAPANESE
RICE FARMERS.

Treasures of Zhongshan

The early Chinese state of Zhongshan, which flourished and then vanished over two thousand years ago, has produced treasures from the tombs of its rulers on the northern banks of the Hutuo River in modern Hebei Province that rank among the finest works of art from ancient China.

The rise and fall of Zhongshan is intimately tied to the history of the Warring States period in China (472–221 BC), the second part of the Zhou Dynasty, when power was in the hands of regional overlords, most of whom had at most only the slightest respect for the imperial throne based at Luoyang. In the early fourth century BC the lords of Zhongshan threw off the yoke of the state of Wei by which they had been subjugated some twenty years earlier. They established their capital at Lingshuo, and for the next few decades Zhongshan enjoyed a period of prosperity, becoming a major power in the region with 1,000 war chariots at its command. The Zhongshan people, while sharing many aspects of their culture with the majority Huaxia peoples of the Central Plains, also derived much of their identity from a northern nomadic people called the White Di. The fusion of nomadic and settled cultures in the Zhongshan state was to produce some of the most animated art styles to emerge from this period in Chinese history.

Of the thirty Zhongshan tombs investigated at Lingshuo two are royal. Between them they produced over nineteen thousand artefacts. One of the tombs was that of King Cuo, the third of five kings of Zhongshan to rule at Lingshuo, who died about 310 BC. The king was buried at the bottom of a 15-m shaft at the centre of a tomb that extended nearly 100 m north to south, and only slightly less east to west. When the tomb was excavated, particular excitement was generated by a series of splendid bronzes inlaid with gold and silver. Animals were represented in these pieces, including tigers and dragons. One of the tigers is consuming a deer, its powerful jaws, claws and hindquarters leaving the fate of the deer in no doubt. A writhing mass of dragons, phoenix and deer adorns the base of a support for a rectangular tray. The combination of casting, riveting, welding and inlaying in the manufacture of this piece is a reflection both of the artistic skill of those who produced it and also their patron's appreciation of and desire for luxury items. Other treasures from these tombs include a bronze plate incised with a plan of the underground royal palace, again inlaid with gold and silver. A bronze trident, perhaps a royal standard, was another symbol that referred back to the nomadic origins of Zhongshan. A fine bronze lampstand was also recovered from the tombs. Over 78 cm tall, it held fifteen oil lamps. Birds sit in its branches while monkeys cavort around them to the delight of two human onlookers on the ground. Fine jade pendants and jade figurines with hairstyles reminiscent of those of the White Di were also found.

After its defeat at the hands of neighbouring states Qi and Yan in 296 BC, Zhongshan did not re-emerge on to the tableau of Chinese history until the Western Han period (206 BC–AD 9). In 1968, in Mancheng County, Hebei Province, near a limestone mountain named Lingshan ('Mountain of the Mausoleum'), soldiers of the People's Liberation Army stumbled across a large cave containing many bronzes, jades and pottery vessels. Archaeologists were summoned and soon discovered a second tomb carved out of solid rock. What the soldiers had mistaken for a cave was in fact a huge tomb, 52 m long, over 36 m wide and 7 m high. The tombs consisted of a series of chambers forming a cruciform shape, entered by a long underground passage. On either side of the passage were two long and narrow rooms, the northern one containing foodstuffs and utensils, the southern

one for horses and chariots. A total of ten chariots and thirty horses were placed in the two tombs. The entrance passage led directly into a great central chamber. Once lined with wood, this chamber contained many figurines and rows of pottery, bronze and lacquer vessels.

Sealed off behind a white marble door was the burial chamber itself. Lying on a white marble bed, exposed now that the wooden coffin had collapsed, lay the best preserved jade burial suit yet discovered in China. From inscriptions on the bronze vessels, and through what was known about Zhongshan at this time, archaeologists surmised that they had discovered the tombs of Liu Sheng, Prince Jing of Zhongshan, one of the sons of Emperor Jing Di (154–141 BC), and his wife Dou Wan. It was known that Liu Sheng had died in 113 BC.

Liu Sheng's jade suit was made up of 2,498 pieces, each carefully shaped to fit the part of the body they were intended to cover, and joined to each other at the corners by thin gold threads, the finest of which were less than one-tenth of a millimetre in diameter. Over a kilogram of gold was needed to tie Liu Sheng's suit together. All this effort was intended, unsuccessfully, to prevent the body from decomposing. Along with the jade burial suits, the deceased had been interred with over two thousand eight hundred objects, including some splendid inlaid and gilt-bronzes, continuing the tradition of luxurious grave goods seen in the tombs of earlier rulers of Zhongshan.

The tombs of the rulers of Zhongshan demonstrate the desire that regional rulers had for prestige in death as well as in life, and their need to be accompanied into the afterlife by all the luxurious trappings of their worldly existence. The demands of these elite patrons stimulated the creativity of their artisans and resulted in the production of objects that still today are regarded as being of remarkable artistic merit.

Left: THE INLAID BRONZE TIGER SHOWN EATING A DEER ENCAPSULATES THE VITALITY OF MUCH ZHONGSHAN ART.
Following page: THE MULTITUDE OF JADE PIECES, SEWN TOGETHER BY OVER A KILOGRAM OF GOLD THREAD, WERE INTENDED TO SECURE SOME KIND OF IMMORTALITY FOR LIU SHENG.

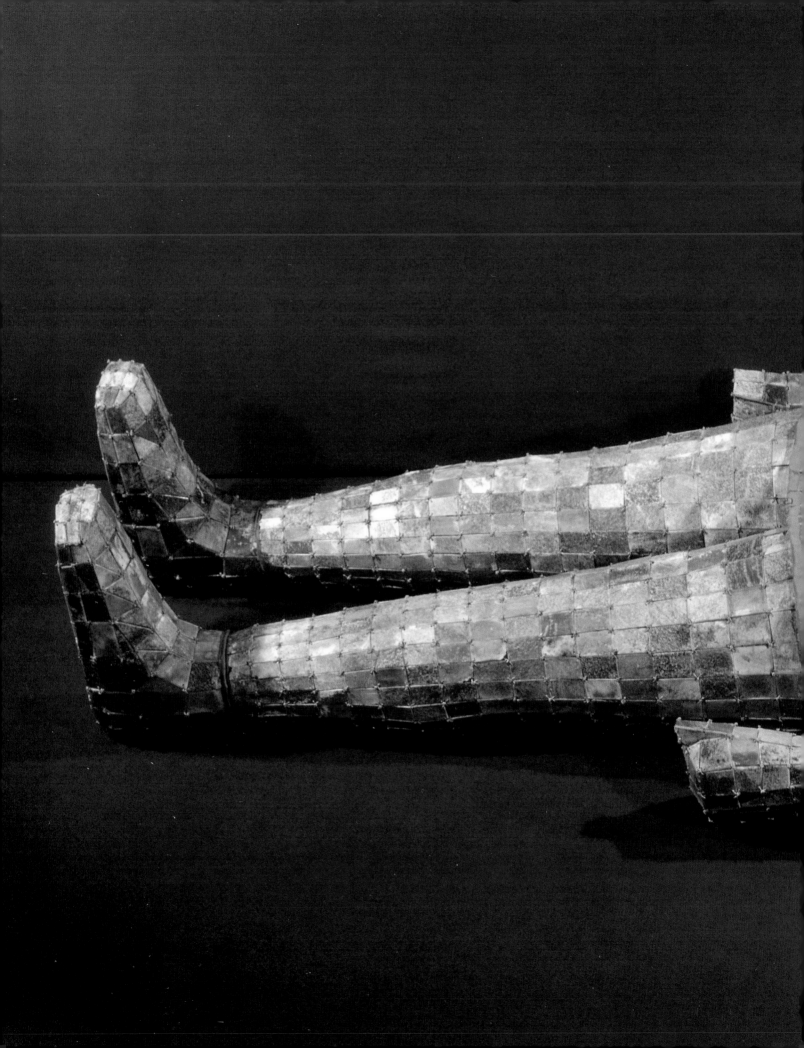

Ancient Scripts from East Asia

Most treasures discovered by archaeologists are mute testimony to the greatness of bygone ages. On occasion, however, a discovery is made that provides a more direct voice from the past, such as the 2,000-year-old letters written by Roman soldiers posted at Vindolanda on Hadrian's Wall in northern Britain (see p. 182). At the other end of Eurasia a series of recent such discoveries is casting new light on what people in the early empires of East Asia were doing and thinking.

Excavations carried out by archaeologists from the Hunan Provincial Museum from 1971 to 1974 at Mawangdui, 3 km east of the city of Changsha, uncovered three remarkable tombs, the burial ground of the family of Li Cang, prime minister of Changsha and marquis of Da in the second century BC. Over a thousand objects were recovered, including books painted on silk, bamboo strips detailing the contents of the tombs, fabrics, musical instruments, statues, a wealth of lacquerware and many other treasures. In Tomb 3 were books written on silk, comprising over twenty titles long thought to have been lost in antiquity, written down in some 120,000 ideographic characters. Works included versions of the Taoist philosophical tracts of Lao Zi, which differ in a number of respects from other extant versions. Another was the Confucian classic, the *I Ching* or Book of Changes, the book that sets out the origin of all things as lying in the interaction of two powers, the masculine and positive yang and the feminine and negative yin, ideas that have influenced Chinese thinking through the ages. Astronomy, astrology, calendrics, medicine and horses are among the subjects of other volumes. In addition, maps and charts show the area around Changsha, with rivers, cities, villages and garrisons, even population numbers and distances. These extraordinary finds are of the utmost importance for understanding the state of knowledge and thought at the beginning of the great Han empire.

In 62 BC, the Han emperor Xuan Di sent 300 troops to a place called Qoco, modern Turfan in Xinjiang, China's most westerly province. The hot and arid conditions that prevail in the Turfan basin, at 46 m below sea level the lowest place in Asia, have preserved unique records of subsequent Chinese activity at this outpost on the Silk Road. The silk routes along which camel trains moved precious goods between China and the west flourished in the Western Han (206 BC–AD 24) and Tang (AD 618–907) periods, when powerful rulers of a unified Chinese empire based at Chang'an were able to extend their western borders. The western reaches of the Great Wall of China passed this way, and the desert has preserved military documents from the wall garrisons. Tombs at Astana and Karakhoja, near the now ruined desert city of Qoco, contained the remains of thousands of documents written on silk. These documents had been used as material to dress the dead and for mattresses and pillows. They include personal correspondence, business contracts, literary classics and official documents. Trade flourished in the markets of Turfan and many transactions are recorded: one customer bought nearly 23 kg of silk and 283 gm of gold. In the Tang Dynasty the movement of travellers was strictly controlled. Travel permits have been discovered, one documenting a trader's journey from Turfan to Hami.

The Heijo palace lies at the centre of the eighth-century capital of Japan in Nara. The city was laid out on a grid pattern, in imitation of the great Tang capital at Chang'an, as Chinese influence spread throughout much of East Asia. Until excavations at the site began in 1961, it was considered that most historical documents relating to this early stage in the development of the Japanese state, notably the court histories *Nihongi* and *Nihon Shoki*, were already well known and that there was little more historical evidence of the period to discover. So when forty-one wooden tablets, or *mokkan*, bearing ink inscriptions, were found at the site in 1962, scholars were delighted. Since then, more than thirty-five thousand such tablets have been recovered from over a hundred sites. The majority of these tablets are between 10 and 30 cm long, although some are over a metre in length. Most are about 5 mm thick, but a good proportion are just shavings, planed off so that the tablet can be reused. The subjects with which the tablets deal are very varied: some relate to the movement of goods and people; others are records from government offices; there are labels to accompany goods for market or taxes; passports and even the announcement of the search for an escaped horse. Some bear the same characters, repeated over and over again, used for handwriting practice by government officials striving to improve their calligraphy.

These written treasures provide invaluable new information about the realities of everyday life and the state of language and knowledge in the early empires of East Asia.

Right: EXTRAORDINARY CONDITIONS HAVE PRESERVED WRITTEN TREASURES FROM ANCIENT EAST ASIA: BAMBOO WRITING STRIPS *(top left),* SOMETIMES BOUND INTO BOOKS *(bottom left)* FROM HAN CHINA (AD 225–220). WOODEN TABLETS FROM THE HEIJO PALACE SITE, NARA, JAPAN, RECORD DRIED SHARK AND SALT *(left)* AND HANDWRITING PRACTISE *(right).*

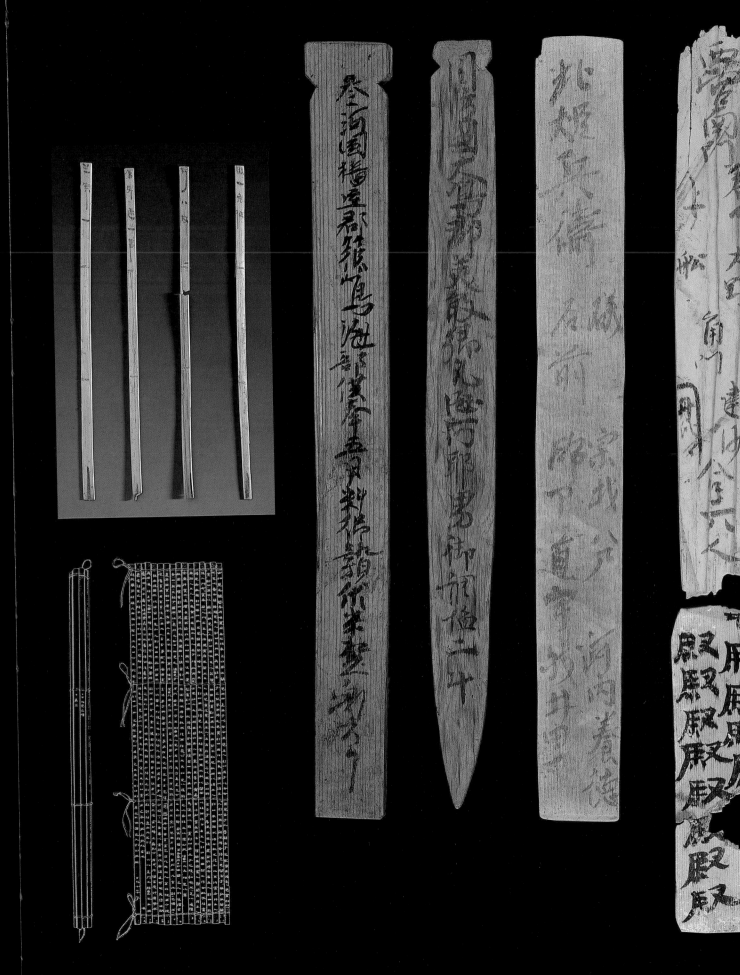

The Funeral Masks of Tashtyk

The clay masks of Siberia's Tashtyk Culture are remarkable examples of likenesses made to fit over the face of the deceased. As such, and especially in view of their rarity – only a few dozen masks and fragments have survived – they are priceless relics that allow a glimpse of the actual appearance of these little-known people.

The Tashtyk Culture flourished in the Minusinsk Basin, in southern Siberia, from the first century BC to the sixth century AD. Primarily pastoralists, these people buried their dead in burial vaults and graves. The deceased were transformed into mummies with their organs and ashes inside them, but it is the masks that really make the Tashtyk funerary practices stand out. The first specimens were found in 1883 by the Russian archaeologist Alexander Adrianov.

The early stage of the culture is characterized by simple pit burials, which occur in cemeteries of up to several hundred graves, each holding two to four bodies. The graves take the form of rectangular holes, 1.5–3 m deep, with their floor and walls covered with birch bark. A framework of logs was placed on the floor; then, after the dead were placed inside, the whole thing was covered with logs, birch bark and soil, with a very low mound on the surface.

The culture's later phase is characterized by burial vaults (though they coexisted with the simple graves for some time). These were marked on the surface by oval mounds of stones and earth, usually in groups of two to four, either next to the cemeteries of pit graves or far from them. These vaults range from small (for ten to forty people) to very large (for a hundred people or even more). They are rectangular, about 1 m deep, but covering an area of 16–90 sq m. The walls, floor and ceiling comprised complex constructions of logs, consolidated with stone slabs. The very big examples also had a special entrance, with stairs or a passage. The whole thing was covered with birch bark, and the surface mound took the shape of a small pyramid. After the vault had gradually been filled with bodies, it was set alight, presumably to cut all links between the world of the dead and that of the living.

Obviously, graves could only be dug in the warm season in the Siberian climate, so dead bodies must have been kept somewhere during the cold season, and two methods were developed for storing them: mummification and cremation. In cases of cremation, the ashes were subsequently inserted into a mannequin. Mummification was carried out on women and teenagers, but only very rarely on men. Both mummies and mannequins received masks. The ashes of cremated men were collected into bags of leather or birch bark. The mannequins (known as 'funerary dolls') were made of leather, and filled with dry grass; the bag of the deceased's ashes was inserted, and then the doll was dressed in real, everyday clothes. Genuine hair or a scalp was sometimes attached, and a face was designed that imitated the masks on the mummies – masks are very rare on the early dolls and, where they exist, they are much cruder, apparently showing not a real person but a generalized human.

In the pit graves, both mummies and mannequins had pillows of wood, stone or wool beneath their heads, and were accompanied by numerous wooden vessels (there are also one or

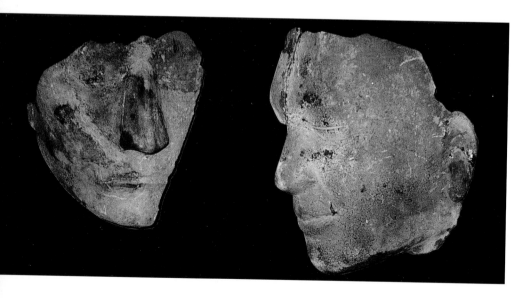

Above: TASHTYK MASKS IN MINUSINSK MUSEUM, SIBERIA.

Left: FUNERARY MASK OF A WOMAN,
TASHTYK CULTURE.

wrinkles and hair on the inside), or sometimes sculpted after death.
Made of a mixture of porcelain clay, gypsum, limestone powder
and quartz sand, they were painted red and black; a few late
specimens also had green and light blue paint applied sparingly.
Women's masks had red spirals or other patterns on the forehead,
temples, cheeks and chin, while males had black patterns on a
solid red background. These patterns may perhaps represent
tattoos that the deceased bore in life.

Occasionally, towards the end of the period, eyelashes, bead
necklaces and pendants were also represented. While some masks
were just of the face, others were bigger and included the ears and
neck, too. Moreover, it appears that, towards the end of the
period, the ritual of cremation was spreading to all adults, and
that masks were being placed not only on mummies but also on to
nearly all dolls. The technique was changing slightly: the people
had begun to make casts, to sculpture the masks right on the dolls'
faces, and even to make whole sculpted busts.

It has been suggested that the masks may have been made to
prolong the life of the deceased's soul, or – as in some communities
in northern Siberia, which buried their dead with the face wrapped
in a fur mask – to wall the deceased off from the world of the
living. But whatever their purpose, the Tashtyk masks represent
beautifully crafted examples of sophisticated and realistic
sculpture.

two clay specimens) grouped at their feet, containing meat, drink
and grain for the afterlife. The graves have also provided abundant
details about clothing and decoration in this culture. The vaults,
having been burned, obviously provide far less detail, but they
contain a wide variety of clay vessels and many charred wooden
objects such as tableware, art objects, boxes, tables and chests.

The mummies' masks are thought to be faithful, individu-
alized likenesses of the people whose faces they covered,
especially as they display not only Mongoloid but
also European features, as is still typical of
the Shor and Khakass people in the
area today. They were
either made on
the face as death
masks (some have
imprints of

Above: RECONSTRUCTION OF TASHTYK GRAVES, AFTER BARANOV
AND VADETSKAYA.

The Dead Sea Scrolls

Above: SINCE THEIR DISCOVERY, SCHOLARS HAVE BEEN PATIENTLY RECONSTRUCTING THE OFTEN-FRAGMENTARY SCROLLS.
Left: THE CAVE – RIDDLED HILLS AROUND THE DEAD SEA.
Below: MANY OF THE SCROLLS WERE PLACED FOR SAFE-KEEPING IN CLAY JARS SUCH AS THESE.
Opposite page: PART OF THE GREAT ISAIAH SCROLL.

The story of the discovery of the Dead Sea Scrolls, perhaps the most famous archaeological find from the Holy Land, is a classic of the 'accidental-discovery-by-small-boy' genre. According to the story, which has undoubtedly been elaborated in the retelling, in 1947 a shepherd boy, Mohammed Dib of the Ta'Amira bedouin tribe, was looking for a lost lamb in the steep cliffs of the north shore of the Dead Sea. A speculative stone thrown into a small cave produced not the expected noise but a metallic rumble. Mohammed returned with two friends to this cave, which they found to contain clay jars, which they eagerly smashed expecting to find gold treasure within. They must have been disappointed to find that the jars held not gold but scrolls of leather and papyrus.

With no great expectation of reward, the better-looking of the fragments were taken to Bethlehem from where they found their way, via antiquities dealers, into the hands of various collectors. These included the Orthodox archbishop of Jerusalem, in whose possession various items were noticed by visiting American scholars. The most remarkable of the items held by the archbishop was the earliest known copy of the Book of Isaiah in the form of a 7-m-long leather scroll.

The recognition of the importance of this material led to a systematic search of the caves above the Dead Sea, in which further fragments were found. Interestingly, a more widespread archaeological survey of the Dead Sea area resulted in the discovery of the site of Khirbet Qumran, which seems to have been a sort of Jewish monastic community of a sect called the Essenes. Founded some time towards the end of the second century BC, this sect seems to have lived by a specific set of rules, and had as one of their main activities the copying of biblical texts – excavations at Qumran revealed a scriptorium where such copying took place. It is likely that the community fled or was disbanded around AD 68, at the time of the First Jewish Revolt against the Romans.

It would have been natural for the community to hide their most precious possessions – their holy books – and it is tempting to think that the Dead Sea Scrolls, none of which is later than about AD 70, and which included not only biblical texts but also a rule book for a community called the 'Manual of Discipline', are the hidden library of the Essenes.

Treasures from Early Korean Royal Tombs

Below: A GOLD CROWN FROM ONE OF THE ROYAL TOMBS AT KYONGJU. MADE OF CUT SHEET GOLD AND 27.5 CM HIGH, THE CROWN IS ADORNED WITH A SHOWER OF CURVED JADES.

The tombs of the rulers of the kingdom of Silla dominate the centre of the Korean city of Kyongju, their capital for nearly a thousand years. These royal burials were designed to foil even the most determined looters, with the result that many of them have remained intact. One of the most important, known as the Tomb of the Heavenly Horse, contained over one hundred and forty funerary objects made up of over eleven thousand component parts.

The tomb comprised a wooden chamber, built at ground level, around which was laid a protective layer of cobbles set in clay, over which was thrown up a tall earthen mound some 57 m in diameter. Inside the burial chamber was a stone platform, on which was placed a coffin. Gold and birch-bark caps adorned the platform, but it was inside the coffin that the real treasures lay. Along with the body of the king, which had long since decomposed, were the items he was to take with him to the afterlife. The kings of Silla were buried in lavish style, with large quantities of gold. The occupant of the Tomb of the Heavenly Horse had a fine gold crown, pendants, a ceremonial girdle, bracelets and rings. On his feet he wore a pair of gilt-bronze shoes, probably originally lined with silk. Also in the burial chamber was a chest containing metal vessels, pottery and riding equipment, including saddles and birch-bark saddle-flaps, on each of which were painted the eponymous winged white horse.

The kingdom of Silla, traditionally founded in 57 BC, was one of several states that arose on the Korean peninsula in the first century BC. The discovery of the aptly named Gold Crown Tomb in 1921 brought Silla to the attention of archaeology, and the exquisite goldwork that characterizes many of the royal tombs has ensured lasting fame. Korean goldsmiths became expert in the use of thinly rolled gold foil and fine gold wire, a technique perhaps learnt from craftsmen from the Chinese commandery at Lelang, which finally fell in AD 313. As well as gold, armour, farming tools, storage jars, iron ingots and pottery were all committed to the burials as grave goods. Silla was the most successful of the early Korean states, taking over the iron-rich enclave of Kaya in AD 562, followed by Paekche to the west in 663. In 668, with the assistance of armies from Tang China, Silla overcame its northern neighbour Koguryo, which is famous for its many lavishly painted tombs, so unifying the Korean peninsula for the first time.

Silla society was rigidly hierarchical, the kings coming from the two highest ranking lineages and the rest of the population being divided into six ranks, three aristocratic, three commoner. The rulers of Silla appreciated luxury objects from abroad as well as the products of their own goldsmiths. Glass was especially highly regarded. A cobalt-blue cup from Syria was found in the Tomb of the Heavenly Horse, while a Chinese stemmed cup of brown and white glass, an Iranian faceted cup and a Syrian glass

Above: THE SILVER CROWN, ORIGINALLY ENCRUSTED WITH PRECIOUS STONES, ILLUSTRATES THE PRIVILEGED WORLD OF EARLY KOREAN ELITE SOCIETY.

wall paintings was being repaired, the tomb of King Munyong is one of very few royal burials from Paekche on the Korean peninsula to have survived intact. Unlike the impenetrable tombs of Silla, most Paekche royal tombs were looted in antiquity.

Paekche was founded in 18 BC by people fleeing the onslaught of the state of Koguryo in northern Korea. Paekche fostered close relations with the Liang Dynasty, which ruled the southern part of China from AD 502 to 557. The brick tomb of King Munyong was constructed just like those of the Liang Dynasty and, along with the Chinese ceramics it contained, reflects the considerable degree of southern Chinese influence on the kingdom. The arched burial chamber was entered via an entrance passage. Both were constructed using hard-fired grey bricks decorated with lotus designs, some of which were inscribed stating how they were made to resemble bricks in Liang-controlled areas of China.

The items with which King Munyong and his consort were buried at first appear a little modest in comparison with the splendour of the Silla tombs. And yet some five thousand gold objects were recovered from the tomb. The fine porcelain lamps that lit it, the fearsome tomb-guardian of Chinese derivation and the funerary furniture show a degree of craftsmanship that compares favourably with their more showy counterparts in Kyongju. The heads and feet of the king and queen rested on elaborately decorated wooden pillows, that of the king being decorated with gold sheet hexagons. The royal couple were buried in clothes covered in gold floral ornaments and small beads. A fine bronze mirror, a gold hairpin in the shape of a bird, a pair of gold earrings and gold ornaments for the now-perished silk crown lay near the final resting place of the king, whose only mortal remains comprised a single tooth. The queen wore a girdle from which hung a long silver pendant and a pair of small glass figurines and a pair of silver bracelets. Like her husband, all that was left behind for posterity of the queen's body was a tooth. Most importantly, two inscribed stone plaques leave no doubt as to the identity of the occupants of the tomb: 62-year-old King Munyong, who died in May 523, and his queen, who died in February 529.

ewer were recovered from the great twin-mounded Tomb of Hwangnam-ni. The ewer had been repaired using gold wire before burial, indicating the high regard in which this object was held by its owner. This same tomb also contained some of the finest examples of silverware from Silla, including a cup decorated with repoussé zoomorphic designs, like those found on the hilt of the sword of King Munyong of Paekche.

The brick tomb of King Munyong of the kingdom of Paekche in south-west Korea sits on a low hill on the northern edge of the city of Kyongju, the capital of Ungjin established in AD 47. Discovered by accident while the drainage around a tomb with

The Treasure House of Ancient Japan

A magnificent wooden building located behind Nara's famous Todaiji temple, the Shosoin, was the storehouse for the treasures of the emperors of ancient Japan. Although the objects are now housed in a modern, air-conditioned building, the Shosoin and its treasures remain as eloquent testimony to the cosmopolitan elegance of the Nara court.

During the Nara and Heian periods (eighth to twelfth centuries AD), each province and county of Japan had its own *shosoin* for the storage of rice and other goods collected as tax. Over time, however, these provincial *shosoin* have all been lost, leaving only the large building originally owned by the Todaiji temple in Nara. The Nara Shosoin is a wooden construction built of Japanese cypress, some 33 m long, 9.4 m wide and 14 m high. The floor is raised nearly 3 m off the ground by forty massive wooden pillars. The building, which dates from the mid-eighth century, is divided into three sections known as the North, Central and South. The North and South sections are built in the distinctive *azekura* log-house style. The Shosoin was owned by the Todaiji temple until the end of the nineteenth century, but is now controlled by the Imperial Household Agency.

There are two main categories of objects in the Shosoin. The first category comprises items used by Emperor Shomu (724–49), which were dedicated to the Todaiji by his widow Empress Komyo in 756. The second category is objects owned and used by the

pearl inlay of a musician on a camel. A white cut-glass bowl was
almost certainly made in Persia, and is similar to a bowl excavated
from a sixth-century tomb mound attributed to the Yamato king
Ankan. A wooden bow used for a game in which balls were shot
instead of arrows has charming ink paintings of ninety-six circus
performers along its length. A series of elaborately carved masks
was used in *gigaku* dance performances, which involved a set stock
of characters including a lion, a drunken Persian king and a
barbarian from South-east Asia. Preserved in the Shosoin are 170
of these masks.

The influence of the Silk Road is visible in the materials and
motifs used for the Shosoin treasures. A group of knives has
handles made of rhinoceros horn, which would have been
imported from China. The figures and animals found on a variety
of objects show strong links with the artistic traditions of China
and Central Asia. A folding screen, for example, depicts a beautiful
woman standing under a tree. Although this motif is of Persian
origin, the woman is dressed in the fashions of Tang China.

The Shosoin treasures were rehoused in a specially built
modern storehouse in the early 1960s. An annual exhibition of a
selection of the treasures has attracted huge crowds to the Nara
National Museum every autumn since 1949, and 1998 marked the
fiftieth anniversary of the exhibition.

Todaiji in various Buddhist ceremonies and rituals. The majority of
these also date to the eighth century but were probably donated to
the Shosoin several centuries later during the middle of the Heian
period. Detailed records also preserved in the Shosoin list many of
the treasures, and where and when they were used.

The Shosoin treasures number at least ten
thousand, any more precise figure being complicated
by disagreements over how to count composite or
fragmentary items. They include furniture, musical
instruments, masks, mirrors, rugs, clothing, ceramics,
glassware, screens, medicines, incense burners and
other Buddhist paraphernalia, maps and documents,
and weapons and armour. Although most of the objects
were made in Japan, some show the influence of exotic
places far off along the Silk Road – China, India and
Persia.

Among the most famous of the Shosoin treasures are a
five-stringed *biwa* lute made of sandalwood with a mother-of-

Ikor and the Ainu Bear Ceremony

Objects that one society regards as treasure may have quite different meanings and values in another place and time. An example of this phenomenon is provided by the Ainu ikor – swords, lacquerware, brocades and other items that were imported from Japan and China and used in the Ainu bear ceremony.

The Ainu are the indigenous people of Hokkaido, the northernmost island of Japan. Biologically, the Ainu appear to be derived from the people of the Jomon period and thus may once have lived throughout the Japanese islands. The term 'Ainu Culture', however, is usually reserved for Hokkaido and neighbouring regions from about the twelfth century AD. From this time, intensive trading and other contacts with the Japanese and the peoples of Manchuria led to major changes in late prehistoric Hokkaido, which resulted in the basic pattern of Ainu Culture as known ethnographically. From the early medieval era, the Ainu also began to expand out of Hokkaido into southern Sakhalin and the Kuril Islands.

A central feature of Ainu Culture is the *iomante* or bear ceremony in which a bear cub is captured and raised before being ritually killed and eaten to ensure the continued plentiful supply of game. Bear rituals of various types were widely distributed across ancient North-east Asia. In Japan, the Jomon period has produced some evidence for what have been interpreted as 'sending-back' rituals in which – as in the *Ainu iomante* – the souls of hunted animals were sent back to the spirit world.

At least three Jomon sites, Higashi-kushiro, Mawaki and Idogawa, have regular alignments of dolphin, boar and deer skulls that may represent such ceremonies. During the Satsumon and Okhotsk Cultures that immediately preceded the Ainu period in Hokkaido, bear rituals became more developed. Okhotsk Culture pit houses are particularly well known for their piles of bear skulls,

but the precise relationship with the *Ainu iomante* is still a subject of debate.

The Ainu bear ceremony in its modern form seems to have become established by the eighteenth century. From around this time, paintings produced by Japanese visitors to Hokkaido illustrate the various stages of the *iomante* in great detail. These paintings also show the way Chinese brocades and beads and Japanese swords and lacquerware were used as offerings to the

THE BEAR CEREMONY PLAYED A CENTRAL ROLE IN AINU SOCIETY AS SHOWN IN THESE JAPANESE ILLUSTRATIONS.

bear, arranged on the altar set up around the dead animal. These ikor treasures were obtained through trade with the Japanese and Manchurians. The Ainu traded animal furs, dried fish and other marine products, and eagle feathers for arrows in exchange for the ikor, as well as for more utilitarian items such as iron pots.

Archaeological study of the *ikor* is hampered by the fact that brocades and lacquerware are not usually well preserved in Ainu sites. Furthermore, many *ikor* appear to have been too valuable to bury in the ground. Instead they were handed down from generation to generation, perhaps only entering the archaeological record when they were replaced by new treasures.

The *iomante* is held during the winter. It is a major ceremony involving all the members of a particular Ainu village and often people from nearby settlements as well. The *ikor* were offered as 'gifts' to the bear to take back to the spirit world. At the same time, however, these gifts also helped to promote the social status of the individuals who gave them. Ainu who gave many treasures became the most respected members of their communities since they were regarded as being the most respectful towards the spirits. That the accumulation of *ikor* did not lead to even greater social divisions within Ainu society can perhaps be explained by the disruption to Ainu society caused by Japanese merchants and by the fact that Ainu groups on Sakhalin usually moved to new settlements during the winter, making it inconvenient to collect too many possessions.

Treasures
of
Australasia

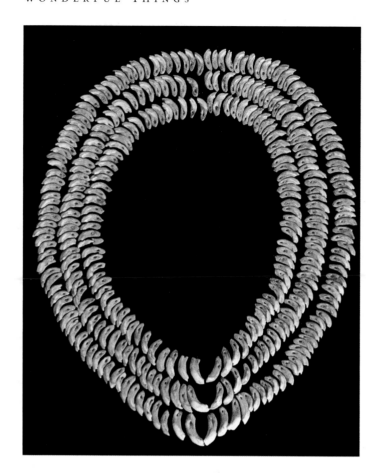

Left: A NECKLACE MADE FROM MORE
THAN THREE HUNDRED KANGAROO AND
WALLABY TEETH FOUND IN A 7,000-YEAR-
OLD BURIAL NEAR COOMA, NEW SOUTH
WALES.

Valuable Goods in Australia and the Pacific

The societies of Australia and the Pacific did not use metal before the arrival of Europeans in the region. The European idea of treasure, centred as it is on precious metals such as gold, is therefore not appropriate here. Nevertheless, these societies did, and often still do, give value to highly prized objects, perhaps because they were made from particular materials or required great skill to make. Like gold in European society, these objects were more likely to continue in circulation than to enter the archaeological record, unless under very exceptional circumstances.

Valuables are rarely found in archaeological sites in Australia and the Pacific. They were often made of perishable materials: examples include possum-skin cloaks in Australia, and bird-of-paradise plumes in New Guinea. Moreover, they were much more valuable for trading purposes. Commonly, valuables circulated in complex exchange networks. A key feature of these systems was that wealth was not simply hoarded. The participants acquired prestige through the ability to pass on precious commodities. Occasionally, valuable objects are found in association with burials. A recent example was an elaborate necklace of 327 pierced kangaroo and wallaby teeth found in the grave of a young man and an older woman interred together about seven thousand years ago near Cooma in New South Wales. The necklace required the killing of at least one hundred and twenty-six kangaroos and wallabies. Two comparable examples of burials with necklaces made from large numbers of Tasmanian devil teeth are known from the Darling River area. These necklaces must have been precious items, expensive to make in terms of labour and time.

Stone for making implements and weapons was very important to people without metal. Some raw materials were particularly highly valued and might be traded over very long distances. In New Zealand, greenstone, or nephrite, was used for tools, such as adzes and chisels, weapons, such as clubs, and for personal adornments. It was worked by sawing it into a rough

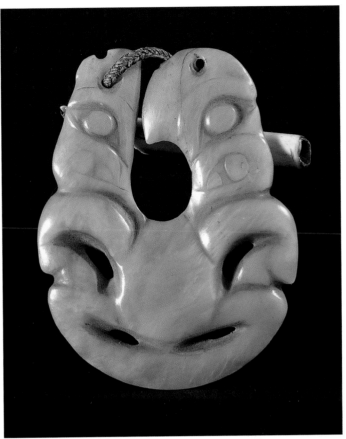

Above: VALUABLE PERSONAL
ADORNMENTS SUCH AS HEI
TIKI (*above*) AND HEI MATAU,
OR FISH HOOK, PENDANTS
(*above right*) WERE MADE OF
GREENSTONE. BOTH OF THESE
WERE ORIGINALLY OWNED BY
MAORI CHIEFS.

shape. The artefact was then further shaped by grinding and
finished off by polishing. These techniques seem to have been
perfected only in the last few hundred years, and greenstone seems
to have been particularly esteemed during the most recent period
of Maori prehistory. Indeed, it has been suggested that the desire
for greenstone may have contributed to the increase in warfare at
this time.

In south-eastern Australia, too, greenstone (andesite, or
amphibole hornfels) was highly valued for making ground stone
hatchets. Raw material from quarries such as Mount William in
Victoria was traded very widely. In some cases, Aboriginal people
travelled considerable distances to obtain stone from the owners of
the quarry. In the nineteenth century, the anthropologist A. W.
Howitt recorded that three pieces of greenstone could be obtained
in exchange for a possum-skin cloak. Such cloaks were very
valuable items, as they were intricately decorated and required a
considerable amount of skill and labour to produce. Greenstone
and other valuables circulated in elaborate trading networks, and
might travel very long distances. In Arnhem Land, in the Northern
Territory, the Ngilipitji quarry was a highly valued source of stone
for making blades for spearpoints. Parcels of these blades have
been recorded hundreds of kilometres from their source.

Wooden Combs from Kauri Point Swamp

In the early 1960s, archaeologist Wilfred Shawcross made a remarkable discovery while excavating in a swamp at Kauri Point in New Zealand's North Island. The waterlogged deposits preserved a range of organic materials, including a unique collection of ornamental wooden combs. It seems likely that the site was a repository for the safe disposal of tapu, *or sacred, objects.*

Above: THIS TATTOOED MAORI MAN WEARS AN ORNAMENTAL COMB IN HIS TOPKNOT AND AN EAR PENDANT AND A HEI TIKI.
Right: THE COLLECTION OF WELL-PRESERVED WOODEN COMBS EXCAVATED FROM KAURI POINT SWAMP IS UNIQUE.

Kauri Point *pa* is a fortified settlement on a peninsula that juts into Tauranga Harbour. The site is defended on one side by a narrow, steep-sided gully with a swamp at the base. Shawcross excavated in this swamp in the hope of finding organic artefacts preserved in the waterlogged deposits. The results were very successful and provide a glimpse of an important aspect of Maori life.

The main structure in the swamp was a small rectangular enclosure or platform that had been built out into the swamp. This was associated with a dense concentration of artefacts, including fragments of obsidian, wooden combs, pieces of gourds and wooden vessels, and musical instruments. Many of the artefacts had been deliberately broken. The obsidian flakes seem to have been placed in bags. These objects were deposited in the swamp over some two hundred years beginning about AD 1500.

The wooden combs are a unique collection, and Shawcross's study of them provided the clue to his interpretation of the site. Over three hundred almost complete combs and large fragments were found, as well as more than a thousand individual teeth. The oldest combs had square tops, while the more recent ones were rounded. The combs were carefully carved from single pieces of wood. Some of the combs were decorated with designs typical of Maori art, including spiral designs and a motif known as a *manaia*, interpreted as a bird's head or bird-headed man.

Shawcross turned to ethnographic accounts of Maori society for an interpretation of the Kauri Point swamp site. He proposed that the site was a sacred spring used as a repository for objects that had become *tapu*. In Maori belief, objects might become *tapu* in a variety of ways and then have to be disposed of safely and reverently. A *wahi tapu*, or sacred place, would be used for this purpose. Water was important in some ceremonies, and sacred places associated with water were known as *wai tapu*, or sacred springs. Many early European accounts of Maori culture described men wearing ornamental combs of bone or wood in their topknots. In Maori religious belief, the head and hair were considered sacred. Complicated ceremonies surrounded haircutting; equipment used in haircutting thus also became sacred. Shawcross argued, therefore, that the combs found at Kauri Point had become tapu through contact with human heads and were consequently disposed of. There are several reasons why obsidian flakes might have become *tapu*. Use for cutting hair is clearly one possibility. Alternatively, people commonly used stone flakes to cut themselves as a sign of mourning; this, too, would render the stone sacred. Shawcross also suggested that the other artefacts could have become *tapu* in a number of ways. For example, the gourds, baskets and other vessels might have held food offerings.

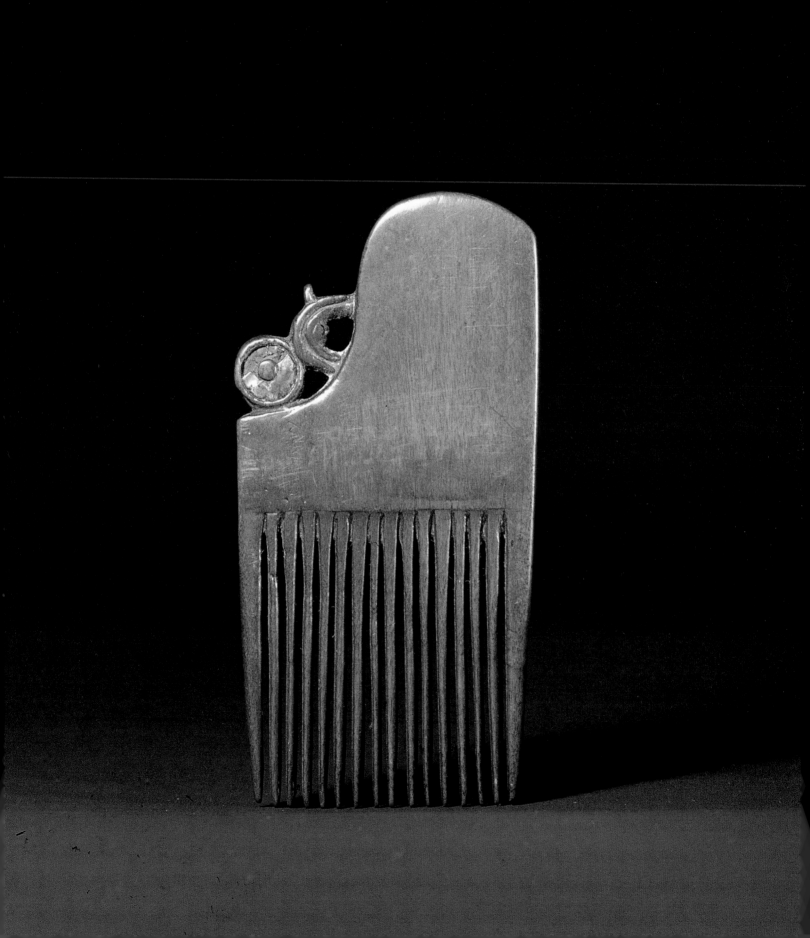

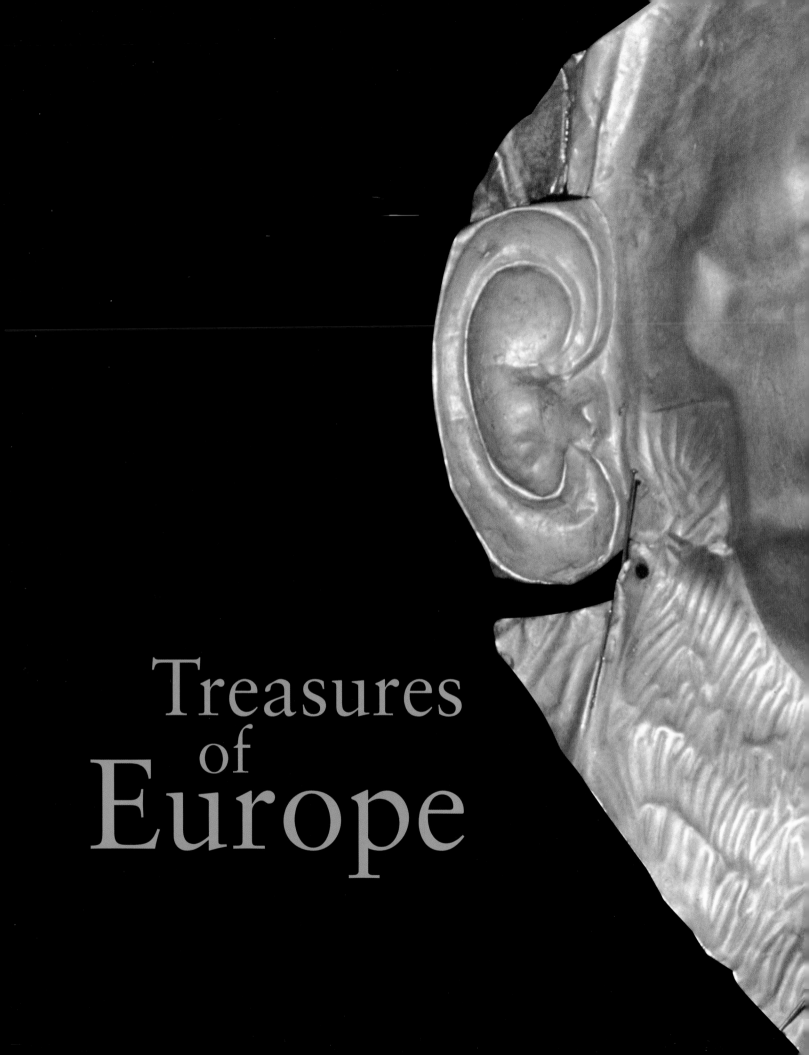

Treasures
of
Europe

Early Ice Age Masterpieces

The oldest known figurative portable art objects have been unearthed from several ancient sites in central Europe and dated by radiocarbon to more than thirty thousand years ago. Scholars are impressed and even somewhat baffled by the fact that these very early artistic creations emerge not as primitive and fumbling efforts, but as masterpieces of sophistication and skill.

This is a phenomenon that stands in bold contrast to human technology, which evolved along a slow and tortuous path from crude stone tools to spearthrowers and wheels over a period of two million years. One of the most important finds has turned up within the past decade, and archaeologists are still trying to understand these original art treasures.

The historic context of this critical event seems to lie in the northward migration of modern humans during the last Ice Age. Early modern human populations had appeared in Africa and the Near East as much as a hundred thousand years ago, but neither they nor their contemporaries in Europe – the Neanderthals – have revealed much evidence of artistic interest or talent; or at least, very little has survived or been discovered. Roughly forty thousand to thirty thousand years ago, modern humans entered Europe and gave birth to the first material expressions of figurative art. Although they also left behind evidence of elaborate body ornamentation and burial ritual, their most formidable achievement is unquestionably a remarkable collection of sculptures, which includes representations of animals, humans, and imaginary beings that combined aspects of both humans and animals.

The first examples of this art came to light in 1931 at the Vogelherd Cave in southern Germany. Here, in the lowest level occupied by modern humans, archaeologists found six animal sculptures carved from mammoth ivory. The artists had carefully selected the ivory from the interior of the tusk, shaped the form with stone tools, and polished it with hide or some other soft material. The sculpture of a horse 5 cm long required an estimated forty hours to complete. Although rendered with considerable skill and accuracy, the carvings are not literal representations of their subjects, but reflect the eye of the artist. The head and body are accorded great attention, while the limbs and feet are relatively neglected. In addition to the horse, which is the most beautiful of the collection, the Vogelherd sculptures include mammoths and lions. At the nearby Geissenklösterle Cave, sculptures of bear and bison have also been found, as well as another mammoth and a small ivory bas-relief of a human with raised arms.

Even more striking than the animal sculptures is a statuette recovered from Hohlenstein-Stadel – another cave in southern Germany – dated to 32,000 years before the present. At 28 cm high and carved from mammoth ivory like the Vogelherd sculptures, the statuette represents an anthropomorphic figure with a feline head. Debate still rages as to whether the body is that of a male or a female, but be that as it may this figurine is one of the most astounding creations of the Ice Age, reminiscent of the lion-headed deities of Ancient Egypt, tens of millennia later.

It should also be noted that all of these carvings are in mammoth ivory, a particularly difficult material to work with – indeed, it is so hard that for any kind of carving it needs to be softened by soaking or long-term storage, to accelerate its ageing and facilitate working.

In 1988, a new statuette of comparable age was discovered during salvage excavations on a hillside overlooking the Danube in Austria. Sculpted in green serpentine, which must have demanded special care and skill, the 7.2-cm-high *Dancing Venus of Galgenberg* is actually quite unlike the 'Venus figurines' of later in the Ice Age. Instead of a fully rounded figure, this one is flattish, its shape largely predetermined by the stone, which occurs in slabs. The right arm and the legs are supported at both ends, while the left arm seems to be folded back at the elbow. Bodyweight is supported on the left leg, while the right leg rests on a slightly higher support. The right hand is placed on the hip, and this pose causes the left breast to be depicted almost in profile, while the right is in very low relief because of the stone's flatness. The vulva is marked – a feature rare in Ice Age depictions of females.

The Galgenberg figure is more or less anatomically accurate except for the thickened limbs, which are probably as thin as the artist dared carve them without making the sculpture unduly fragile. Overall, this carving is the result of considerable techno-logical skill, as the stone is rather delicate and brittle, and the head, left arm and breast could easily have broken off. In addition, the two openings (under one arm and between the legs) would have required a delicate boring operation.

It is difficult to believe that these carvings were not preceded by a very lengthy tradition, the material remains of which have eluded us so far, presumably because the majority were produced in organic materials such as wood that have not survived. Some of the sculptures appear to have been fashioned as personal ornaments, which may have carried some social significance: for example, some of the Vogelherd animals – the horse, mammoth and a feline – have perforations at the front and hind legs, and may have been worn as pendants, which would account for the wear and polish on them. Marks seem to have been added to them at times whose purpose remains a complete mystery, while serving to underline the importance accorded to these carvings over a period of time.

Above left: IVORY HALF-RELIEF FROM VOGELHERD, GERMANY, OF AN ANIMAL WHICH HAS BEEN VARIOUSLY INTERPRETED AS SOME KIND OF BIG CAT, A HYENA OR EVEN A YOUNG RHINO.
Above: DANCING VENUS OF GALGENBERG.

Art Treasures
of the
Ice Age
Steppe

Between 25,000 and 14,000 years ago, the earth experienced its last major Ice Age. Massive glaciers spread across portions of the northern hemisphere and a vast glacial steppe dominated northern Eurasia. It is in this forbidding and somewhat bizarre landscape that the second great revolution in human art took place.

If the earliest forms of art were highly restricted in time and place (see p.126), the wave of creativity that accompanied the return of the glaciers witnessed the most widespread and enduring artistic tradition in human history. This was probably caused, at least in part, by the relative homogeneity and longevity of the Eurasian Ice Age steppe.

Just as the art of Medieval or Renaissance Europe must be understood in its social context, it may be necessary to appreciate the peculiar environmental setting in which the artists of this period found themselves. The forests of modern Eurasia were greatly reduced, and cold, dry landscapes with few trees prevailed across much of the northern half of the Old World. The animal inhabitants of this environment reflected a curious mixture of grassland, tundra and woodland species, including now extinct forms such as the woolly mammoth and cave lion. In some areas, the scarcity of trees forced people to build shelters from the bones and tusks of mammoths, and to burn animal bones in their hearths to heat them. The 'mammoth houses' of eastern Europe are as much a hallmark of this epoch as the art.

Left: THE *VENUS OF WILLENDORF,* CARVED IN LIMESTONE.

Besides the cave paintings, which on present evidence are predominantly confined to western Europe, the most famous art of the period is the collection of female statuettes usually referred to as 'Venus figurines'. If animal representations dominate the earliest Ice Age art (and the cave paintings), depictions of women – generally without clothing – seem to be the most common theme in the sculpture of the time. Female statuettes have been recovered from caves and campsites as far west as the French Pyrenees and as far east as central Siberia. The earliest known examples of these statuettes have been dated by radiocarbon to 28,000–29,000 years ago – almost as old as the first art (see p. 126) and apparently before the onset of the last Ice Age – while the youngest of them may not date to more than 21,000–22,000 years before the present. Thus the 'Venus figurines' may have endured as a stylistic convention for as much as eight thousand years.

Above: DETAIL OF AN IVORY FIGURINE FROM MAL'TA, SIBERIA.

There is, however, a great deal of variation in these figurines, especially with respect to geography. Also, the artists employed a wide variety of media, including mammoth ivory, limestone and fired clay or loess soil. The classic style is represented by the well-known *Black Venus* from the site of Dolní Vestonice in Moravia. This statuette is 11.5 cm high, and rendered in fired loess. Little attention was devoted to the facial features (in this case confined to the eyes), arms and legs. Instead, the artist concentrated on the large, pendulous breasts, protruding abdomen (with prominent navel) and shapely buttocks. The equally famous *Venus of Willendorf* from Austria exhibits a similar style, although this sculpture, which is also roughly 11 cm tall but modelled in stone, reveals more attention to the limbs and seems to be adorned with some form of headgear or braided hair. Many of the statuettes found in Russia and the Ukraine reflect this central European style, and a number of examples have been recovered from ancient campsites like Kostenki and Gagarino on the Don River.

Further east, a very different style of female figurine is found. From the campsites of Mal'ta and Buret' near Lake Baikal, over thirty whole or fragmentary statuettes have been recovered. Carved in mammoth ivory, the Siberian figurines reflect much less emphasis on the breasts and abdomen, and often the outline of the former is simply engraved on the torso, rather than being modelled in three dimensions. They also exhibit more facial details, and some are shown fully clothed. These differences suggest that the Siberian statuettes may bear very little relation to the European 'Venus figurines'.

Much speculation has surrounded the meaning of this art. Although the figurines are not found in graves, they are generally believed to have had some religious or ritual significance, perhaps related to fertility or hunting magic. Some have argued that the climate and economy of the Ice Age steppe would have placed a premium on efficient storage of body fat, creating a plump feminine ideal. Other scholars have stressed the social importance of these and other forms of imagery, suggesting that they reflect the growth of ethnic communities based on shared symbols; Marxist prehistorians of the 1930s believed that the women represented the leaders of matriarchal societies. These explanations may overlook the obvious fact that artists have betrayed an eternal fascination with the female form.

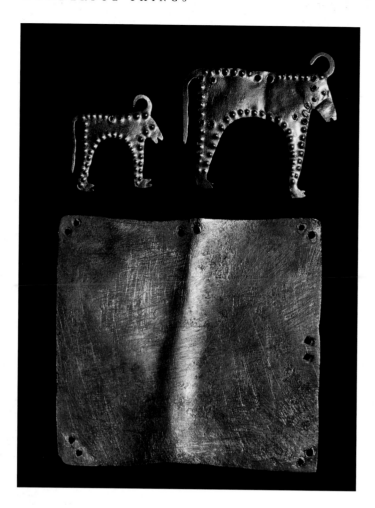

Power, Prestige and Gold at Varna

The Copper Age cemetery at Varna in north-east Bulgaria, dating to between 4500 and 4000 BC, provides the richest collection of burials of this period in eastern Europe. They are unique in their volume of gold, copper and other luxury items and have led archaeologists to wonder what sort of society might have produced such a site.

During this period, Europe was populated by simple agriculturalists who were becoming increasingly proficient in firing pottery at high temperatures. They were soon able to transfer this ability to working with metals, with the result that copper and gold artefacts began to appear in burials as offerings from the Balkans north to Slovakia and Poland.

The Varna cemetery was discovered in 1972 during the excavation of a cable trench. The site is located on the northern edge of a lake that was once a bay on the Black Sea. Between 1972 and 1986, about 7,500 sq m were excavated, which constituted about 75 per cent of the estimated original size of the cemetery. Within this area, nearly three hundred graves were found that dated to the end of the Copper Age in this region, although one-fifth were 'symbolic graves', or cenotaphs, without actual human remains. The burial rite was similar among all the graves in the Varna cemetery. Rectangular pits were dug, ranging in depth from 30 cm to 2.5 m, with sloping sides. Some of the graves had skeletons in an extended position, while others had contracted burials, with the knees drawn up to the chest and the head bent forward. The cenotaphs, of course, have no bodies in them. Only a handful of the burials lacked grave goods, while some contained hundreds of objects.

Gold artefacts, which constitute the most distinctive aspect of the Varna cemetery, occur in sixty-one of the graves. Curiously, most of the gold is found in the cenotaphs, while only a few of the graves with skeletons were similarly furnished. Three of the cenotaphs – Graves 1, 4 and 36 – were extraordinarily rich. Grave 1 contained 216 gold objects, which together weighed over a kilogram, while the 339 gold objects in Grave 4 weighed over 1.5 kg. Grave 36 had the most gold items – 857 – which together weighed 789 gm. Three other cenotaphs – Graves 2, 3 and 15 – contained gold-ornamented clay masks with male features.

In most of the Varna burials with skeletons, the body was placed in an extended position. Perhaps the richest of these was Grave 43, which contained the skeleton of a man who was about forty to fifty years old and about 1.75 m tall. Accompanying the skeleton were nearly a thousand gold objects weighing over 1.5 kg, along with other items made of copper, stone, clay and the shell of the marine mussel *Spondylus* (probably from the Aegean Sea). One of the gold objects is termed a 'sceptre', in which a wooden handle had been sheathed with gold and topped with a stone macehead. The skeleton in Grave 43 also had large rings around the upper

Above: PLAQUES AND ANIMAL FIGURES MADE FROM SHEETS OF GOLD.
Right: ONE OF THE GRAVES AT VARNA SHOWING PLACEMENT OF THE ORNAMENTS, INCLUDING LARGE GOLD BRACELETS.

arms, numerous beads that had been strung together, and circles of gold sheet that ornamented the corpse's clothing. Some burials at Varna contained skeletons in a contracted position; but as there seems to be no difference between the grave goods found with the contracted burials and those in the extended position, the significance of the variation is unclear.

While the gold artefacts are clearly the most memorable category of finds at Varna, it is important to remember that there are also significant numbers of copper, flint and shell objects found in the burials. Copperworking developed in the Balkans around 4500 BC, and mines in the Carpathian mountains supplied the ore for this metal. The widespread use of copper reflects the increased ability to control high temperatures in the technology during this period. Many of the copper artefacts at Varna are hammer-axes, while others are pins, rings and other ornaments. A variety of flint tools are found in the graves, made from long blades of high-quality material. Beads and arm-rings of *Spondylus* shell were also found, particularly in the graves with the masks.

The spectacular finds at Varna have been interpreted as indicating that different individuals had varying degrees of access

to status, power and wealth. Besides being used for ornaments, gold was incorporated into other artefacts that also had symbolic significance, such as the maces and masks. Moreover, it was used to highlight significant parts of the body, such as the face and genitals. It is clear that the gold and other high-quality artefacts had considerable prestige value. The volume of gold found at Varna is by far the earliest concentrated accumulation of this metal, not to be equalled again until the Royal Cemetery at Ur in Mesopotamia about one and a half thousand years later (see p.68).

Ongoing research is aimed at understanding the society that produced the Varna cemetery. Nearby in north-east Bulgaria are large settlements, such as those at Ovcharovo and Polyanitsa, with densely packed houses laid out in a regular plan and separated by narrow alleys. The houses are of relatively uniform size and give no hint of social differentiation by themselves. These sites are also surrounded by fortifications, indicating that there was conflict among these peasant communities. Wealth and power typically breed rivalries and alliances, and alliances are generally based on exchange, often of luxury items. One possible interpretation of the Varna finds might be that the lavish burial rite represents a 'working out' of the consequences of the death of these individuals for the allied groups they represent. In such a scenario, the grave goods would have been contributed by various factions to demonstrate their continued affiliation. At the moment, this is only speculation, but it is a plausible explanation for the sudden appearance of such a volume of metal and other luxury items.

On the other hand, it has recently been argued that the wealth of the Varna cemetery may reflect the spiritual world of the community that maintained it, rather than Copper Age economic or social structure. Such acts of ancestral veneration, in this view, emphasize the connection between the founding members of the community and their living descendants. The cenotaphs may have commemorated individuals who died away from home. In this light, the Varna cemetery may be seen as an extreme case of a much wider pattern of rich burial in south-east Europe rather than as a reflection of social competition and differentiation.

Prepalatial Jewellery from Mochlos

Below left: LARGE NUMBERS OF STRIPS OF SHEET GOLD, WORN AS DIADEMS, WERE FOUND IN THE PREPALATIAL GRAVES AT MOCHLAS.

Below right: EXAMPLES OF THE GOLD JEWELLERY FROM THE PREPALATIAL TOMBS AT MOCHLOS.

In 1900, Sir Arthur Evans discovered the remains of a vibrant and prosperous civilization that flourished on Crete some two thousand years before the birth of Christ and was characterized by labyrinthine palaces and bustling towns. Evans named this civilization Minoan after King Minos, the legendary ruler of Crete. The Early Bronze Age antecedents to this civilization are obscured by the passage of time. At first glance it appears to have been an impoverished society whose works of art were limited to a primitive style of pottery and a few objects of metal; but this apparent poverty is belied by a series of elegant stone vases, possibly the artistic and technological highpoint of the Early Minoan civilization, and the first tentative contacts with Egypt and the Levant

Excavations in 1908 of a small cemetery on the island of Mochlos, just off the north-east coast of Crete, shed the first light on the remarkable prepalatial civilization that existed on the island in the Early Bronze Age. Richard Seager, the American excavator, was staggered by the wealth he found in the tombs, which imitated the dwellings of the nearby settlement. For five weeks 'the cemetery continued to yield a rich harvest of vases and small objects', namely metal weapons, ivory seals, and most memorably a wealth of gold jewellery. Two tombs in particular stand out both for the massive concentration of wealth buried within them and for their impressive architecture and ornamental façade of purple and green schist and grey-blue limestone orthostats (upright stones).

The jewellery from the tombs at Mochlos is the best example of prepalatial jewellery known on Crete, and dates to around 2300–2100 BC. In addition to numerous beads from at least eleven necklaces, Seager found about one hundred and fifty items of personal adornment and a single silver cup. Further excavations at the site in the 1970s increased the known corpus of jewellery, but only added a second silver cup. There is a surprising profusion of gold unmatched in other Early Minoan sites on Crete. The basic materials used are sheet gold, gold foil and fine gold wire.

Technically the goldwork is elementary, and even appears backward in comparison with that from other regions. The Cretan goldsmiths had not yet mastered soldering, and so there is no use of decorative techniques such as filigree and granulation, which are used to such effect on the gold from Troy (see p. 64). On the other hand the jewellers made intricate gold chains, and there is proficient application of dot repoussé decoration, achieved by pressing gold foil over a mould or using a pointed tool to punch a design into the sheet gold. In addition to the extensive use of gold there are beads of semi-precious stones (chalcedony, rock crystal,

carnelian, amethyst and steatite), shell and small discs of faience, the earliest known use of this material on Crete. Gold, drum-shaped beads decorated with floral patterns imitate fish vertebrae, recalling the primitive ornaments worn by the forebears of the inhabitants of Mochlos.

The most outstanding pieces of jewellery are the delicate hairpins fashioned as daisies, crocuses and sprays of leaves, and the diadems, which are very reminiscent of the elaborate headdresses found in the Royal Cemetery of Ur (see p. 68). Diadems were commonly used throughout the Near East and Aegean in the Early Bronze Age, and would have functioned as a symbol of authority, to designate someone with special spiritual or secular powers. Although the gold sheet diadems from Mochlos are very delicate, they show signs of wear and were obviously used during the lifetime of their owner, probably being worn on ceremonial and festive occasions. They were decorated with simple patterns or figured scenes – a pair of eyes, opposed dogs and horned quadrupeds – in dot repoussé. These diadems were complemented by an array of golden jewellery: fragile bracelets, necklaces of gold and stone with leaf-shaped pendants hanging from delicate gold chains, and gold sheet discs and stars sewn on to clothing; but it is noteworthy that there were no dress pins or earrings.

Clearly, the inhabitants of Mochlos devoted a great deal of attention and much of their wealth to personal adornment. These exquisite pieces of jewellery were not made specifically for funerary display, but were worn by their owners during their lifetime and buried with them at death. The burial of such large quantities of gold is a remarkable statement of the prosperity of Mochlos and the complex social hierarchy that had developed at the site. In effect, the inhabitants of Mochlos were removing an important, valuable and rare resource from circulation by placing it in the tombs of the dead. Despite the enormous quantities of gold deposited in the tombs at Mochlos, silver is only rarely found in the cemetery, and in fact there are only two silver vases. These would have been exceptionally important grave gifts as, in the ancient world, silver was more valuable than gold.

Mochlos was a small but thriving and affluent settlement ruled by local chiefs, the religious and secular leaders of their people. Their power and wealth were marked in life by their fine gold jewellery, and in death by elaborate burial in large tombs that became the focus of the spiritual life of the community. They derived their fortune and position from their control of Mochlos, with its excellent harbour and advantageous position at the end of the Aegean maritime trade routes. Immediately to the north are the Cyclades, a circle of tiny, but mineral-rich islands that were probably the source of the gold and silver found buried in the tombs at Mochlos.

Amber and Jet: Treasured Accessories from Prehistoric Europe

Rich burials of the Early Bronze Age in Europe have given up some of the greatest treasures of prehistoric decoration. Important men and women were buried with an array of elaborate accessories, most notably finely worked amber beads and necklaces, and buttons made out of the smooth black stone, jet. The woman interred in the barrow in the Wilsford cemetery in Wiltshire in south-west England, south of Stonehenge, wore one of the finest amber necklaces of antiquity, a multitude of circular beads strung together and separated by rectangular spacers.

Amber occurs naturally in the Baltic Sea and off the coast of Jutland in Denmark. In addition, blocks the size of bricks have often been washed up on the coast of East Anglia. The natural qualities of amber were recognized by the early hunter-gatherers of northern Europe, who fashioned amber pendants in the shape of animals and birds. Early farmers ritually deposited hoards of amber in the ground, perhaps as offerings to the gods. Hoards of up to thirteen thousand pieces of amber have been discovered in Denmark. One such votive hoard, discovered in the Sortekoers Mose, West Jutland, contained nearly one thousand eight hundred amber beads buried in a pottery vessel. In this neolithic period amber was treasured by the people who lived in the amber-producing districts and they kept it for themselves, burying it with the dead or offering it to the spirits.

In contrast to this local consumption of amber, by the time bronzeworking was spreading through Europe, a trade in amber grew up that was to link the Baltic with the Mediterranean, and in which it is possible to discern links between the wealthy princes of Wessex and the rest of Europe. Indeed, once amber appeared outside its natural area of

Left: AN AMBER NECKLACE FROM UPTON LOVELL, WILTSHIRE. AMBER WAS AN ESPECIALLY TREASURED IN EUROPEAN PREHISTORY.

distribution, desire for it appears to have stimulated other, major changes. The bronzeworking Unetice Cultures of Germany and central Europe developed a special penchant for the resin, and it was quite probably the exchange of bronze from these regions for amber that set in train the Bronze Age in northern Europe. In turn, the control of the amber trade bolstered the social status of elite groups in central Europe, reinforcing the growth of social differentiation so visible in the rich graves of the period. Amber objects, including plaques, plates, buttons and pendants, are found from as far north as the Knowes of Trotty in the Orkney Islands, and south to Mycenae (see p. 146).

Apart from beads and necklaces, amber was occasionally used to make cups. A complete example was discovered in an Early Bronze Age grave from Hove, in Sussex, along with a polished stone battleaxe, a bronze dagger and other items. The beauty of the warm, translucent glow of the amber captivated archaeologists just as it must have those involved in the burial ceremonies nearly four thousand years ago. Another amber cup, more fragmentary than that from Hove, was found in a grave at Clandon in Dorset. These cups are part of a tradition of placing drinking equipment in graves.

Amber was not the only highly prized material for accessories in the Early Bronze Age. Jet is a hard, black lignite that can be very highly polished to give a deep, black shine. In 1887, a crouched inhumation burial was excavated at Mount Stuart, Bute, in Scotland. The burial was that of a young woman, whose skull had perhaps been trepanned in a piece of prehistoric surgery. A pottery food vessel was laid at her feet and around her neck had been placed a splendid jet necklace. Over a hundred beads were recovered, along with four trapezoidal spacer-plates and other pieces, all originally strung together to form one of the finest jet necklaces ever discovered. Jet occurs naturally on the coast of East Yorkshire in the north of England, and would have been a rare resource. Other, similar, black materials that were utilized by Bronze Age craftspeople included shale, which occurs in Kimmeridge in Dorset. This was probably the source of a fine

Above: A JET NECKLACE FROM MOUNT STUART, BUTE, ONCE WORN BY ONE OF EUROPE'S EARLIEST ELITES.

shale cup from a barrow on Farway Broad Down, excavated in 1869. This cup, like those made of amber, was probably made on a lathe, and it had been placed near a little heap of cremated bones that lay on a pavement of burnt flints, before the barrow mound had been thrown up over the whole lot.

These discoveries of amber, jet and shale in graves of the Early Bronze Age are testimony to the high value placed on these special materials by the emergent elite classes of prehistoric Europe, who treasured them for their lustre and rarity. For modern archaeologists, they are treasures that tell of the appearance of controlled trade and exchange, and of wealthy individuals who were able to control the production and consumption of prestige objects.

Bush Barrow and the Treasures of Bronze Age Goldwork

In 1808, William Cunnington set about the excavation of a large burial mound on Normanton Down, Wiltshire. Little did the distinguished and experienced antiquarian know that he was about to encounter one of the key figures in the construction of one of the greatest prehistoric monuments in the British Isles, Stonehenge, which lay about a kilometre to the north-east of the barrow.

Cunnington and his patron, Sir William Colt Hoare, were among the greatest of the eighteenth- and nineteenth-century antiquarians who laid the foundations for the modern study of archaeology. They were adept at opening barrows (burial mounds), and realized that they had discovered something rather out of the ordinary. The layout of the burial in the Bush Barrow was rather unusual for the rich graves of the Early Bronze Age Wessex Culture. The body of a tall man lay stretched out on his back, his feet pointing north. He was lying directly on the old land surface, instead of being placed in a pit dug into the ground as was more normal. On and around his body was a carefully placed set of objects that confirmed his importance. On his chest was a gold lozenge-shaped plate, a smaller gold lozenge lying outside his right thigh, next to a ceremonial mace. In his right hand was a small bronze dagger, above which, and parallel to his right arm, were two larger daggers, their pommels towards the man's head. Behind these lay a further gold object, thought to be a scabbard hook. Next to his right shoulder the diggers found a bronze flanged axe. Some 40 cm behind his head a large number of bronze rivets and some badly corroded, thin bronze strips lay intermingled with slivers of wood. This object has been variously regarded as the remains of a shield, a helmet and, more recently, a surveying tool, akin to an alidade.

The Wessex Culture was defined by the renowned British

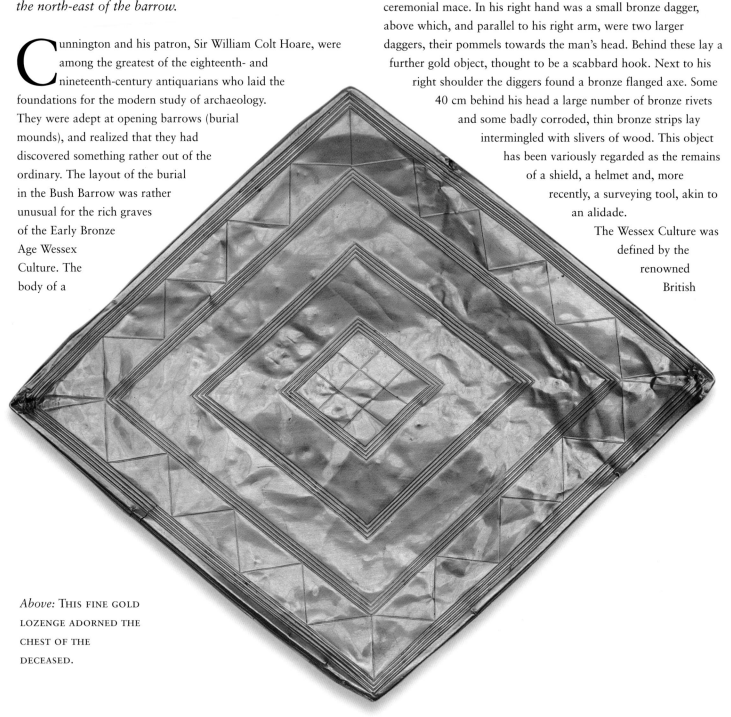

Above: THIS FINE GOLD LOZENGE ADORNED THE CHEST OF THE DECEASED.

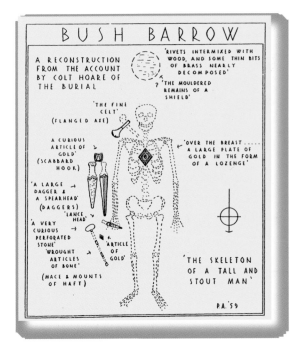

Left: THE BUSH BARROW BURIAL AND GRAVE GOODS (AFTER ASHBEE P., 1960, THE BRONZE AGE ROUND BARROW IN BRITAIN). *Right:* THE 'SCABBARD HOOK' FROM THE BUSH BARROW, AND *(below)* GOLD OBJECTS FROM WILSFORD, WILTSHIRE.

prehistorian Stuart Piggott in 1938. Piggott identified a series of approximately one hundred very rich burials, interred beneath the burial mounds so characteristic of the chalk downlands of the Wessex region of south-west Britain. The burials were distinguished from previous burial forms by the exotic objects that accompanied the deceased, most notably objects of bronze, gold and amber. There was a uniformity to these burial assemblages that allowed Piggott to regard the incumbents of these tombs as the elite rulers of small states that had shared values regarding prestige goods, and probably shared stakes in the control of the production and distribution of these treasured items.

Only one in seven of these tombs actually contained any gold, but the quality of work invested in the gold objects of the Wessex graves far exceeded any other British goldwork of the time, with the possible exception of a fine gold cape from Mold in North Wales. Detailed studies by specialists in the archaeology of metalworking have suggested that much, if not all, of the Wessex goldwork was from the workshop of a single master goldsmith. The niceties of the tooling around the edges of the large lozenge, for example, are shared by many of the finest gold finds. If this is in fact the case, the florescence of the Wessex Culture can perhaps be dated to a single working lifetime.

The treasures from the Bush Barrow have affinities with Europe, in particular with Brittany in north-west France, that attest to extensive cultural contacts in the Early Bronze Age, at least between elite groups. Along with other rich burials in the Wessex group, including that at Upton Lovell, and Clandon in Dorset, the Bush Barrow contains items of a character and sophistication shared with French counterparts that make it one of the most important prehistoric sites in Europe. At the time of the Wessex Culture, Stonehenge was undergoing its third phase of development, with huge local sarsen stones being shaped and set up around the reused bluestones from the Prescelli Hills in Wales. The continental links displayed by the objects from the Bush Barrow show how the people who built Stonehenge maintained contact with other parts of Europe.

The treasures of the Bush Barrow and their treatment at the hands of conservators have in recent years provoked considerable controversy over how antiquities of this class power in the age of Stonehenge. The significance of the Bush Barrow and its occupant, however, is unquestioned. Many problems remain unresolved, including his relationship with what was happening at Stonehenge.

Bronze Age Hoards of the Carpathian Basin

The practice of placing finely made bronze artefacts in buried caches was common throughout Europe in the second millennium BC, but it was especially pervasive in the Carpathian Basin. Around 1500 BC, the prehistoric inhabitants of modern Hungary, Slovakia and Romania deliberately buried numerous bronze artefacts.

Fuelled by the rich Transylvanian ore deposits, bronze metallurgy was refined to a remarkable level of expertise by the smiths living in riverside settlements and hilltop fortified sites. Their wares frequently survive to be discovered not as stray finds in habitations or as offerings in burials but as deliberate buried deposits both inside settlements and in the surrounding countryside.

Three of the most spectacular Bronze Age hoards of the Carpathian Basin come from the site of Kosziderpadlás, about 70 km south of Budapest in Hungary, and have given their name to a series of deposits throughout Hungary and Slovakia. 'Koszider type' hoards are remarkably rich and diverse in their individual composition, yet strikingly similar across this region. They consist typically of a sample of the weapons, tools and ornaments of the Carpathian Basin in the mid-second millennium BC. Common artefact types include daggers, disc-butted and shaft-tube axes, and swords decorated with incised spiral and geometric patterns; spiral bracelets, armlets, and anklets with rolled ends; and shaft-hole axes. A particularly distinctive form is the bronze 'ivy-leaf' pendant, in which two opposing semicircular arcs enclose smaller interior arcs curving in the opposite direction.

Slightly earlier than Koszider is the Hajdúsámson hoard in north-east Hungary, which was discovered in 1907 during the digging of a drainage ditch. The major element of this hoard was a bronze, solid-hilted sword that was placed pointing towards the north; twelve shaft-hole axes had been placed across the sword with their blades pointing west. The deliberateness of the placement of these items clearly indicates that this was an offering with considerable meaning rather than a hurried attempt to hide possessions from raiders. The sword and several of the axes were finely decorated with incised lines and scrolls.

Around the same time, goldworking also flourished in the Carpathian Basin. A spectacular treasure consisting of hair-rings, a necklace, spirals and beads was found at the fortified village of Barca in eastern Slovakia. Large hoards are also known from Transylvania at the Romanian sites of Tufalau, Smig, Graniceri and Ostrovul Mare. One of the most remarkable gold artefacts of this period is the bracelet from Bilje in northern former Yugoslavia, which was found in 1840. Now in the Natural History Museum in Vienna, the Bilje bracelet weighs 205 gm. The part that surrounds the arm consists of three ribbed bands, on to which are attached two gold plates with curving ends (reminiscent of the 'ivy-leaf' pendants, in fact). These are decorated with repoussé bosses and fine incised lines.

Another dramatic gold find of this period is a series of cups from Bihar on the Hungarian-Romanian border. They were stamped from single sheets of gold large enough to include a lip and a handle, and decorated with incised lines. The craftsmanship of these pieces reflects the remarkable skill of the indigenous metallurgists of the Carpathian Basin.

The people who buried the bronze and gold artefacts in the Carpathian Basin lived in settlements whose debris often accumulated to form mounds, or tells, although by Koszider times many of these had been abandoned. Elsewhere, they surrounded hilltops with ditches to construct fortified villages. In the nearby countryside, they raised crops and livestock. Many of their dead, especially individuals of higher status, were buried under small mounds, or tumuli. Much of their wealth was acquired from trade along the rivers of this region, and the combination of this trade and the agricultural productivity of the bottomlands yielded the riches that are found in the hoards.

But why bury such wealth? Many archaeologists believe that it had some sort of votive purpose, although we have no idea of the Bronze Age deities to which such offerings were made. The practice of burying valuables in hoards continued throughout the second millennium BC, even as the prehistoric communities changed their burial rites and settlement patterns. It was not until the advent of iron that hoards ceased to be deposited with such frequency throughout the Carpathian Basin.

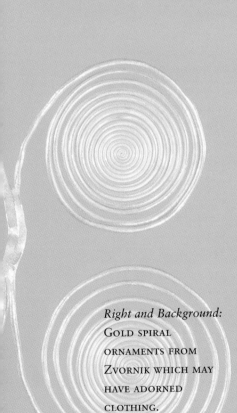

Left: THE HEAVY GOLD
BRACELET FROM BILJE.

Right and Background:
GOLD SPIRAL
ORNAMENTS FROM
ZVORNIK WHICH MAY
HAVE ADORNED
CLOTHING.

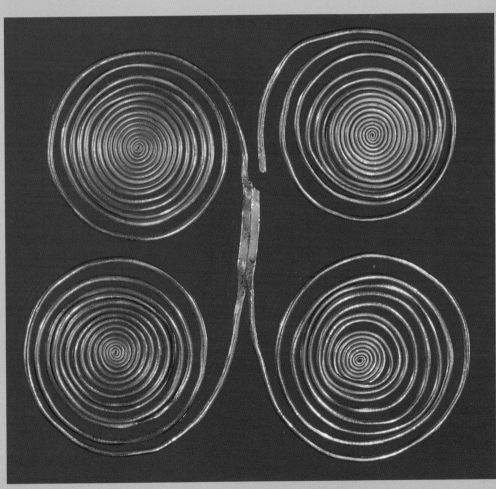

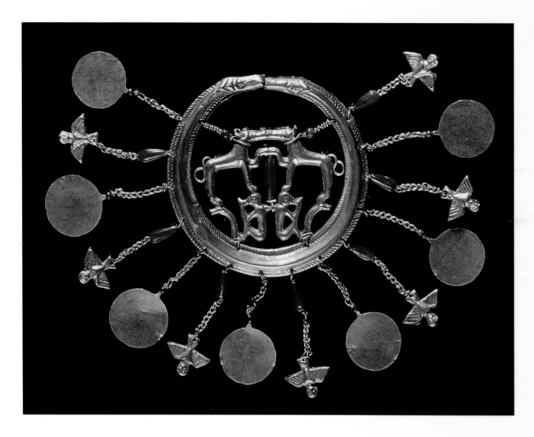

The Aegina Treasure

In 1891, the representative of a Greek firm of sponge importers offered the British Museum a dazzling hoard of gold treasure that had reportedly been found in a tomb on the island of Aegina. The British Museum bought the treasure in 1892, and Sir Arthur Evans acquired four Mycenaean vases, allegedly found with the treasure, which he gave to the Ashmolean Museum in Oxford.

The hoard of jewellery is unique in the Greek world, and for a long time proved very difficult to date because of the uncertain circumstances surrounding its discovery. Scholars suggested dates ranging from the Late Bronze Age (fourteenth and thirteenth centuries BC), contemporary with the four pots in Oxford, to as late as the seventh century BC, and some suggested it was possibly even of Phoenician manufacture. According to other scholars it was not a homogeneous collection, but instead an eclectic mix of Mycenaean and later elements, typical of a tomb looter's hoard.

There is considerable circumstantial evidence to suggest that the treasure was indeed found on Aegina. The probable location of its discovery is a Mycenaean cemetery in a vineyard on Windmill Hill, just north of the modern town of Aegina and close to the so-called Temple of Aphrodite. This cemetery was explored in 1904 by the Greek archaeologist A. Keramopoullos, who identified four burial chambers of Mycenaean date. Was it in one of these that the treasure was found? Certainly, a letter to the British Museum, written in 1914 by the former governess to the sponge dealer's family, confirmed that the treasures were 'found in an old tomb of a priestess of the temple of Venus' together with much pottery that had not been taken to England. The governess had herself been given some jewellery, including 'two pieces of cornelian with carved fingers on it', which she agreed to sell to the British Museum. However, while accepting the stories surrounding the discovery of the treasure, the leading expert on Greek jewellery, Reynold Higgins, found it difficult to relate the treasure to the latter part of the Mycenaean period but instead preferred to place the jewellery in the Minoan tradition, a couple of centuries earlier.

The hoard is a remarkable collection of jewellery made of gold and semi-precious stones, and the techniques used are typical of Minoan craftsmanship. The jewellers used sheet metal, which was embossed by pressing the metal on to a steatite mould. Additional decorative details were added in filigree (fine wires of gold soldered on to the gold background) and inlay of lapis lazuli – a technique introduced to Greece from the Near East, where it is first attested in the Royal Cemetery of Ur around 2500 BC

Opposite page: ELABORATE
HOOPED EARRING OF GOLD
AND CARNELIAN WITH PAIRS
OF GREYHOUNDS AND
MONKEYS AT THE CENTRE.

Above: THIS GOLD PENDANT, WITH THE SO-
CALLED 'MASTER OF THE ANIMALS' STANDING
ON THREE LOTUS FLOWERS, IS A CURIOUS
MIXTURE OF EGYPTIAN AND MINOAN
ICONOGRAPHY.

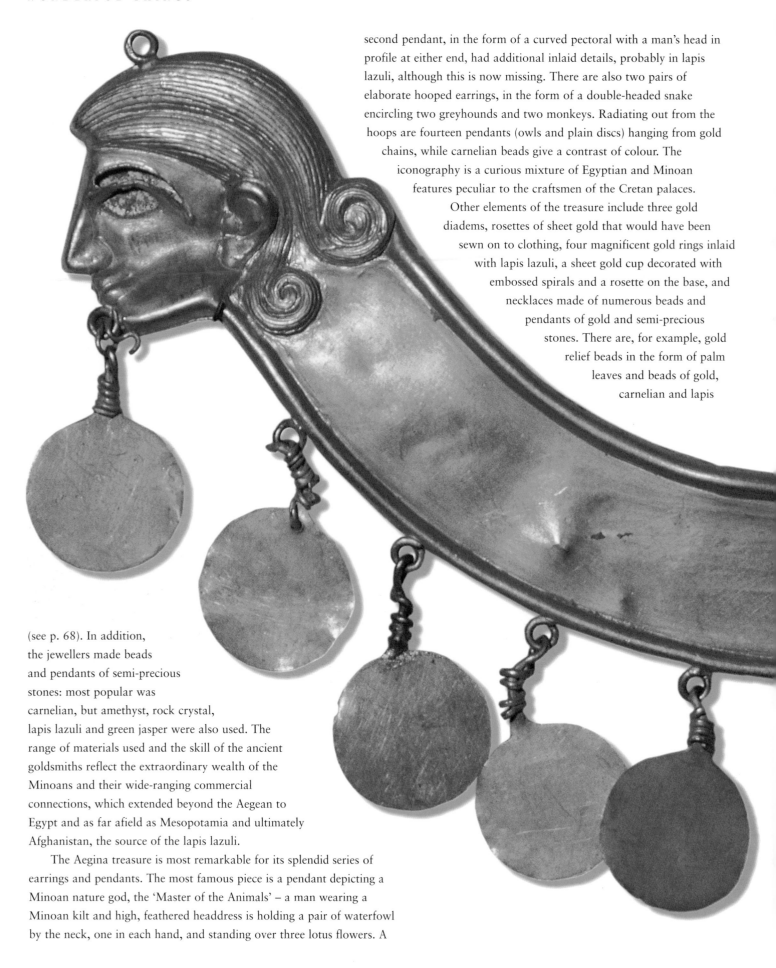

second pendant, in the form of a curved pectoral with a man's head in profile at either end, had additional inlaid details, probably in lapis lazuli, although this is now missing. There are also two pairs of elaborate hooped earrings, in the form of a double-headed snake encircling two greyhounds and two monkeys. Radiating out from the hoops are fourteen pendants (owls and plain discs) hanging from gold chains, while carnelian beads give a contrast of colour. The iconography is a curious mixture of Egyptian and Minoan features peculiar to the craftsmen of the Cretan palaces. Other elements of the treasure include three gold diadems, rosettes of sheet gold that would have been sewn on to clothing, four magnificent gold rings inlaid with lapis lazuli, a sheet gold cup decorated with embossed spirals and a rosette on the base, and necklaces made of numerous beads and pendants of gold and semi-precious stones. There are, for example, gold relief beads in the form of palm leaves and beads of gold, carnelian and lapis

(see p. 68). In addition, the jewellers made beads and pendants of semi-precious stones: most popular was carnelian, but amethyst, rock crystal, lapis lazuli and green jasper were also used. The range of materials used and the skill of the ancient goldsmiths reflect the extraordinary wealth of the Minoans and their wide-ranging commercial connections, which extended beyond the Aegean to Egypt and as far afield as Mesopotamia and ultimately Afghanistan, the source of the lapis lazuli.

The Aegina treasure is most remarkable for its splendid series of earrings and pendants. The most famous piece is a pendant depicting a Minoan nature god, the 'Master of the Animals' – a man wearing a Minoan kilt and high, feathered headdress is holding a pair of waterfowl by the neck, one in each hand, and standing over three lotus flowers. A

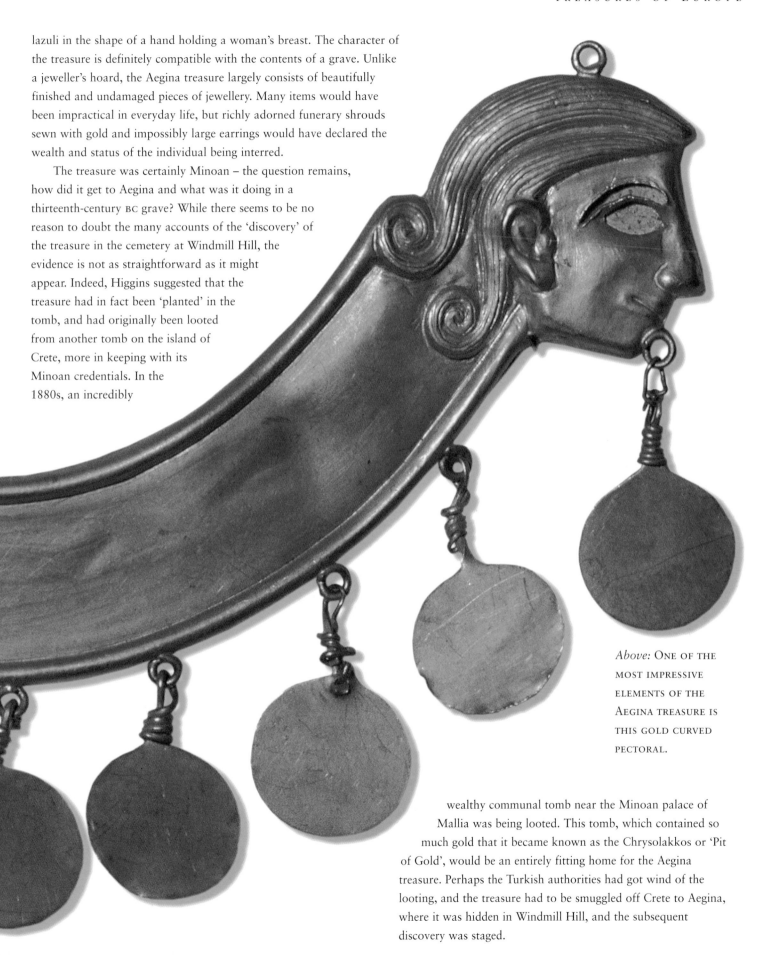

lazuli in the shape of a hand holding a woman's breast. The character of the treasure is definitely compatible with the contents of a grave. Unlike a jeweller's hoard, the Aegina treasure largely consists of beautifully finished and undamaged pieces of jewellery. Many items would have been impractical in everyday life, but richly adorned funerary shrouds sewn with gold and impossibly large earrings would have declared the wealth and status of the individual being interred.

The treasure was certainly Minoan – the question remains, how did it get to Aegina and what was it doing in a thirteenth-century BC grave? While there seems to be no reason to doubt the many accounts of the 'discovery' of the treasure in the cemetery at Windmill Hill, the evidence is not as straightforward as it might appear. Indeed, Higgins suggested that the treasure had in fact been 'planted' in the tomb, and had originally been looted from another tomb on the island of Crete, more in keeping with its Minoan credentials. In the 1880s, an incredibly

Above: ONE OF THE MOST IMPRESSIVE ELEMENTS OF THE AEGINA TREASURE IS THIS GOLD CURVED PECTORAL.

wealthy communal tomb near the Minoan palace of Mallia was being looted. This tomb, which contained so much gold that it became known as the Chrysolakkos or 'Pit of Gold', would be an entirely fitting home for the Aegina treasure. Perhaps the Turkish authorities had got wind of the looting, and the treasure had to be smuggled off Crete to Aegina, where it was hidden in Windmill Hill, and the subsequent discovery was staged.

Mycenae 'Rich in Gold'

Homer's descriptions of Mycenae 'rich in gold' were dramatically brought to life by the excavations of Heinrich Schliemann in 1876. Schliemann discovered the remains of an ancient civilization that flourished a thousand years earlier than the time of Pericles, and he named it 'Mycenaean' after the capital of the legendary King Agamemnon. In 1876, he found the graves of the ancient rulers of Mycenae in a circular enclosure just south of the famous Lion Gate. A second grave circle was excavated in 1951 by the Greek archaeological service. Schliemann's burial enclosure is now known as Grave Circle A and the more recently excavated one as Grave Circle B, but the burials in Circle B predate those in Circle A.

Within the area of Circle B were twenty-six graves – rectangular shafts cut into the bedrock – but there were only six graves in Circle A. Each grave housed several burials of men, women and two children. Indeed, some nineteen burials were recorded in Circle A. The wealth of Circle A in particular is astounding and the most striking aspect of the funerary furniture is the sheer quantity of gold – at least 13 kg in the three richest graves alone. It appears that the wealth deposited with individual burials increased through time. While the earliest burials in Circle B were relatively poor, only equipped with simple grave goods, the richest burials in Circle B (Graves Alpha, Gamma, Delta, Epsilon and Omikron) contain objects comparable in wealth to those of Circle A. Most notable among the grave goods from Circle B is a vase in the shape of a duck, made of rock crystal.

While the relationship between the two grave circles is unclear, it is evident that the graves in both circles belonged to the early rulers of Mycenae, possibly from two competing families. The individuals buried in Circle A were interred with a remarkable funerary display of incredible wealth, which is unsurpassed in Graves III, IV and V. The male members of the Mycenaean aristocracy achieved their status through their prowess as warriors and were buried with a fine range of weapons. These include a magnificent set of daggers, the blades of which were decorated with scenes of hunting or warfare in gold and silver inlaid in niello. These were not functional weapons, but intended entirely for show. Women of high status were adorned with elaborate jewellery. They wore necklaces of amber, which reached Greece from the Baltic via a tortuous trade route, and agate and diadems of gold decorated with embossed circles and rosettes. Spirals of solid gold were made into hair ornaments, necklaces and bracelets.

Clothing was fastened with large bronze pins with heads of rock crystal, and there is one example of a silver pin with a gold head in the form of a female figure beneath a palm tree. Circular ornaments of sheet gold decorated in repoussé work were strewn over the burials. Crosses and floral-shaped ornaments of sheet gold decorated in repoussé were found with some of the burials. These were not discovered *in situ*, and so it is difficult to ascertain how they served to ornament the burials, but they were possibly elements of fancy diadems. Gold signet rings with scenes of warfare and hunting were also found. Unique among the finds is a set of five masks of sheet gold that covered the faces of the most important male burials in Grave IV of Circle A – and one of electrum in Circle B. The finest of the gold masks Schliemann identified with the face of King Agamemnon (see page 124).

The richest of the graves is Grave IV in Circle A, which housed the burials of two males and two females, possibly their consorts. In addition to the fine array of weapons and jewellery, the burials were equipped with many large copper vessels and vessels of plate gold and silver. While the copper vessels appear for the most part to be utilitarian cauldrons and ewers, many of the plate metal vases seem to have had a ritual function. Among these there was a silver vase in the form of a bull's head with golden horns and a gold rosette on its forehead, and a gold vase in the form of a lion's head. In addition to these ceremonial vases, there were beautiful drinking sets, cups, goblets and jugs of plate metal, often with ribbed decoration or embossed spiral ornamentation. These include a two-handled goblet with golden birds soldered on to the handles – a vase that Schliemann identified with the cup of King Nestor of Pylos, described in Homer's *Odyssey*.

Much of the funerary furniture appears to be the work of Cretan artisans, whose work was highly valued throughout the East Mediterranean, as far afield as Egypt, at the beginning of the second millennium BC. The military flavour of much of the artwork implies that this material was commissioned by the warriors of Mycenae, and was not imported from Crete. The grave circles at Mycenae represent a sudden flowering of wealth following a long period of stagnation and poverty in Greece. The source of the wealth of the warriors and their consorts buried in the grave circles can only be guessed at. Some archaeologists have suggested that the gold was loot from piracy or was payment to mercenaries. But the deposition of such massive quantities of gold, silver and copper in tombs – removing valuable mineral wealth from circulation – implies that there was a continuous supply of such wealth for the aristocracy of Mycenae.

Right: ENORMOUS QUANTITIES OF GOLD WERE FOUND IN THE SHAFT GRAVES INCLUDING LARGE NUMBERS OF PLATE METAL VESSELS, SUCH AS THIS CUP WITH ARCADED DECORATIONS FROM TOMB V IN CIRCLE A.

Dowris and the Irish Goldsmiths

Between 1000 and 600 BC there grew up in the lower valley of the River Shannon in the centre of Ireland one of the greatest metalworking traditions in prehistoric north-west Europe. In the years leading to the advent of iron-using cultures, in what is perhaps Ireland's first golden age, the bronze- and goldsmiths of north Munster in southern Ireland created works of sophistication whose influence was felt from Iberia to Denmark.

Some of these treasures have come into the hands of archaeologists following the chance discovery of great hoards of metal objects, often deposited in watery places, possibly to appease the gods in times of environmental and political uncertainty. Over one hundred and fifty such hoards are now known from the Late Bronze Age. One of the greatest of these hoards comes from Dowris in County Offaly. The Dowris hoard comprised over two hundred bronze

objects, many of which embodied the high degree of technological achievement for which the bronzesmiths of the last stages of the Irish Bronze Age are famous. No less than forty-four bells or rattles, as many spearheads, forty-three axeheads and over twenty extraordinary horns or trumpets had been dumped into the ground along with a collection of enigmatic crotals (pendants or weights resembling a bull's scrotum), perhaps related to a cult of bull worship, introduced to Ireland from the Continent.

The Dowris hoard has given its name to the last period of the Irish Bronze Age, a period of economic expansion and impending change. The bronzesmiths of the time were expert in both casting bronze and working with sheet metal. Although Ireland had long exported metal to Britain, the Dowris phase represented something of an industrial revolution in prehistoric metallurgy. In casting, clay moulds replaced those made of stone. New working methods included soldering and annealing. Many new forms of tool were developed by bronzesmiths who worked from fixed centres: sickles, knives, hammers, chisels and gouges were all produced along with thousands of looped and socketed axeheads. The changes were not all peaceful, however, and for the first time large numbers of weapons appeared in Ireland. Over six hundred swords have been discovered along with spears and shields.

The trumpets and great bronze cauldrons that set the north Munster area apart from the rest of Ireland may indicate the holding of great communal feasts. The people of the Dowris Phase lived partly in single farmsteads, such as Ballindery 2, and partly in larger settlement centres, some defended by ditches and palisades, as at Navan Fort. Still others lived in small lakeside settlements called crannogs, such as Clonfinlough. They used wheeled transport and draft horses to make their way through the forested countryside, and laid brushwood trackways across the soggy bogs. They practised a mixture of agriculture and hunting.

As well as bronze, the metalworking shops of the Dowris Phase produced some of the most exquisite gold objects of the Bronze Age. Some seven hundred gold items, mostly ornaments, are known from this phase. They include garment fasteners, hair-rings, neck ornaments that would often have complemented amber necklaces, collars, gorgets (throat armour) and bracelets, many fine examples of which come from other hoards in central Ireland. One of the best comes from County

Right: ITEMS FROM THE DOWRIS HOARD, DISCOVERED IN THE 1820S, INCLUDED CAULDRONS, TRUMPETS AND ENIGMATIC CROTALS.

Above: THIS FINE GOLD MODEL SHIP FROM BROIGHTER ECHOES THE MARITIME CONTACTS BETWEEN IRELAND AND IBERIA IN THE LATER BRONZE AGE.

Clare, where over one hundred and forty gold items were found in the Mooghaun hoard, the largest assemblage of Bronze Age gold ornaments from a single context in north and west Europe.

The large numbers of gold objects produced in the Dowris Phase were matched by a great increase in the amount of gold used in individual pieces. One garment fastener from Dunboyne in County Meath, an object with two conical terminals joined by a bow-shaped bar that operated as a kind of metal double-button holding together two buttonholes in a piece of clothing, weighed 1.2 kg. Such large objects must surely have been for ceremonial or display purposes rather than for simple everyday wear. Other gold items included hollow boxes and balls. Most of the gold items were made of bar or sheet gold, but other techniques were also developed at this time, including cladding surfaces with gold foil, in particular decorated pin heads, like those from Ballytegan in County Laoghais. The apogee of the Dowris goldsmiths' craft can be seen in the fine lock rings, which were made by soldering together gold threads no more than a millimetre thick. Some of these were made of up to ten separate pieces of gold.

Not all hoards were intended for permanent deposition. At the crannog of Rathtinaun in County Sligo, a wooden box was discovered containing a collection of feminine items, its location carefully marked by wooden sticks for later collection.

The hoards waned with the appearance of ironworking, which was to usher in a new age of Irish prehistory. Yet, even though times changed, many ritual practices remained, as testified by the finds of many other votive hoards from the Iron Age, notably the Broighter hoard, with its gold model ships.

Vix and Treasures of the European Iron Age

In the sixth century BC, the Celtic chieftains of south-east France and south-west Germany became enamoured of luxury items from the Mediterranean world. The investigation of the hillfort at Mont Lassois, France, and the associated rich burials at Vix produced sensational results confirming the scale of inter-Alpine contacts.

Below: DRINKING SETS LIKE THIS, WITH FINE CERAMICS AND BRONZES, ATTEST TO THE FASHION FOR MEDITERRANEAN SOCIAL FASHIONS IN IRON AGE WESTERN EUROPE.

Mont Lassois, a 109-m hill that protrudes from the upper valley of the River Seine, commands the land route from the Seine region to the corridor formed by the Rivers Rhône and Sarrone that leads down to the Mediterranean. In the later part of the sixth century BC, Mont Lassois was the residence of a powerful Celtic chief, who defended the hill with substantial ditches and palisades and an elaborate entrance way. Excavations of the defences and entrance way in the early 1950s produced many thousands of pottery sherds and metal fibulae (safety pins) and provided an assemblage of artefacts unrivalled at that time from a hillfort in France, and that enabled archaeologists to date the site's occupation relatively precisely. In addition to the local pottery, the excavators noted the presence of large quantities of wine amphorae that must have been brought in, presumably full of wine, from the newly flourishing Greek trading centre at Massilia, modern Marseilles.

In January 1953, in temperatures of between −1 and +2°C and their investigations hampered by snow, the archaeologists, led by local schoolteacher René Joffroy, decided to open the large burial mound at Vix that lay near the foot of the hillfort. The mound was some 42 m across and 6 m high. Undaunted by the scale of the undertaking, and not even imagining what awaited them within, the archaeologists dug into the mound to reveal the remains of a subrectangular wooden burial chamber. Inside the chamber, which had long since collapsed under the weight of the earth mound above, the body of a woman lay on the remains of a dismantled wooden wagon. The body was adorned with jewellery including a fine gold torc (neckring) of Greek manufacture, weighing about 450 gm. Nearby lay the remains of horse trappings and some bronze bowls.

The torc was not the only evidence that this Celtic princess came from a society with strong links with the Mediterranean world. Her grave was also furnished with all the necessities for a Greek-style symposium, or wine-drinking party. This included fine pottery cups, painted with black figures from Attica and a beautiful bronze wine flagon made in Etruria in Italy. In the north-west corner of the burial chamber, however, lay the greatest treasure, for which Vix has become justly famous: namely, a huge bronze krater or wine-mixing bowl. This krater, the largest bronze to survive from the ancient western world,

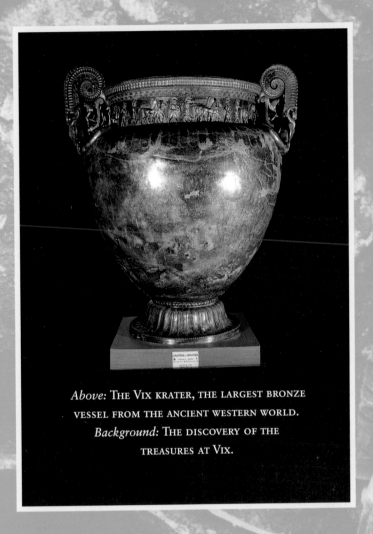

Above: THE VIX KRATER, THE LARGEST BRONZE
VESSEL FROM THE ANCIENT WESTERN WORLD.
Background: THE DISCOVERY OF THE
TREASURES AT VIX.

was in rather a pitiful state when Joffroy first set eyes on it. Weighing over 208 kg, it took the archaeologists no fewer than three days to extract it from where it had lain, battered and neglected, for over two and a half millennia.

After two bouts of restoration, the Vix krater was returned to its original glory. The body of the vessel had been cast as one piece, and had a diameter of 1.27 m. It rested on a foot of beaten bronze, itself weighing over 20 kg. The krater was decorated around the neck by a series of embossed friezes showing processions of Greek hoplite footsoldiers and horse-drawn chariots. It boasted two magnificent voluted handles, each over 55 cm high, weighing 45 kg apiece. Lions and snakes adorned the handles, which were complemented by the monstrous visage of a snake-haired gorgon on the surface of the krater. The body of the vessel was further ornamented by a variety of designs including spirals, palmettes and diamonds. The krater was probably made in Sparta, in Greece, or at Tarentum, a Greek colony in southern Italy. It was then transported in pieces by sea, most likely to Massilia, before heading by boat up the Rhône to its final destination north of the Alps, where it was reassembled for use in the sumptuous rounds of feasting and gift-giving that characterized the relations between paramount chiefs and their subordinates.

During the sixth century BC, hilltop-defended settlements in eastern France, Switzerland and Germany were often associated with rich burials outside the defences. These burials often contained luxury items that originated in the Mediterranean world. At Eberdingen-Hochdorf one of the grandest burials of all was decked out with gold ornaments that appear to have been made especially for the funeral. The tomb also housed a large cauldron containing the remains of a liquid, possibly mead, and locally produced, gold-encrusted drinking horns. Textiles had been hung from the walls of the chamber, and there was a bronze couch on wheels, made in Etruria or elsewhere in Italy. At the Heuneburg,

one of the greatest of the European hillforts, it was not only the burial goods that were of Mediterranean inspiration, but also some of the architecture. In addition, other exotic imports, silk and chickens made their European debut here.

If feasting and gift-giving endowed prestige in life, prestige in death was gained through the conspicuous consumption of highly valued imported wine sets, through removing them from this world by burying them in the tombs of the elite. Mediterranean traders were doubtless pleased to be able to meet the demand for such luxury items, in exchange for furs and hides, gold and foodstuffs, perhaps including the smoked hams for which the region subsequently became famous, as described by classical authors. The other form of currency for which there was great demand in the Mediterranean world was slaves.

Vix and its great krater are evidence for a society partly driven by a desire for prestige goods. The world of the princess, entombed on the wagon at the foot of Mont Lassois with her treasures, was one greatly touched by the expansion of Mediterranean influence and trade.

Ancient Classical Sculptures

Left: MARBLE STATUE OF THE GODDESS APHRODITE FROM THE ISLAND OF MELOS IN THE AEGEAN.
Opposite page: DETAIL FROM THE GREAT ALTAR OF ZEUS AT PERGAMON SHOWING THE BATTLE BETWEEN THE GREEK GODS AND THE GIANTS.

In the Middle Ages travellers and scholars started to recognize the remains of the earlier classical sites, which were yielding quantities of ancient art. For example, Buondelmonti, during a visit to the Greek island of Delos in the early fifteenth century, attempted to place the archaic colossal statue of Apollo, originally dedicated by the Naxians, back on its base. Elsewhere on the island he recorded 'a crowd of other statues executed with marvellous art, and yet others buried under little mounds'.

Not all sculptures fared so well. Take, for example, the sculptures from the mausoleum of the emperor Hadrian. According to one ancient source, the base was decorated with groups of ancient sculpture – some of them copies of original Greek sculptures – which were dismembered by the defenders of Rome against the attack of the Goths in AD 537. Other sculptures were deliberately removed by Christians, disapproving of pagan gods, while others in marble were taken down and destroyed to make lime. There is a story of a fifth-century priest in Arles who was injured by falling marble in the theatre, perhaps during the course of removing marble to decorate the new Christian basilica. Some of the destruction of ancient sculpture was thorough: a statue of Venus at Nîmes was found in 103 pieces. However, when a statue of the hero Hercules was found at Avignon in the fourteenth century, orders were given for it to be reburied.

The popes and the Italian nobility chose to decorate their palazzi with sculptures found on their estates. One of the most celebrated was the *Laocoön*, found in January 1506 near Santa Maria Maggiore in Rome and installed by Pope Julius II in the Belvedere of the Museo Pio-Clemintino. It was the pope's architect who recognized the group showing the Trojan priest Laocoön and his two sons being bound by two snakes that had emerged from the sea as they prepared to make a sacrifice. This work formed part of the scheme of the Palace of Titus at Rome – though the bronze original may have been made at Pergamon in western Turkey – and was described by Pliny as being 'the most worthy [of sculptures] of admiration'. So famous was the statue that it was handed over to the French under the Treaty of Tolentino in 1797, only returning to Rome in 1816. The group so caught the public imagination that Charles Dickens was able to conjure up the *Laocoön* as a simile when Scrooge attempted to put on his stockings.

Left: BRONZE
STATUE OF
ATHENA FROM A
GROUP OF
STATUES FOUND
IN THE PIRAEUS.

The Grand Tour gave an added incentive for gentlemen travellers to collect ancient sculpture that could then be sent home and displayed in their homes. Such displays could be seen in English country houses such as Holkham Hall in Norfolk - home of Thomas Coke, later Earl of Leicester – and Newby Hall in Yorkshire. The demand by English collectors for classical sculpture was so great that in the later decades of the eighteenth century dealers such as Gavin Hamilton were searching the ruins of Hadrian's Villa at Tivoli for suitable works of art. Ostia, the port of Rome, also attracted the antiquities dealers. It was from here, probably in 1775, that Hamilton extracted a fine, semi-draped statue of Venus that he sold for £600 to Charles Townley; the statue is now in the British Museum.

With the rise of museums in Europe, collections of sculpture were acquired for display in each country's national museum. There was a wholesale removal of sculptures from Mediterranean sites to feed the classical tastes of the European public. Thus the pedimental groups from the temple of Aphaia on Aegina, representing the sieges of Troy, were discovered by C. R. Cockerell and sold to Prince Ludwig of Bavaria; they are now on display in Munich. Fragments of the relief sculptures from the Great Altar of Zeus at Pergamon had been acquired from the eighteenth century, but most were removed in the nineteenth and were sent to Berlin. Perhaps the most celebrated was the collection of the sculptural decoration of the Parthenon from the Athenian acropolis by Lord Elgin, which was despatched to London; other fragments from the same temple were sent to Paris where they underwent repair. Yet Elgin was not alone in Greece at this time. E. D. Clarke had earlier managed to remove one of the massive caryatids from the grand entrance to the sanctuary of Demeter at Eleusis in Attica and to present it to Cambridge University where it was initially displayed in the University Library. The statue had been known to some of the earliest travellers to Greece, but it was Clarke who managed to persuade the local Orthodox priest to assist with its extraction from a dung heap.

The *Venus de Milo*, a statue showing the semi-naked goddess Aphrodite, was discovered by a peasant on the Aegean island of Melos in the spring of 1820. A French naval officer, along with the French vice-consul, acquired the work on behalf of the French ambassador to the Sublime Porte at Constantinople, the Marquis de Rivière, who in turn presented it to Louis XVIII. The statue, made from two blocks of marble, was found with an inscribed base, which, if it belongs, showed that the statue had been made by a sculptor from Antioch on the Maeander. The popularity of

Above: CHARLES TOWNLEY AMONG HIS
CLASSICAL SCULPTURES.

the statue has much to do with European politics at the start of the
nineteenth century. In 1815, with the defeat of Napoleon, the
French were forced to return the marble statue *Venus de Medici* to
Florence, and thus the *Venus de Milo* was presented to the public
as a far superior sculpture than the one they had just had to
relinquish.

As national museums competed with each other during the
nineteenth century, large-scale operations were mounted to acquire
complete compositions. One of the long-standing sculptured
monuments was the Mausoleum of Halikarnassos, one of the
seven wonders of the ancient world. This monumental tomb had
been constructed in the mid-fourth century BC for the local dynast,
Mausolus. Some of the leading Greek sculptors of the day –
Skopas, Bryaxis, Timotheos and Leochares, according to Pliny in
his *Natural History* – were involved with the project. The site of
the tomb seems to have been rediscovered in the late fifteenth
century, when the Hospitaller Knights of St John had been
rebuilding the fortifications of their castle at Bodrum (at the site of
the ancient Halikarnassos). Some of the pieces were exported to
Italy and formed part of private collections in places such as

Genoa, but the rest were either built into the castle, enhancing its
'classical' feel, or destroyed.

Although the earliest British attempts to acquire the marbles,
in the form of three-dimensional and relief sculptures, had been in
1816 when a permit had been obtained for their removal from the
castle, it was not until 1846 that Sir Stratford Canning, the British
ambassador to the Sublime Porte (at Constantinople), was able to
load them on to a Royal Navy ship. They were eventually
presented to the British Museum. Further investigations were
conducted by Charles Newton during the 1850s, and the site of
the Mausoleum was found.

Most of the ancient bronze statues were recycled, either as
tastes changed or just for the base metal. Thus visitors to ancient
sites can often be met with a mass of empty statue bases where
such statues once stood. One of the few ancient bronze statues to
have survived on land was the *Charioteer*, which was found during
French excavations at the sanctuary of Apollo at Delphi in 1896. It
survived because it had been toppled and buried during an ancient
earthquake. The figure shows a young man in long garb still
holding the reins. The original group would have included the
horses and chariot. Fragments of the inscribed statue base show
that it had served as part of a dedication by the Sicilian tyrant
Polyzalos of Gela, whose team of horses had won the chariot race
in the Pythian games at Delphi in either 478 or 474 BC.

However, the Roman taste for Greek art meant that
consignments of Greek sculpture were sent back to Italy. Some of
these shipments never made it, and with the rise of sport diving in
recent years a number of ancient sculptures have been found.
These include a bronze statue of Zeus (but often identified with
the sea-god Poseidon) off Cape Artemision, at the north end of the
island of Euboia. A fifth-century BC shipwreck off Porticello in the
Straits of Messina was found to contain the bronze head of a
Greek philosopher.

In 1959, during excavations in the Piraeus, the port of Athens,
a group of bronze statues of mixed date was discovered. One of
the earliest, perhaps dating from the late sixth century BC, appears
to show the god Apollo. It takes the form of sculpture commonly
known as a *kouros*. In its left hand are what appear to be the
remains of a bow, and on its outstretched right hand would
originally have been a phiale, or shallow cup, which would have
indicated the making of an offering or libation. Other pieces
include a larger than life-size Athena, and two of Artemis; these
may date to the fourth century BC, or perhaps be later Hellenistic
copies of classical originals. As the archaeological context has been
dated to the first century BC, it has been argued that the works
formed a consignment ready for shipment to Rome but were
caught up in Sulla's attack on the city in 86 BC.

Shipments from Greece also included replicas of famous Greek
works for the Roman market. There are descriptions of statues in

the Athenian agora being regularly copied, and bands of sculptors worked to meet demand. One of the most interesting of these groups was discovered in the Piraeus. It consisted of several marble relief panels showing scenes of the battle between the Greeks and the Amazons. In fact, the individual scenes were part of one particular work, the relief shield from the great gold and ivory statue of the Athena Parthenos by the sculptor Pheidias, which was housed in the Parthenon. Although the original has been lost, the scenes shown on the Piraeus panels can be clearly identified from Roman marble copies of the complete shield (such as the Strangford Shield now in the British Museum, or another shield found at Patras in the Peloponnese). Clearly, some cultured Roman wished to have 'Parthenon' reliefs decorating his villa.

THE RIACE BRONZES

Bronze statues were a common sight in the ancient world. Such sculptures were often erected to commemorate famous victories in the great athletic festivals of the Greek world such as at Olympia and Delphi. Likewise, the public spaces of many of the cities contained monuments to famous citizens. Although we can read classical descriptions of such bronze sculptures, notably by Pausanias who wrote a travel guide to Greece in the second century AD, hardly any of these statues survive today.

A number of bronze statues have been found underwater, and the likely explanation for this is that they had been removed from their original locations by Romans who had acquired a taste for Greek sculpture. In 1972, two large bronzes were found off Riace Marina in southern Italy. This pair seems to come from a group of naked but armed military figures, and the assumption is that it was part of a victory monument in some Greek sanctuary from which it had removed. No doubt the statues were on their way to some Italian villa when the ship they were aboard got into difficulty, and the statues were jettisoned to try to lighten the vessel's load; a study of the seabed found no indication of a shipwreck. In style they appear to belong to the mid-fifth century BC, and some scholars have tried to associate them with some of the well-known sculptors of that time. Some scholars have suggested that they may have formed part of the group of Achaian heroes at Olympia made by Onatas of Aegina, though this is hard to prove; certainly, one of the statues from the Olympia group was reported by Pausanias to have been taken to Rome by the emperor Nero. The skill of the Greek bronzesmith can be seen in the inlaid eyes, the coppered lips and the silvered teeth. One of the figures originally wore a Corinthian helmet, but this has become detached.

Right: A BRONZE CHARIOTEER FROM A VICTORY MONUMENT DEDICATED AT DELPHI.

ONE OF TWO BRONZE GENERALS
FOUND IN THE SEA OFF RIACE IN
SOUTHERN ITALY.

Celtic Prince

One of the most important archaeological finds in Europe for decades was made in recent years: an almost perfectly preserved statue of a Celtic 'prince', 1.82 m tall and weighing 227 kg, and about two thousand five hundred years old.

I t was discovered by archaeologists excavating a Celtic grave site near Glauberg, north-east of Frankfurt. The reddish-brown sandstone image, complete except for its feet, is clad in carved armour, crowned with a laurel wreath, and holding a sword and shield. Gold jewellery found in the nearby grave matches that shown on the statue. Archaeologists believe the figure was originally placed on the grave, and was then later moved and buried, which explains how it survived in such good condition when other grave sites were plundered.

Until this discovery it was not known that the Celts made statues of this size. The new figure bears a remarkable resemblance to the four faces carved in bas-relief on each side of a stone pillar from Pfalzfeld, in the Rhineland, dating to 450–350 BC, which have the same extraordinary headgear, the three-leaf motif on the brow, the beard and the three-leaf palmette beneath the chin.

Celtic Torcs

In 1990, a $10-million hoard of gold and silver artefacts, said to be the biggest discovery of treasure in Britain this century, was unearthed from a 16-ha field in Norfolk, eastern England. Being treasure trove, it was declared the property of the Queen and handed to the British Museum.

This same field, at Ken Hill near Snettisham, first rose to prominence in 1948 when, having previously been used for growing lavender, it was ploughed to greater depth in preparation for a cereal crop. Three hoards of torcs (Iron Age neckrings, made of braided wire) were found, and two more were unearthed by the plough in 1950. These early finds included the great gold Snettisham Torc, one of Britain's finest antiquities. Oddly, the field had since been left undisturbed by metal-detector enthusiasts, although marked on maps as the site of that discovery, and despite other sporadic finds being dragged to the surface by the plough over the years. It was generally assumed that the site had been virtually wrecked by ploughing.

In 1989, however, Cecil Hodder, an eighty-year-old former RAF squadron leader, explored the field with a metal detector after harvest, and found a coin together with four small fragments of torcs. The following year he made a more systematic search and hit the jackpot: the fragments of a bronze vessel in a pit about 30 cm below the surface. Inside were 587 pieces of broken metalwork weighing 9.5 kg, including at least fifty more torcs, seventy ingot rings and bracelets, three straight ingots and several coins. After he reported this find, the British Museum was called in and investigated the whole field, stripping away topsoil and excavating a 1.2-ha area. By Christmas, another five hoards had been detected, including dozens more torcs: twenty-five bronze specimens were mostly fragmentary, but thirty-eight others of gold and silver were beautifully preserved. Indeed, they are in such fine condition that one, which had been compressed when buried, sprang back to its normal shape when removed from the small, rock-cut pit of the kind in which all the hoards had been placed.

Some of the pits contained neat, closely packed 'nests' of torcs with coins and bracelets. The deepest contained particularly fine neckrings: four gold, seven gold/silver alloy (electrum) and one silver. The Museum's five hoards yielded sixty-three torcs (nine gold, fifteen electrum, fourteen silver and twenty-five bronze).

Altogether, therefore, this one field has yielded seventy-five complete and a hundred fragmentary torcs; more than a hundred ingot rings/bracelets; and 170 coins. The combined weight is over 29 kg. The Snettisham deposits were probably not votive: the field was not a recognizable sanctuary, and Iron Age artefacts in bogs or rivers, which are generally reckoned to be offerings, almost never include torcs. It is thought by some specialists that the site may instead have been some sort of tribal treasury or bank, and whoever hid this bullion hoard intended to retrieve it.

Neckrings were important items of jewellery, display and prestige in the Celtic world. Many sculptured figures of the period wear them (both humans and gods), and the Roman statue of the *Dying Gaul* wears nothing else. The historian Polybius said that Celtic warriors went into battle adorned with little more than torcs, while other writers specified that both men and women wore gold neckrings: Queen Boudicca, whose tribe, the Iceni, lived in the Snettisham region, was also described by the Roman historian Dio Cassius as wearing a great gold neckring. Excavations in Celtic cemeteries in Europe have often revealed torcs on adults, especially women. However, neckrings have never been found in such hoards in Britain before, and no site in mainland Europe has ever produced more than half a dozen torcs.

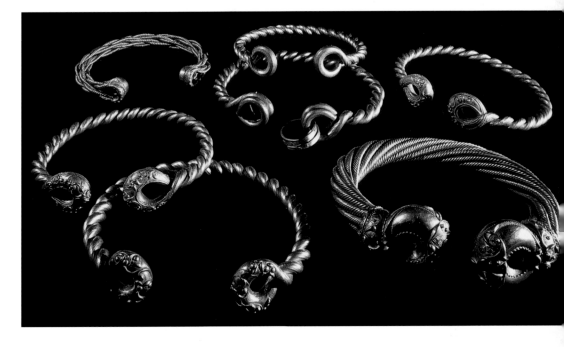

Above: TORCS FROM SNETTISHAM, IPSWICH AND NEEDWOOD FOREST.

The Lady of Elche

The limestone bust known as the 'Lady of Elche' is probably the best known and most spectacular object to have come down to us from the pre-Roman past of the Iberian peninsula, and more specifically from the Iberian Culture of the last five centuries BC. Thought to date to the late fifth or early fourth century BC on the basis of its style, the sculpture was found by chance on 4 August 1897 at the Iberian town of La Alcudia (modern Elche, in Valencia, Spain) during agricultural work, and hence little is known of its archaeological context. The discoverer was a fourteen-year-old boy, Manuel Campello Esclápez, who was helping his family on the farm. His pick came up against a stone that turned out to be the face of a figure. The sculpture, once unearthed, was at first baptized the 'Moorish Queen'.

The bust, 56 cm high (it was made in this form – it is not the broken or cut top part of a statue), is more or less life-size and may have been hidden intentionally, as it was protected by a semicircle of stone slabs and stood on two slabs, with its back against the city wall. This cist-like arrangement was filled with sand from the beach, which helped preserve the polychrome decoration of the sculpture. Today, traces of red paint can still be seen on its lips, mantilla and cloak.

The sculpture is thought to be the portrait of a real person – perhaps an aristocrat or a priestess – rather than an idealized goddess figure, as it has a slight asymmetry instead of physical perfection. Nevertheless, the lady (some have suggested it may be a male, but most scholars agree it is a female) has fine features: a slim, straight nose, delicate lips, almond-shaped eyes and an expression of deep concentration. The form of tiara above her head could be mounted on something like the present-day Spanish ornamental comb, making a kind of mantilla held to the brow by a diadem. At both sides of the head are big, disc-shaped cases, which were probably metal in reality, and which seem to have held her hair, which was plaited and coiled into a spiral; the cases are held to the diadem by a double strap. This kind of complex headdress

was described by Artemidorus, a Greek traveller who visited Iberia around 100 BC. In fact, such outfits seem to have been quite common in this period, as shown by finds of their remains: one in silver filigree, from Extremadura, is now in Madrid's National Archaeological Museum, while another similar specimen was found at the Iberian necropolis of El Cigarrelejo, in Murcia.

The cloak covers the sculpture's back and shoulders, and extends to the front, where it opens to reveal three necklaces made up of two kinds of pendants (miniature amphorae and medallions) on a sort of shawl or toga, below which can be seen an inner tunic fixed to the neck by a small, ring-shaped fibula.

The sculpture has a coarse finish at the back, indicating that it was intended to be placed against a wall; and it contains an almost spherical cavity, 18 cm in diameter and 16 cm deep, which has been the subject of different interpretations. It is not big enough to be considered a funerary urn, so the hole may have held some kind of offering, relic or talisman. At the time of the bust's discovery, the cavity showed absolutely no traces of its usage, and certainly no sign of blackening as might be expectedif it had contained ashes like other sculptures of the Iberian Culture. Yet the object was clearly finished, as shown by its polychrome painting.

A few days after the discovery, the sculpture was sold to French archaeologist Pierre Paris for 4,000 Francs, and taken to the French capital where it was exhibited for many years in the Louvre. It returned to Spain in 1941, as part of a whole list of Spanish antiquities and a Murillo painting that were presented by France in exchange for a Velázquez, an El Greco and an eighteenth-century tapestry. The sculpture was then displayed in the Prado in Madrid, but since 1971 the Lady of Elche has been the star attraction of the National Archaeological Museum. It is a true Spanish icon, which has inspired artists ever since its discovery and whose image has appeared on postage stamps, banknotes, and even lottery tickets and telephone cards!

The Panagyurishté Treasure

Although ancient literary sources and inscriptions often refer to the widespread use of gold and silver plate in the ancient world, it is rare to find such pieces. Inheritance, reworking and theft have all helped to remove the evidence from the archaeological record. However, it is on the fringes of the Greek world that examples of the real wealth of the Greek cities have been found. Some of the best pieces have been discovered in the area known as Thrace (the equivalent of north-east Greece and Bulgaria) where Greek silver seems to have been used alongside locally made pieces.

Some of these treasures have been found in tombs. For example, the grave mounds at Duvanli contained several stunning Greek silver vessels decorated with gilded figures. These include a kantharos (a stemmed drinking cup) with scenes of Dionysos, and a phiale (a shallow cup) with a chariot racing scene. An exotic piece was a rhyton consisting of a long, curved, fluted horn, ending with the front of a horse. Given that Athenian pottery was found in the same groups, it has been proposed that the silver

Right: GOLD RHYTON IN THE FORM OF A RAM FROM THE PANAGYURISHTÉ TREASURE.

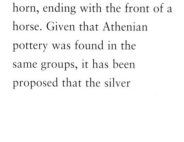

plate was in fact the upmarket version of the widely found red-figured pottery. A similar mix of Athenian pottery with silver plate from the Greek world was found in a grave mound at Dalboki.

Yet one of the most superb hoards of Greek plate was found at Panagyurishté in Bulgaria, and consisted of over 6 kg of gold vessels. This hoard, perhaps dating to the fourth century BC, contained a number of unusual relief jugs ('head vases') and rhyta. The rhyton was a special drinking vessel that was common in the Persian world; an earlier silver example, a calf's head decorated with satyrs, was found at Rachmanli in Thrace. There are four in this hoard, representing different animals: a stag, a bull, a ram and a goat. In the neck part of each rhyton was a relief scene that suggests they were made in the Greek world, even if their last resting place was in barbarian Thrace. The iconography is purely Greek, including scenes with Herakles and Theseus, Dionysos and his female companions the Maenads (particularly appropriate for a drinking vessel), and a Judgement of Paris.

One of the three relief jugs is a representation of the goddess Athena, wearing a helmet surmounted by a sphinx and a griffin. This distinctive headdress may well have been intended to evoke the enormous gold and ivory statue of the goddess, known only through descriptions and Roman marble copies, that was made by the sculptor Pheidias and placed in the Parthenon at Athens. The other two may represent the mythical warrior women, the Amazons. Such pieces are quite rare, and a silver version, two heads back-to-back, appears to come from a precious hoard at Tell el-Maskhuta in Egypt.

On the amphora – in fact designed to be a drinking vessel – from the treasure there is a scene that represents two heroes defending a door. Although the scene may represent a story such as 'The Seven against Thebes', the pose of the two men recalls the famous statues in the Athenian agora, the *Tyrannicides*, representing Harmodios and Aristogeiton. This might suggest that the workmanship was that of a goldsmith familiar with Athenian statuary. One of the more striking pieces was a gold phiale decorated with three rows of heads representing blacks.

The Panagyurishté phiale also carried two inscriptions, one in the equivalent of Attic silver coins (drachmae) and the other in Persian gold; interestingly, it was clearly made to weigh 100 Persian darics (a Persian gold coin weighing around 8.46 gm). Such an inscription is suggestive of the gold phiale, valued at 16 Athenian minas (the equivalent of 100 darics), once owned by the Greek Demus who had acquired his cup from the great king of Persia.

The Rogozen Treasure

Perhaps one of the most impressive finds of ancient treasure in recent years was the 1986 discovery at Rogozen in Bulgaria of what appeared to be two buried sacks of silver. The two deposits contained 165 pieces, and together they weighed 19.91 Kg. As this represents 3,600 sigloi (a Persian unit of weight, commonly used for silver plate), it has been suggested that the hoard may have been collected, perhaps in the fourth century BC, to form a sort of tribute and for some reason was never recovered. The plate consisted of what seem to be vessels made in the Greek world and others that were made in Thrace (now north-east Greece and Bulgaria), probably in the region of Vratsa, and sometimes lifting motifs and forms from their classical counterparts.

A number of the pieces carried ownership inscriptions. A phiale (a shallow cup) and a jug appear to have been the property of one Satokos. This name is known from the Greek historian Thucydides to have been used by one of the Thracian kings in c. 431–430 BC. A larger group of ownership names, all on phialai, refer to Kotys. Each inscription seems to be qualified by a place name, which, it has been argued, indicates the origin of the plate: the different places mentioned are Beos (twice), Apros (twice), Sauthaba, Ergiske (three times) and Geistoi (twice). Kotys is also a Thracian (Odrysian) royal name, and these inscriptions have been linked to Kotys I (383–359 BC). A third royal name is that of Kersebleptes, which is linked to the topographical name of Ergiske. Such an individual is known to have been one of the successors of Kotys I. Together these inscriptions have led to a theory that the hoard was a royal one, perhaps accumulated over one hundred years.

One of the most eye-catching pieces in the hoard is a gilded silver phiale decorated inside with a scene in high relief. The cup also carries an ownership inscription: 'belonging to Didykaimos.' The bearded figure on the right appears to be grabbing at a woman on the left whose clothes are falling off her. The man is identified by various attributes such as a lion skin, a club and a quiver; he is the hero Herakles, and his pose would suggest that he has been drinking. The woman is identified as Auge by a Greek inscription above her head. The myth represented concerns the priestess Auge, the daughter of King Aleos whose banquet Herakles had been attending. The inscription above Herakles is one of the few ancient Greek jokes to survive. The craftsman, instead of putting the name of the hero, has merely written the Greek for 'it's obvious'; in other words, if you don't recognize this figure from his attributes, an inscription won't help you. This may have been a joke at the expense of the Thracian acquiring the cup who perhaps could not read the Greek inscription.

One of the other apparently Greek pieces from the treasure was a phiale decorated with four pairs of lion-griffins around the central boss. The piece weighed the equivalent of 50 sigloi (a Persian unit of weight). Some of the other phialai from the hoard were made in a Thracian style. There are some decorated with the heads of women, which in format recall the layout of the heads of blacks on the gold phiale from Panagyurishté (see p.162). A further phiale was decorated with the heads of cattle.

Some of the jugs in the treasure were decorated with relief scenes. Although based on classical iconography, the execution suggests that they were made by Thracian silversmiths. On one jug there are two representations of the Great Goddess seated on the back of a panther, and clutching a bow and arrow. Between the pair is the hunting motif, common in eastern art, of a lion holding a stag by the throat. The Great Goddess, again holding a bow, appears on another jug, this time seated in a chariot pulled by winged horses. A more classical theme is represented on a further jug. In three identical scenes, Herakles, holding a club, is being attacked by an Amazon, one of the group of female warriors. Another jug has a more everyday scene showing a boar hunt, with two spearmen on horses. A further group of jugs is more plain, and merely decorated with stylized petals around their walls.

A typically Thracian item from the treasure is a silver gilt, biconical beaker. The wall is decorated with a frieze of semi-mythical animals; one has elements of a stag and a goat, as well as having eight legs. The shape of the cup finds parallels with two found in the Agighiol tumulus in Romania, and probably dates to the mid-fourth century BC. A further biconical cup, reported to have been dredged up in the Danube, is now in the Metropolitan Museum of Art in New York; there is a suggestion that it may also come from Agighiol. All four beakers carry the motif of the eight-legged, goat-bearded stag. The stylistic inference is that the Rogozen beaker was not locally made, but rather came from the area to the north of the Danube. It has been suggested that it might have been an example of a looted piece of plate, or possibly a diplomatic gift between the elite.

Above: THIS IS THE MOST SPLENDID PHIALE IN THE ROGOZEN TREASURE. THE *OMPHALOS,* OR CENTRAL BOSS, IS DECORATED WITH A ROSETTE OF LONG PETALS ALTERNATING WITH SPIKELIKE LEAVES. FOUR PAIRS OF CONFRONTED LION-GRIFFINS WITH THEIR HEADS TURNED BACKWARD ALTERNATING WITH GILT PALMETTES ARE REPRESENTED IN THE WIDE OUTER FRIEZE. POSSIBLY THIS PHIALE WAS MADE BY A GREEK MASTER FROM ASIA MINOR. ITS ORIGIN IS INDICATED BY THE PAIRS OF CONFRONTED GRIFFINS, A CHARACTERISTICALLY ORIENTAL MOTIF, AND THE COMBINATION OF ANIMAL AND VEGETAL MOTIFS. THE REPRESENTATION OF ANIMALS IN PROFILE WITH ONLY TWO LEGS VISIBLE, AND THE TREATMENT OF THEIR TAILS AND WINGS EITHER GEOMETRICALLY, OR IN A WAY THAT SUGGESTS VEGETATION, IS ALSO TYPICAL OF THE METALWORK AND SCULPTURE OF ASIA MINOR. THIS GREEK PHIALE WOULD HAVE ARRIVED IN THRACE THROUGH EXCHANGE, OR AS A GIFT OR WAR BOOTY.

Etruscan Tombs

The Etruscan cemeteries of modern Tuscany in Italy long attracted the attention of early travellers who wondered at the rock-cut tombs, which were often filled with fine pottery imported from the Greek mainland. The tombs of Etruria were so productive – one early writer suggested that pottery was collected from them like truffles – that Josiah Wedgwood was to name one of his ceramic factories 'Etruria' after the find spot of so many of the fine 'vases' that were to become the models for his own designs. Lucien Bonaparte, Prince of Canino, dug on his lands around Vulci, and the tombs were to provide material for the growing classical collections of many of the newly established museums of Europe. One estimate from the 1830s suggested that more than three thousand four hundred Greek pots were recovered from tombs in the area in a single year.

Above: REPRESENTATION OF LARTHIA SEIANTI FROM A TERRACOTTA SARCOPHAGUS LID IN AN ETRUSCAN TOMB AT CHIUSI.

O ne of the most famous nineteenth-century travellers and explorers of the region was George Dennis. During the 1840s he was to make several journeys through the region, which was to be described in his book *The Cities and Cemeteries of Etruria* (1848). This was an exciting time when numerous important finds were being made, perhaps one of the most important being the Regolini-Galassi tomb at Cerveteri, which had been opened in 1836. This tomb contained a number of exotic imports including gilded silver bowls that were probably made in the eastern Mediterranean. These were decorated with scenes such as lion hunts. In 1850, the British Museum acquired the contents of the Isis tomb at Vulci, which held such exotic objects as a carved ostrich egg and a faience flask bearing hieroglyphic inscriptions. The Bernardini tomb at Palestrina included a gilded silver bowl that was decorated not only with incised scenes of eastern origin but also with snake-like attachments around the outer rim.

During the excavation of Etruscan tombs it was recognized that a proportion of the items in some of the earliest came from Egypt or the Near East. The movement of such objects, which included exotic metalwork as well as ivory, is probably best explained in terms of Phoenician contact. The Phoenicians, who originated on the eastern seaboard of the Mediterranean, established 'colonies' in North Africa (such as Carthage), western Sicily and elsewhere in the western Mediterranean.

The high quality of paintings, in particular those found in the tombs around Tarquinia, captured the imagination of the British public in the second half of the nineteenth century and also stimulated great interest in central Europe, especially Germany, as they provided dramatic insight into the mysterious Etruscan culture. For example, the tomb of the Leopards was decorated with a musician playing a double-flute. One of the most celebrated tombs was the tomb of the Reliefs at Cerveteri, known since the early nineteenth century, which in effect had been cut from the rock to form a banqueting chamber, with drinking cups and other ornaments 'hanging' from the walls. However, instead of living banqueters, corpses would have been placed around the room in niches carved as couches complete with cushions. The tomb itself probably dates from the early third century BC.

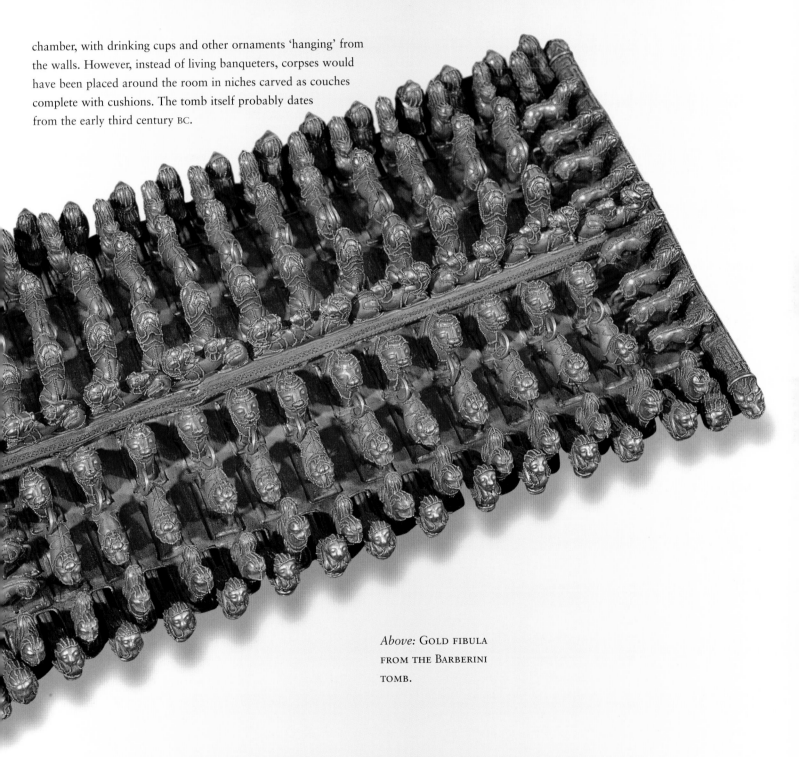

Above: GOLD FIBULA FROM THE BARBERINI TOMB.

The Hildesheim Treasure

One of the most important hoards of Roman silver was discovered in October 1868 during the construction of military earthworks near the town of Hildesheim in Germany. The hoard consisted of over sixty individual pieces ranging from large mixing bowls to drinking cups. There was also a silver folding tripod table and a lampstand. The pieces appear to have been a complete dining service that was buried in a time of danger.

Right: TWO SILVER DRINKING CUPS FROM THE TREASURE.
Below: SILVER EGG PLATE.

Although some of the pieces may date back to the Republican period, it is thought that the group was buried during the time of Augustus. The owner had considerable means and is likely to have been one of the Roman officers who was involved in the campaigns against the Germanic tribes. It is perhaps significant that the find was made outside the frontiers of the Roman empire, halfway between the Rhine and the Elbe.

Literary and epigraphic records of domestic silver plate suggest that a set (*ministerium*) would consist of two elements, the silver for drinking (*argentum escarium*) and the silver for eating (*argentum potorium*). Elements of both are present in the Hildesheim treasure. Within the treasure were a number of sets. For example, a set of four silver cups, each weighing about 320 gm, were decorated with inlaid niello ivy wreaths on the upper wall; a set of identical, but much smaller, cups was also found in the treasure. A pair of silver relief cups was decorated with theatrical scenes; both tragic and comic masks fill the decor. The setting is wooded and two stone-built and garlanded altars are shown, each surmounted by a statue. A more simple drinking cup was decorated with other emblems of the drinking-god Bacchus including the thyrsus. The festival emphasis is made by the way that garlands are draped around the cup.

One of the more impressive pieces was a silver cup with a gilded medallion in the centre. This showed a seated figure of the goddess Minerva, looking back over her shoulder. Other such medallion cups from the treasure include one with a scene showing the hero Hercules strangling two snakes. A pair of relief dishes from the treasure shows the eastern goddess Cybele with her consort Attis.

A ladle (*simpulum*) from the treasure had a handle in the form of a branch, over which a vine was growing, a suitable motif for an object used in a drinking service. The main vessel from a drinking set such as this was a large krater for mixing the wine and water, again decorated with vine tendrils. Some of the pieces from the treasure were inscribed with their weight. For example, each of a set of three trays was inscribed with an annotation that shows the combined weight of the three to have been 'two pounds, five ounces, and four scruples', the equivalent of 795.9 gm. The trays are in fact slightly lighter than the average 263.3 gm, and this has been explained by the loss of rectangular feet at the corners.

Hoards from Pompeii

*With the eighteenth-century excavations of the cities
destroyed by the great eruption of Vesuvius in AD 79,
unprecedented views of the Roman world started to emerge.
Many of the celebrated objects from the excavations at
Pompeii, as well as the nearby town of Herculaneum, have
included intricate wall paintings and mosaics, together with
major pieces of public art such as sculpture. However, the
circumstances of the burial of the cities allowed everyday
objects to be discovered* in situ. *Thus for the first time it
was possible to gain a glimpse of Roman luxury.*

U nlike ruined houses and settlements that were normally
robbed of their precious treasures, Pompeii and
Herculaneum have yielded a sizeable proportion of items
in gold and silver that were abandoned as their owners tried to flee
the destruction. It is clear that silver plate was in regular use in the
homes of the elite. Its presence has been explained in part by the
taste for Greek silver plate acquired during Roman expansion into
the Greek lands of the East Mediterranean. This taste even became
formalized in Roman art, as the tomb of a Roman magistrate

(*aedile*) at Pompeii, C. Vestorius Priscus, was even decorated with
a scene showing a table laid out with a set of silver plate that
included cups and jugs.

Although some plate may have been recovered in the weeks
and months after the eruption of Vesuvius – this may explain the
presence of a group of corpses carrying a lantern in the remains of
the villa of Diomedes – some complete sets were discovered during
the excavations. The first such set, consisting of 109 pieces as well
as gold jewellery and over a thousand gold coins, was not
discovered until 1895. It was found in the ruins of a villa at
Boscoreale, to the north-west of Pompeii (see p.176). This villa
seems to have formed the centre of an agricultural estate as it
contained wine presses, an olive press and a large room for storing
wine. The treasure itself was hidden in the wine-pressing room,
and beside it was the body of a woman.

The treasure seems to have been accumulated over time. The
earliest piece appears to have been a stemless silver cup with a
gilded central boss. Inside were engraved bands of lotus leaves. A
series of Greek letters may be traces of a 'signature' by the Greek
craftsman. Similar cups have been found elsewhere in southern

Above: SILVER DRINKING CUP.

Above left: SILVER DIPPER WITH RELIEF MARINE SCENE
ON THE HANDLE.

Italy and Sicily. For example, a pair was found in the burial of a Celtic warrior, along with other silver plate, at Montefortino in central Italy in 1895; the treasure was later acquired by the Metropolitan Museum of Art in New York. As this was part of a cemetery of Gauls, it has been suggested that these cups were part of a hoard of looted silver, perhaps made in the late fourth century BC. Like the Boscoreale cup, both these cups have a central cone, which has certain stylistic links with Etruscan bronze cups. Three similar cups, now in Berlin, were discovered at Paterno in Sicily. Together, these cups suggest that they were created within the context of the Greek colonies of southern Italy, perhaps at the end of the fourth century BC. If so, this makes the Boscoreale cup over three hundred and fifty years old before it was buried.

A particularly fine example of silver plate is the pair of silver kantharoi (stemmed drinking cups) with relief decoration. Both seem to have been the products of the Imperial Augustan court. The first shows the emperor Augustus seated on a folding chair, surrounded by troops and lictors (carrying bundles of rods). Before him kneel a group of figures who, from their dress (animal skins) and beards, can be identified as barbarians; they have presumably either been defeated in battle or have submitted in the face of Rome. Augustus is presented with the children of the tribes and extends his hand in an act of clemency. This image may reflect one of Augustus' trips to the German frontier, either in 15 or 8 BC. On the other side of the kantharos Augustus is seen enthroned and surrounded by deities. In his hand he holds a globe on which the goddess Venus places the representation of Victory, indicating how

Augustus' rule encompasses the whole world. Elsewhere Roma, the personification of Rome, stands over a pile of captured enemy weapons. Behind Augustus a procession of figures is led by the god of war, Mars; these are likely to be representations of the captured peoples and provinces who now submit to Rome thanks to the prowess of Augustus' armies.

The second cup shows the official sacrifice that was made at the start of the campaign. A bull is about to be struck by an axe in front of a garlanded temple. On the reverse is the triumphal scene after the campaign, which shows Tiberius (Augustus' successor) mounted on a chariot. It has been argued that all four scenes may have been based on a now lost major monument that celebrated Tiberius' victories in AD 12. The use of such imagery on drinking vessels may be explained as being a special commission by a member of Augustus' court. No doubt contemporary with these cups is the pair found in the grave of a member of the local social elite at Hoby in Denmark. Though the style is clearly Augustan, the iconography shows the incidents from the Trojan War: first, the appeal by King Priam for the body of his son Hektor, and second, the story of Philoktetes.

A further pair of kantharoi from the hoard shows a squatting boar in relief. He rests before an amphora lying on its side. The boar may be about to be killed as there is a large knife nearby. The piece appears to have been made by a Greek, as it carries a Greek inscription naming the craftsman, Sabinus. An unusual relative of these kantharoi is a silver 'saucepan' or 'skillet', with elaborately fluted walls. The handle is decorated with swans' heads and a

Left: SILVER SKYPHOS.
Right: GOLD AND MOTHER-OF-PEARL NECKLACE.

thyrsus, the emblem of the god of drinking, Dionysos. Such vessels are likely to have been used for serving hot liquids.

Within the hoard were a pair of dishes with a relief medallion (*emblema*). Such dishes appeared in the third century BC, and as such may have been considered collector's items. The complete dish has the bust of a man in high relief; in the second, only the bust of a woman survives, probably as it became detached from its bowl. It has been suggested that the man and woman may have represented a husband and wife, perhaps ancestors of the owner of the villa at Boscoreale. The complete bowl appears to carry an ownership inscription relating to somebody called Maxima; sets of plate from the same hoard have the abbreviated name 'Max' and 'Maxi'. A further relief medallion bowl appears to be a personification of Africa, as the gilded female figure seems to be wearing an elephant headdress and is holding a horn of plenty, and other wild animals are shown. This bowl is also interesting as it is inscribed with a complex weight inscription. This records the weight for the emblem and bowl together (2 Roman pounds, 10 Roman ounces and 6 scruples), and then the two parts separately. This is a good reminder that plate was not just for display, but was also an important way to hold wealth in the ancient world.

Among the other plate were some silver eggcups. These would almost certainly have been used to serve boiled eggs as a starter at a Roman banquet. Only three were found; interestingly, one of them carries an inscription that may record an abbreviation of the name of the owner, 'M', and an indication of three items. A set of four bowls, each one resting on three lions' paws, were inscribed with the name of the owner, Pamphilus, identified as an Imperial freedman, and then the weight of the four items – 4 Roman pounds and 4 scruples.

Although silver was widely used for drinking vessels, it was also applied to articles used for beautification. In particular, mirrors could be made from silver; one side would carry a design in relief, and the flat, polished surface of the reverse could be used to view the person's reflection. Silver mirrors are known to have been used in Etruria as well as in Greece during the classical period. One of the mirrors from the Boscoreale treasure has a relief medallion showing a seated Leda and the swan (the god Jupiter in disguise). The quality of the work has led some scholars to associate the mirror with the work of the Republican craftsman Pasiteles, who, according to the writer Pliny, was well known for such works. A second mirror from the treasure was decorated with the bust of a Maenad, one of the followers of Bacchus. This was inscribed with the name of the silversmith, M. Domitius Polygnos.

A major hoard from Pompeii was discovered in 1930 in an underground chamber in the house of Menander. The plate, consisting of 118 items, had been carefully packed, along with some jewellery and coins, in a wooden chest. This treasure has several parallels with the Boscoreale treasure. For example, the silver 'skillet' has a handle that is highly decorated with a hunting scene. Likewise, four eggcups were found. It also contained a mirror consisting of a plain disc. Along with this treasure were found several pieces of jewellery, including a gold *bulla*, an amulet worn by the sons of Roman citizens and dedicated in the household shrine when the boy came of age and adopted the *toga virilis*. Together these hoards provide an important glimpse of the real private wealth of the Roman world.

Right: SILVER MIRROR FROM THE HOUSE OF MENANDER.

The Boscoreale Treasure

Although gold and silver vessels are well known from the writings of ancient classical authors, very few pieces survived the barbarian invasions of the Roman empire. It was the eruption of Vesuvius in AD 79 that preserved some of the most important glimpses into the wealth of the Roman world. Early excavations found single items or small groups, but in 1895, during the clearance of a large rural villa at Boscoreale to the north-west of Pompeii (see p. 170), a large hoard of silver plate, containing over a hundred pieces, was discovered.

Above: SILVER MIRROR WITH RELIEF OF LEDA AND THE SWAN.

The owners of the plate had clearly placed it somewhere safe – in the wine vat below the house – and no doubt had hoped to return once the eruption was over. With the treasure was a mass of some one thousand gold coins. Beside the treasure lay the skeleton of a woman, who had perhaps been posted there to keep an eye on the treasure but who succumbed to the poisonous gases that seeped into the subterranean space.

The hoard itself was broken up and can be found in several museums, including the Louvre in Paris and, to a lesser degree, the British Museum in London. The hoard contained unusual pieces, such as a shallow silver dish with a relief head of a man mounted inside. A graffito showed that the cup had at one point belonged to somebody called Maxima. A companion piece is represented by the silver portrait head from a now lost bowl. A bowl from the same hoard had a relief mounted in the centre showing the personification of Africa, complete with elephant headdress. The style suggests that it may have been created during the reign of the emperor Augustus, and thus may have formed part of the family treasure.

Other treasures have also come to light in subsequent years. A second major hoard covered by the debris from Vesuvius was found in the house of Menander (see p. 174) at Pompeii in 1930. This consisted of 188 pieces that had been carefully placed in a chest in the cellar of the house.

A number of large hoards of plate dating from the time of late antiquity have been found elsewhere across the extent of the Roman empire. These include the Mildenhall treasure in Suffolk (see p. 192) with its magnificent plate decorated with Bacchic scenes. In more recent years the Sevso treasure has surfaced on the antiquities market, though sadly its precise archaeological context is still unclear.

Left: SILVER
PHIALE WITH
RELIEF HEAD OF
AN ELDERLY MAN.

Left: SILVER
PHIALE WITH
A RELIEF
SHOWING THE
PERSONIFICATION
OF AFRICA.

Mosaics from Roman Britain

Left: MOSAIC
FROM
FISHBOURNE
WITH CENTRAL
PANEL SHOWING
A CUPID RIDING A
DOLPHIN.

During the digging of foundations for new buildings in towns such as Bath and Cirencester, builders came across the tessellated pavements of the Roman towns. Sometimes they were incorporated into the new structure, such as the pavement that can still be seen in the basement of the Royal Hospital for Rheumatic Diseases in Bath. Moreover, as English gentlemen were unable to take the Grand Tour in the early nineteenth century because of the Napoleonic Wars, they turned to their own country estates to find classical traces of the Roman occupation of Britain. Often they found remains of Roman villas, which not infrequently were found to contain mosaic floors.

The Roman historian Tacitus, in the *Agricola*, mentions that during the first century AD the local elite of Britain were keen to adopt various Roman customs including the use of Latin and the wearing of the toga. With this came the adoption of Roman traditions such as the banquet, and this meant that houses started to incorporate a dining room, or *triclinium*, and it was this room, in which the head of the household would entertain neighbours and friends, that would have been decorated with a mosaic floor. Often the banqueters would be placed around the walls of the room, their couches standing on plain mosaic pavements, facing into the decorated centre, which could serve as a discussion piece.

This setting explains some of the literary allusions that are found in the schemes. For example, the *triclinium* of the villa at Lullingstone in Kent contained a semicircular section showing the Rape of Europa, and in the main part of the *triclinium* Bellerophon and the Chimaera, surrounded by the personification of the four seasons (though autumn is lost). This probably dates to the early fourth century AD. Europa is shown seated on the bull – the disguise of Jupiter – along with two cupids, indicating the association with love and an erotic encounter. This scene, designed to be viewed from the outer edge of the room, was surmounted by a Latin text that can be translated as: 'If jealous Juno had seen the swimming of the bull she would with greater justice on her side have repaired to the halls of Aeolus.' This is an allusion that educated diners would have recognized as coming from Virgil's *Aeneid* (the account of the Trojan hero Aeneas) where Juno, the consort of Jupiter, tried to persuade Aeolus, the god of the winds, to bring down a storm on Aeneas' voyage to Italy after the fall of Troy.

The literary world of the villa owners of Britannia is also indicated by the presence of fourth-century AD mosaics at the Low Ham villa in Somerset. These were discovered in 1938 when a farmer dug a pit to bury a dead sheep. The mosaic comes from the *frigidarium* (the cold room of a set of baths), and was intended to be viewed from the outer edge. The baths themselves indicate the spread of Roman culture as it was adopted by the local elite in Britain. The scenes are derived from Books 1 and 4 of the *Aeneid*. The earliest scene is that of the Trojan fleet, represented by three ships, which has just landed near Carthage; on board can be seen some of the sacred objects that had been saved from Troy. By the ships Achates seems to be represented, spear over shoulder and holding a diadem, one of the presents for Queen Dido.

The love-match between Aeneas and Dido is indicated in a scene where the pair glance at each other over a cupid (disguised in Phrygian dress, like Aeneas) and the goddess of love, Venus. The next stage represents a hunting scene from Book 4. This leads to the final scene, where Aeneas and Dido embrace in a cave while sheltering from a storm. At the heart of the mosaic, and directing this encounter, is a naked figure of Venus attended by two cupids. This interest in Virgil from members of the provincial elite is even reflected in the wall paintings from the villa at Otford in Kent, which contain a quote from Books 1 and 12.

Some villas were decorated with highly elaborate mosaics. The largest known pavement from Roman Britain came from a fourth-century villa at Woodchester in Gloucestershire. At the centre of this mosaic was Orpheus, and around him were the mesmerized animals. The Woodchester mosaic contains elements that scholars now recognize as reflecting the work of a school of mosaicists, working, perhaps, from the nearby town of Cirencester. This school was likely to have been responsible for the mosaics at Chedworth villa, on the edge of the Cotswolds. These probably date to the fourth century, including the mosaic in the *triclinium* decorated with scenes of satyrs (companions of the god Bacchus) and nymphs, and the four seasons (though one is lost) in the corners. Other British schools of mosaicists seem to have operated from Dorchester and also in the Humberside region.

One of the largest residences from Roman Britain was found at Fishbourne, just outside Chichester in Sussex. Some scholars have associated the complex with the palace for the Roman client-king Cogidubnus from the earliest years of the Roman occupation. Certainly, the exotic nature of its decoration suggests that it was owned or occupied by somebody who wished to embrace Roman taste, culture and fashion. In fact, most of the mosaics from Fishbourne date to later phases of the complex, although some simple, black-and-white geometric designs do belong to the first-century structure. A mid-second century mosaic includes a marine scene with a cupid riding a dolphin along with various mythical sea-creatures.

Some of the mosaics from Britain reflect the Christian allegiance of the owners of the villa where they were found. One of the most famous of these mosaics was discovered in 1963 at Hinton St Mary in Dorset; it probably dates to the fourth century. The mosaics form two distinct sections, which although contiguous were nevertheless separated by two short stub walls. The main part of the floor consisted of a square mosaic. At each of the four corners was a bust draped in a single cloak, held over the shoulder by a brooch. In three of the four sides, there is a semicircular field with hounds – each wears a collar – pursuing stags and a hind. The fourth side, clearly the point from which the mosaic should have been viewed, merely contains a tree. At the centre of the main section of the mosaic was a circular roundel in which is shown a male bust, wearing two different layers of garments, with the chi-rho monogram (the first two Greek letters of Christos) behind. This can either be explained as an image of Christ or perhaps of one of the Christian emperors.

The smaller pavement contains a representation of a pagan myth, Bellerophon, riding Pegasus, and spearing the Chimaera. Like the main part, it was flanked by two scenes with hounds pursuing game. This iconography is similar to that found at Lullingstone. This imagery might serve as a Christian allegory for the destruction of evil by the force of good. If this is in fact Christian imagery, drawing on

Right: PANEL SHOWING THE HEAD OF CHRIST FROM A MOSAIC FOUND AT HINTON ST MARY.

pagan motifs, then the tree may represent the Tree of Life. The four figures at the corners, normally filled by images of seasons or winds, might represent the four evangelists, Matthew, Mark, Luke and John.

This mix of Christian and pagan motifs finds a parallel in the Frampton villa mosaic, also in Dorset. This was recorded, and then reburied, in the early nineteenth century. The mosaic formed part of the *triclinium*, and those reclining in the apse would have looked down on the face of Neptune and been able to read a Latin inscription: 'The head of Neptune, to whose lot fell the kingdom (of the sea) scoured by the winds, is figured here, his deep-blue

brow girt by a pair of dolphins.' The mosaic in the main part of the *triclinium* included a hunter and scenes of Venus and Adonis. At some stage the *triclinium* seems to have been used for Christian meetings. At the junction between the apse and the main part of the *triclinium* there is a central chi-rho symbol, which makes sense when read not from the apse but from the main body of the room. This might indicate that the owner of the villa allowed the room to be used for Eucharistic celebrations. Some have suggested that the mosaic work might be by the same group of mosaicists as those responsible for the Hinton St Mary mosaic, as well as the Christian mosaics, now lost, from Fifehead Neville, also in Dorset.

Vindolanda: Letters from Rome

'I have sent you…woollen socks…two pairs of sandals and two pairs of underpants…Best wishes to Tetricus and your mess-mates, with whom I hope you are living in the greatest happiness…' This extract from a letter written almost two thousand years ago to a doubtless shivering and grateful soldier near Hadrian's Wall in northern Britain provides a fascinating, behind-the-scenes glimpse of life in that superb fighting machine, the Roman army.

Excavations by British archaeologist Robin Birley since 1969 at the fort of Vindolanda have revolutionized our knowledge of Roman writing habits and of some aspects of army life through the discovery of a unique collection of letters and documents, the oldest evidence of this kind from Britain.

Vindolanda, modern Chesterholm, was first constructed a decade or two before Hadrian's Wall was built a few miles to the north in AD 122–5. The Wall marked the northern margin of a vast empire that stretched to the Euphrates River in Syria. Britain was a latecomer to this empire, having been made a province by Claudius in AD 43. The pre-Hadrianic fort at Vindolanda (Celtic for white lawn), dating to *c.* AD 85–125, was a timber construction, which underwent a number of rebuildings, adapting and enlarging on the original plan, before being replaced by a stone fort around 160.

The earliest timber frontier-station at Vindolanda covered about 1.4 ha; ten years later it was expanded to twice that size, with subsequent phases of remodelling. The variety of evidence recovered from the site – especially organic remains and leather goods – has made it one of the most important for our knowledge of Britain in this period. Finds include abundant worn-out shoes and sandals (often of women and children, indicating their presence here from the earliest occupation onward); innumerable tent fragments, bags, straps, bootlaces and leather offcuts; a complete chamfron (head armour for a horse); hundreds of small fragments of textiles; a child's sock and insole; a wide variety of wooden objects such as tent pegs, bowls, boxes and cups; chair seats and legs; a trestle-table top; bucket staves, lids and bungs; combs, spoons and spatulae; barrel staves and lids, rich in graffiti or brand names; plentiful pottery including Samian ware and amphorae with their painted inscriptions preserved; a whole door; and remains of oak beams, flooring planks and roofing, and of plastered wattle and daub walls *in situ*. The excavators even found a lady's wig made from hair-moss. Metal objects, from spearheads and needles to rings and coins, were found uncorroded, looking as though they were buried only a few weeks ago, and numerous ballista (catapult) bolts have been recovered in all levels.

Each rebuilding of the fort entailed a levelling with clay and crushed sandstone; these substances, together with the straw and bracken used as floor coverings, as well as the by-products of leather tanning and the springs on the plateau that kept the lowest layers permanently damp, all produced a mix creating the ideal conditions for good preservation of organic materials, sealed from water and oxygen by covering layers of clay and turf. The overall effect has been like a deep-freeze. Whole fronds of bracken were found, some of them still green when first exposed, and intact pupae of stable flies were recovered.

However, Vindolanda's most remarkable treasure has been its sample of the enormous quantity of documentation generated by the Roman army and bureaucracy. Before these excavations, not a scrap of this documentation had been found in Britain, and in the rest of the Roman empire our knowledge was almost entirely restricted to papyri from Egypt and Syria.

Birley's first discovery of the Vindolanda documents occurred in the spring of 1973: 'I doubt whether I shall ever again experience the shock and excitement I felt at my first glimpse of ink hieroglyphics on tiny scraps of wood,' he wrote; 'we stared at the tiny writing in utter disbelief.' By the end of 1988 the number of documents had risen to more than a thousand, more than the total of all the inscribed stones on Hadrian's Wall itself. In 1993, the total rose again dramatically, when over three hundred charred tablets were recovered from the bottom of a bonfire, lit by troops in AD 105 to burn unwanted archives before departing the area. The site has now produced a total of almost one thousand six hundred documents.

About 15 per cent (236) are wax tablets in wooden frames, a type already well known from the ancient world, on which texts were inscribed with a metal stylus, examples of which were also found at the site. So far, the Vindolanda specimens have proved impossible to read, since they bear the marks of several different scripts superimposed, though some addresses are legible. It has been found that these tablets could be 'filed' like modern cassettes or disks, with an ink note on the edge to allow rapid identification.

However, the vast majority (1335) are in the form of ink-writing on slivers of wood, only a fragmentary handful of which had previously been known from the whole Roman empire. They had been described by the third-century AD Greek historian Herodian, who referred to tablets 'of the kind made of lime-wood cut into thin slivers and folded face to face by being bent'. This is precisely the kind found at Vindolanda, except that they are made of birch or alder, the most suitable native woods of this region. As on papyri, the ink was applied with a reed pen, and the site has yielded some still functional Roman 'fountain pens' with a thin tube linking little barrels of ink to the nib. The slivers are 16–20 cm long and 6–9 cm wide, with a thickness of 1 or 2 mm; however, many are extremely thin, sometimes less than 0.25 mm. The surface is smooth and very fine-grained, clearly prepared for writing in ink. When fresh, these tablets would have been particularly supple, and could be folded across the grain without cracking. Analysis indicates that they were cut from the sapwood of very young trees, using an especially sharp, long-bladed knife.

Many are tiny fragments of shredded documents, while others are too abraded to read, or had been cleaned for reuse. Nevertheless, around two hundred of the tablets have readable texts, and a few have up to forty-six surviving lines of script.

Many of the tablets were embedded in compacted layers of bracken and straw flooring, which also contained residues of human occupation such as bones, oyster shells, leather, cloth, jewellery, wooden implements, and considerable quantities of human excrement and urine. These were clearly areas of discarded refuse; in fact, some of the letters here have burned edges, and may have originated in bonfires. Other finds were made in the ditch of the earliest timber fort, which lay beneath the later, larger forts: some of their buildings gently subsided into this damp area. Tablets were also discovered in drains, refuse pits and silted-up water tanks. Most, however, were recovered from *praetoria* (commanding officers' residences) and from the floors of buildings.

It was often difficult to extract the fragile fragments and dry them with minimal shrinkage. Many are stuck together and have writing on both sides. Techniques also had to be developed to conserve the ink (made of carbon, gum arabic and water) by soaking the tablets in alternate baths of methyl alcohol and ether for six weeks. Even so, infra-red photography is usually still necessary to distinguish the script. Attempts are also being made to use computers to disentangle multiple superimposed texts. Most of the letters, which

Left: THE FIRST VINDOLANDA TABLET RECORDING THE SENDING OF SOCKS AND UNDERPANTS.

Right: THE LETTER
FROM CLAUDIA SEVERA
INVITING SULPICIA
LEPIDINA TO HER
BIRTHDAY PARTY.

probably came from a variety of British locations and perhaps even Gaul, have a standardized format, using the broad edges as top and bottom, and written in two columns. The writer then scored the wood down the centre, folded the right half on to the left, and wrote the address on the back. Some tablets have matched notches in their edges, probably used for binding strings to maintain privacy.

In some of the documents that are accounts rather than letters, the narrow edges were used as top and bottom, and the lists were written in columns. Sometimes several of these were fastened end-to-end by matching tie-holes, making one long, concertina-like document.

The Vindolanda tablets provide a unique opportunity to study Latin cursive or business script of the late first and early second centuries in a large number of specimens from different hands. This 'Old Roman Cursive' comprises small, simple characters, which can be extremely difficult to decipher, distinguish and read, in contrast to the 'literary' style, which used capital letters. Moreover, writers of Latin cursive used almost no punctuation, often employed abbreviations and sometimes did not even leave spaces between words. This makes the task of decipherment all the harder.

Some patterns have emerged, however. For example, writers of private letters always used the double column format, and began with their own name and that of the addressee in the first line, followed by *salutem* (greetings) in the second line, on the right. Where the letter has been written by a clerk or scribe, the authors often add a line or two in their own hand, much as we do today: for example, 'vale, frater' ('farewell, brother').

Hundreds of different hands are in evidence on the Vindolanda tablets, representing a period of a few decades. Despite this variety, the scripts are closely similar to those found on Egyptian papyri of the same period, indicating that Latin cursive was fairly standardized throughout the empire.

But what of the content of these precious documents? As one might expect, they tell us little of great political or historical events – one could hardly expect them to. Nevertheless, as this period is poorly represented by evidence of any kind, some interesting points have been gleaned from the tablets: for example, one document refers to Marcellus, a man known to have been governor of Britain in AD 103. But in the hundreds of lines of text there is no mention of an emperor or of named gods, and only one of a legion (the II Augusta).

On the whole, however, the tablets provide more mundane insights into army life on the empire's frontier. The official military documents record the activities of particular groups: in one of the duty rosters recovered, 343 men are assigned to the *fabricae* (workshops) to undertake work in the construction of a bath-house and hospital, and in plastering and working at the kilns. Others mention duty in the regimental bakery and brewery, while another refers to the manufacture of shields and swords in the fort's workshop. One *pridianum* (official strength report) reveals that only a third of the garrison was present on a particular day, 250 men of the normal 750; and of those remaining in the camp, almost 10 per cent were sick owing to wounds or conjunctivitis.

Over twenty routine reports by junior officers have been recovered, recording the state of the men and equipment under their command; some of these fragments even give the date and the unit's name. There are many letters to the prefects requesting permission to take leave, suggesting that there were some peaceful times for those on the newly conquered frontier. One extract from an intelligence report or military manual refers most disparagingly to the performance of the British cavalry, described as 'Brittunculi' ('wretched Britons').

Some particularly informative documents list food commodities such as vintage wine and sour wine (for officers and ranks respectively), Celtic beer, barley, fish sauce, lard, salt, spices, wheat and a range of meats: ham, pork, roe-deer and venison. The traditional belief that meat was rarely eaten in the Roman army now looks extremely doubtful, especially as recent archaeological studies of bone remains from Roman forts, including Vindolanda, suggest that a great deal of meat was consumed. We cannot, of course, be sure how many of these remains represent the officers' diet rather than the soldiers' daily rations.

Oddly, the letters – thanks to their addresses – have proved more informative than the official documents about the identity of the units occupying Vindolanda. There were two auxiliary cohorts: the Eighth Cohort of Batavians, a previously unknown unit, probably of 500 men, commanded by Flavius Cerialis (several letters to him have survived) and Flavius Genialis; and the First Tungrian Cohort, a 1,000-strong infantry unit already known from other sources, and led by Iulius Verecundus. Both units probably came from the Low Countries, and it is interesting that the historian Tacitus mentions Batavians and Tungrians in action under Agricola at the battle of Mons Graupius in northern Scotland in AD 84.

The letters include some of recommendation, aimed at obtaining help from influential people (such as Flavius Cerialis) for the bearer. But perhaps the most fascinating letters are also the simplest. The message about socks and underpants is one such, in the very first letter to be found, in 1973. Another, written in a very neat hand to a cavalry officer named Lucius, says: 'a Cordonouis amicus missit mihi ostria quinquaginta' ('from Cordonovi a friend has sent me fifty oysters'). One long letter, with forty-five lines of continuous script, complains that the writer has ordered huge quantities of goods such as cereals and hides, but they have not yet arrived; the writer realizes that the roads are so awful that you can't get any traffic down them, so 'please send them by mule instead'. One decurion wrote to Cerealis, fuming because the commander had paid no attention to his previous demand for more beer supplies: 'cervesam commilitones non habunt quam rogo iubeas mitti' ('the lads have no beer, please send some').

The collection also features private correspondence between officers' wives, including the remarkable archive of Sulpicia Lepidina, wife of Flavius Cerialis. In one famous letter, her friend Claudia Severa invites Lepidina to a birthday party on the third day before the Ides of September. Claudia sends greetings from her husband Aelius (thought to be Aelius Brocchus, commander of a neighbouring fort), and from her little son, and ends the letter with a brief message in her own handwriting, the earliest known example of Latin writing by a woman.

These simple, precious messages come down to us from the ordinary folk of almost two thousand years ago, a kind of everyday commentary on the life of the Roman army that acts as a counterbalance to the contemporaneous Trajan's Column in Rome.

Before the Vindolanda excavations, only half a dozen names had survived of people active in Britain between the recall of Agricola and the arrival of Hadrian. Thanks to these excavations and decipherments, we now have over one hundred and forty names ranging from a procurator and lots of prefects, centurions and decurions to ordinary soldiers, slaves, servants and merchants – and, happily, a few women, too. We even find mentions of Vitalis, a bath-house keeper, and of Abionus, a herdsman. This period and this corner of Roman Britain have thus had their cast of historical characters resurrected from oblivion.

The Treasure
of the Spring
at Bad Pyrmont

*In the nineteenth century, Bad Pyrmont in northern
Germany became famous for its mineral springs. During
renovations at the springs in 1863, the stump of an old
linden tree was found lying across one of the spring outlets.
At its base was a concentration of about three hundred
bronze fibulae (safety pins), three silver Roman denarii
(coins) and a bronze, spiral finger-ring. Nearby were three
vessels, whose handles characterize them as ladles. One of
these was made of bronze and decorated with enamel, while
the other two were wooden.*

Since Bad Pyrmont is located beyond the Imperial Roman
frontier, the collection of fibulae is of considerable interest
because it consists of a mixture of native German and
provincial Roman designs. About forty are Roman while the rest
are Germanic, apparently dating to the third century AD. Such a
hoard reflects the degree to which artefacts passed through the
Imperial frontier and the prestige that these held for the peoples
beyond the frontier.

Similarly, the bronze ladle from Bad Pyrmont is attributed to
workshops in northern Gaul during the second half of the second
century AD. The outer walls of the vessel and the upper side of the

Above left: PART OF THE COLLECTIONS
FROM THE SPRING AT BAD PYRMONT,
INCLUDING THE BRONZE LADLE AND
NUMEROUS FIBULAE.
Above right: A CLOSE-UP OF ONE OF THE
ZOOMORPHIC FIBULAE.

handle are decorated with green and blue enamel within a complex geometrical pattern in the metal surface. The silver coins also come from Imperial mints. One is of Domitian (AD 81–96), another of Trajan (AD 98–117), and the third of Caracalla (AD 211–17). Such a span of time suggests that the coins also functioned as prestige goods. Tacitus writes about this practice: 'The Germans nearest us value gold and silver for their use in trade and recognize and prefer certain types of Roman coins…they like coins that are old and familiar.'

The evidence suggests that the fibulae, ladles and coins found their way as offerings into the spring at Bad Pyrmont during the third century AD. Offerings in springs, pools and bogs are very common during this period in northern Germany and southern Scandinavia. Although we do not yet have a clear idea of the deities to whom these offerings were made, such localities clearly held considerable significance for the peoples of this region as sacred places.

The Portland Vase

One of the most celebrated pieces of Roman glass is the so-called Portland Vase, now in the British Museum. This amphora was reported to have been found in the late sixteenth century within a funerary mound, the Monte del Grano, just outside the Porta San Giovanni at Rome. However, as the vase was also said to have been found in a third-century sarcophagus, itself known since 1594, the story has to be taken with some caution.

The vase itself formed part of a number of Roman collections, including that of Cardinal Francesco Barberini, and was eventually sold around 1780 to a Scotsman, James Byres. He in turn sold it to Sir William Hamilton, then British ambassador to the court at Naples, who passed it on in 1784 to the Dowager Duchess of Portland (hence the name). In 1810, after the vase had been damaged, a loan was made to the British Museum. However, it was not to escape further mishaps. In 1845, a young man went berserk and smashed the vase and its display case in one of the public galleries. Although in some two hundred pieces, the vase was carefully restored and returned to display. In 1945, it was purchased from the Portland family.

One of the reasons for the vase's fame was that scholars have been unsure about the techniques used to make it. Wedgwood even tried to make ceramic versions ('jasper ware') of it after borrowing it from the Duke of Portland. Although there is as yet no agreement about how a cameo glass vessel like this was made, one recent theory is that such decoration was mould-made and that the whole piece was formed in a rotating mould. One of the clues is that inside the vase are 'striations', which have been interpreted as 'rotary scratches' rather than as marks of internal grinding.

The base is made from a separate piece of cameo glass. The figure wears a distinctive Phrygian cap, and this may indicate that he is intended to be Paris, son of King Priam of Troy, perhaps in deliberation as he judges the goddesses Hera, Athena and Aphrodite, a judgement that led to the outbreak of the Trojan War.

There are many different interpretations of the iconography. At the centre of both sides of the amphora are figures of semi-naked women, within a rustic setting indicated by trees. One side appears to be a scene of love, as a young man approaches from the left, while an Eros hovers overhead; next to the woman there seems to be some sort of sea-monster. On the other side the woman is shown in an attitude of mourning; her left hand holds a down-turned torch. One of the earliest interpretations was made by the Prussian scholar Johann Winckelmann, considered by many to be the founder of classical archaeology, who in 1776 suggested that two of the figures could be interpreted as Peleus and Thetis. Although some scholars still follow this interpretation, others have suggested the myth of Theseus and the sea-goddess Amphitrite. If the interpretation is elusive, it seems likely that the imagery was the product of Augustan Rome. Thus one suggestion has been that it represents the coupling of Atia, the mother of Augustus, with Apollo in the form of a serpent.

The Portland Vase is in fact one of several Roman vessels using the technique of cameo glass. Other examples include an amphora found in a tomb at Pompeii (in the presence of Italy's King Ferdinand II), which is decorated with cupids in the main scene. Also from Pompeii are two cameo glass panels from the house of Fabius Rufus, which show scenes linked to Ariadne's meeting with Dionysos, and her initiation into his mysteries.

Opposite page: THE BASE PANEL OF THE PORTLAND VASE, PERHAPS SHOWING PARIS.

Above left: A ROMANTIC ASSIGNATION IN A RUSTIC SETTING.

Above right: A WOMAN APPARENTLY IN MOURNING.

The Water Newton Hoard

This fourth-century hoard is one of the earliest groups of early Christian silver from the Roman empire. It was discovered in 1975 at Water Newton in Cambridgeshire, the location of the small Roman town of Durobrivae.

The hoard consisted of twenty-eight silver items as well as coins, which suggest that the hoard was buried around 350. Several of the pieces carry personal names attached to the chi-rho monogram (the first two Greek letters of *Christos*), perhaps naming the patrons of the plate to the church. In particular, a silver bowl, weighing 662.9 gm, carried a Latin verse inscription, interrupted with chi-rho monograms:

'I, Publianus, relying on You, honour Your holy sanctuary, O Lord.' It has been suggested that these words evoked the Roman Canon of the Mass. If so, this object might have served as a cup for the wine at Eucharist. Other parts of what appear to be part of a set of church plate include several other silver bowls and silver jugs. A strainer, presumably for wine used in the Eucharist, had the chi-rho monogram at the end of its handle, along with the alpha and omega. One of the more unusual pieces was a silver goblet, with two vertical handles. Within the hoard were a number of triangular silver plaques that were decorated with the chi-rho monogram. These may have served as some form of votive for the church, since one carried an inscription: 'Anicilla has fulfilled the vow that she promised.' A single gold disc completed the hoard.

Above: SILVER VOTIVE PLAQUE WITH THE CHI-RHO SYMBOL.

Right: SILVER BOWL INSCRIBED BY PUBLIANUS.

Right: TWO SILVER
RELIEF PLATES FROM
THE HOARD SHOWING
MAENADS, PAN WITH
HIS PIPES, AND A
SATYR.

The Mildenhall Treasure

One of the most magnificent finds from Roman Britain was a hoard of thirty-four silver pieces allegedly found in 1942 at West Row near Mildenhall in Suffolk when deeper ploughing was started. There was apparently a Late Roman villa near the find spot. Items in the hoard appear to have a mixed date, perhaps reflecting the fact that this was a treasure built up over several generations by a family. For example, the covered bowl, decorated with a relief scene

showing centaurs hunting wild boar, lions and panthers, may date from the late third century. Likewise, the flanged bowls decorated with relief scenes are typical of the second and third centuries. However, it seems that some of the larger dishes indicate that the whole treasure was deposited in the late fourth century.

The most stunning piece is the Great Dish, over 60 cm in diameter and weighing 8.25 kg. There are two concentric bands of decoration around the central face of a sea-god, either Neptune or Oceanus, from whose hair and beard emerge four dolphins. Around the face is a band of Nereids – the daughters of Nereus – and various mythical sea-monsters. The main scene shows Bacchic revelry with some thirteen main figures plus various felines. A naked and crowned Bacchus, holding his emblematic staff, a thyrsus, rests his left foot on the back of a

Below: SILVER-COVERED BOWL.

panther. In the midst of the festive Maenads and satyrs, a drunken Hercules, clearly much the worse for drink, is seen collapsing towards his lion skin; two satyrs appear to be trying to support him. Assisting with the revelry is a Pan. A pair of silver platters continues the Bacchic theme. On one, under the watchful gaze of a water-nymph, Pan plays his pipes in harmony with a Maenad on a double-flute. On the other are shown a satyr and a Maenad. Two of the flanged bowls seem to have been made as a pair. The rims of both are decorated with friezes of animals, and in the centre are portrait heads, perhaps of Alexander the Great and Olympias, his mother. Another flanged bowl shows a hunter grappling with a bear. The Christian element of the hoard is emphasized by the chi-rho monogram (the first two Greek letters of *Christos*) flanked by an alpha and an omega, the symbols of the beginning and the end, an allusion to Christ being the first and the last, which appear on some of the spoons. Some scholars have also interpreted the pair

of silver goblets as vessels for the Eucharist, although this identification is far from certain.

A recent, posthumously published account by Tom Lethbridge, then the honorary keeper of Anglo-Saxon antiquities at the Cambridge University Museum of Archaeology and Anthropology, records that the official story was that the treasure was dug out of a field in the middle of a snowstorm. Rumours had been prevalent in the 1930s that the field, adjoining the site of a small Roman villa, had contained Roman treasure. It was when the treasure was offered for sale to an antiquities dealer around 1946 that the British Museum first heard about the find; the finder then reported the hoard to the police and the treasure was confiscated. However, there was a lingering suspicion that part of the hoard had already been smuggled out of Britain. The full story may never be known.

Right: SILVER FLASK WITH EMBOSSED SCENES.

The Esquiline Treasure

This late fourth-century AD hoard of silver was discovered on the Esquiline Hill in Rome in 1793. It spent time in several private collections, including that of the Duc de Blacas, one-time French ambassador in Rome and Naples, before being sold in Paris in 1866. Although most of the hoard was acquired by the British Museum, one silver saucepan in the form of a scallop shell and decorated with a figure of Venus and two putti was acquired by the Musée du Petit Palais in Paris, and a jug in the form of a woman's head went to the Museo Nazionale in Naples.

One of the key pieces in the treasure was a silver casket, decorated with relief panels, and which may have served as a bridal casket. On the lid is a rectangular panel on which, within a wreath supported by two cupids, are the busts of a man and his wife. The two can be identified by a Latin inscription on the edge of the lid, which provides two personal names, Secundus and Projecta, and the prayer, 'vivatis in Christo' ('May you live in Christ'). Projecta has been associated with the woman for whom Pope Damasus (366–84) wrote an epitaph that was displayed in the church of San Martino ai Monti (close by the find spot of the treasure). It has thus been argued that the complete treasure was buried sometime before the Visigothic sack of Rome by Alaric in AD 410.

In spite of the Christian inscription, the iconography of the casket is purely pagan. As on the silver saucepan from the hoard, there is a scene with Venus seated in a scallop shell attended by two sea-monsters on whose backs stand two putti. This deity attending to her toilet is mirrored by Projecta who is shown on the

Above: THE SILVER
CASKET OF PROJECTA.

base of the casket, immediately beneath Venus, seated within the setting of her own home, attended by women. The second main panel on the lid shows a procession towards the baths. These scenes may hint at the preparation of a Roman bride for her wedding. Thus the Christian bride has as her model the pagan goddess of love.

On the casket, one of the female attendants is shown bearing a box for her mistress. A domed silver box, suspended on three chains, formed part of the treasure. The outside is decorated with relief panels showing the Muses. Inside were found five silver flasks, presumably to hold perfumed oils for use during the woman's toilet.

Two pieces of silver plate – a rectangular dish and a circular one – were inscribed, within a gilded wreath, with a monogram that has been interpreted as standing for Projecta Turci. This has allowed scholars to propose that the husband of Projecta was L. Turcius Secundus. Other items in the treasure included four silver-gilt statues representing the Tyche – the representation of Fortune – of four of the main cities of the empire: Rome, Constantinople, Alexandria and Antioch. The high status of the family that owned this treasure is emphasized by the six sets of silver horse trappings from the treasure.

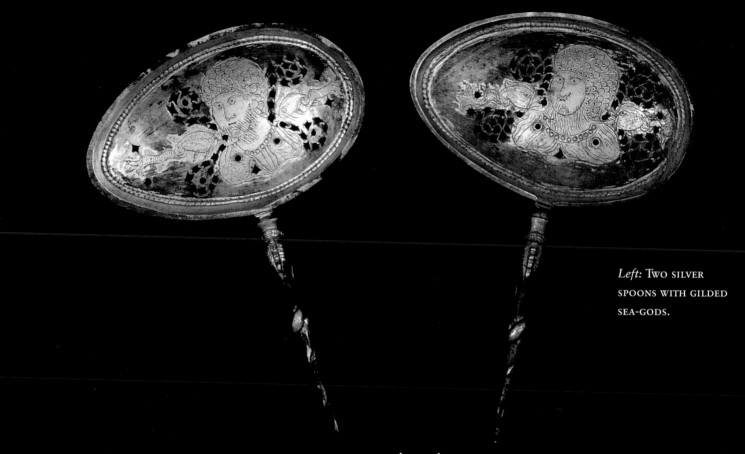

Left: TWO SILVER
SPOONS WITH GILDED
SEA-GODS.

The HoxneTreasure

One of the largest hoards from Roman Britain was found at Hoxne in Suffolk in 1992. It consisted of around two hundred gold and silver objects as well as 14,865 coins. Such a large group of coins helps to pin down the date of the hoard. Altogether some fifteen Roman emperors are represented and, apart from one coin, all were minted between AD 358 and 408. The latest coins belong to the usurper Constantine III, and thus the hoard may be placed from 408 until about 450. Interestingly, a very similar gold coin hoard, covering nearly the same chronological range, was found in the neighbouring village of Eye in around 1780.

The treasure seems to have been deposited in some sort of wooden chest, strengthened with iron fittings, which excavation suggests measured some 60 x 45 x 30 cm. Within this box may have been other containers, some of them perhaps decorated with bone or ivory inlay. Two small silver locks found in the box may have belonged to smaller caskets. The objects themselves seem to have been carefully wrapped and packed, as traces of organic material, perhaps straw, and textiles have been found. Several of the items included personal names. In particular, the name of Aurelius Ursicinus appears, picked out in niello, on ten matching spoons.

One of the most elaborate inscriptions appears on a gold bracelet formed by an open lattice-form of inscription, which reads: 'Lady Juliana, use this happily.' Presumably, this was a special commission from a goldsmith.

As in most other Roman hoards of this date from Britain, there is a Christian element within the Hoxne treasure. There are some twenty-four Christian inscriptions on the objects. These consist of the chi-rho monogram (the first two Greek letters of *Christos*) on two of the spoons, and the monogram cross on two sets of spoons and ladles. Another spoon carries the Christian text, 'May you live in God.'

One of the main groups of material in the treasure consists of gold jewellery, including nineteen bracelets. One of the most unusual pieces is a gold body-chain, weighing around 250 gm,

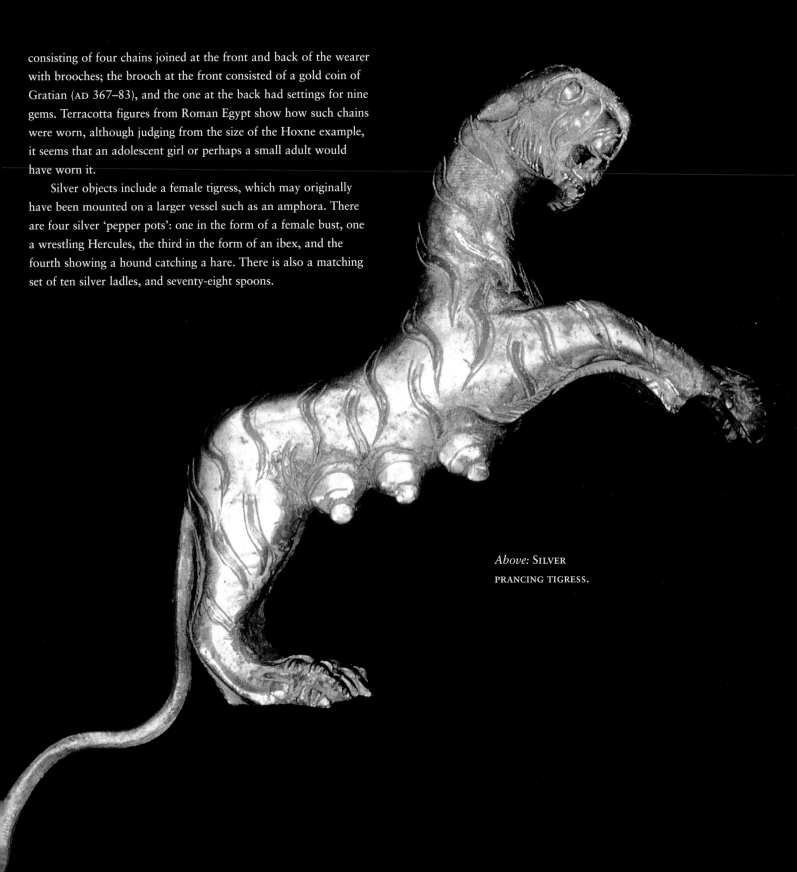

consisting of four chains joined at the front and back of the wearer with brooches; the brooch at the front consisted of a gold coin of Gratian (AD 367–83), and the one at the back had settings for nine gems. Terracotta figures from Roman Egypt show how such chains were worn, although judging from the size of the Hoxne example, it seems that an adolescent girl or perhaps a small adult would have worn it.

Silver objects include a female tigress, which may originally have been mounted on a larger vessel such as an amphora. There are four silver 'pepper pots': one in the form of a female bust, one a wrestling Hercules, the third in the form of an ibex, and the fourth showing a hound catching a hare. There is also a matching set of ten silver ladles, and seventy-eight spoons.

Above: SILVER
PRANCING TIGRESS.

Left: IMPRESSED GOLD FOILS FROM HELGÖ, SWEDEN. THE LOVING COUPLE ON THE FOIL IN THE FOREGROUND HAVE BEEN INTERPRETED AS THE GOD FREY AND HIS WIFE GERD.

The Golden Age of Scandinavia

The period between AD 300 and 550 can truly be called the Golden Age of Scandinavia. While life in continental Europe was disrupted by barbarian migrations and the eventual collapse of the Roman empire, the lands around the Baltic Sea were relatively placid. Important commercial networks emerged to connect the Baltic with other parts of Europe. The islands of the Baltic Sea, including Bornholm, Gotland and Öland, became especially important as trading centres. Much of the wealth that emerged was concentrated into gold obtained from southern and eastern Europe and made into ornaments by Scandinavian goldsmiths. For various reasons, many of these gold ornaments came to be buried – sometimes individually, sometimes in large hoards. Some remarkable examples have been preserved, while many others were melted down before antiquities laws came into effect during the nineteenth century.

The largest Scandinavian hoard of this period, from Tureholm in Sweden, contained about 12 kg of gold and was found in 1774. Although about 90 per cent of the hoard was melted down by its finder, Count Nils Adam Bielke, the part that survived by being purchased by the government contains a number of remarkable specimens, including a gold ring probably worn as a collar. An even more remarkable collar was found at Möne in Sweden, consisting of seven richly ornamented gold rings. A single ring from Trolleberg weighed 1.25 kg.

The hoard from Timboholm in Västergötland contained only unworked gold, presumably a cache of raw materials hidden by a goldsmith. Weighing about 7 kg, the Timboholm hoard was made up of two large gold ingots and about two dozen interlinked spiral gold rings. These were not ornaments for wearing but rather gold

Below: THE GOLD INGOTS
AND INTERLINKED GOLD
RINGS FROM TIMBOHOLM,
SWEDEN, FOUND IN 1904.

that would have been worked further if the owner had not had cause to bury his gold supply.

Gold brooches, known as bracteates, have frequently been found in hoards throughout northern Europe. These are small, coin-sized pendants made from gold foil and often depict human and animal figures. Many are presumed to have some religious significance associated with the Nordic god Odin.

In recent decades, advances in archaeological recovery methods have dramatically increased the number of tiny, ornamented gold foil pieces found at a number of sites throughout Scandinavia. These gold foils, many the size of a little fingernail, are puzzling. They are too brittle and delicate to have been worn as ornaments, and they have no holes for sewing them on to clothing. Yet they have very detailed decoration. A common theme is of a man and woman embracing, while others depict single humans and animals.

The use of water in the sieving of archaeological deposits at the site of Sorte Muld on Bornholm resulted in the recovery of around two thousand three hundred such tiny foils. Another significant find has been at Lundeborg, a trading centre on the Danish island of Fyn, where a concentration of about fifty foils was found. The nature of this find suggests that they were kept in a bag or a small box of perishable materials.

The Scandinavian 'gold rush' reflects the emergence of centres of power and wealth that were the bases of a warrior elite organized around powerful kings. The accumulation of valuables by this elite and competitive gift-giving may have been important in establishing this highly stratified social order, whose trading and warfare also provided the foundation for the emergence of the expansionist Viking state.

Below: THE GOLD INGOTS
AND INTERLINKED GOLD
RINGS FROM TIMBOHOLM,
SWEDEN, FOUND IN 1904.

Right: A THREE-RINGED
GOLD COLLAR FROM
ÅLLEBERG, SWEDEN,
WITH MINUTE HUMAN
HEADS AND ANIMAL
FIGURES BETWEEN
THE RINGS.

Sutton Hoo

The Ipswich Journal *of 1860 carries the first account of investigations of the burial mounds at Sutton Hoo that overlook the estuary of the River Deben in Suffolk. Yet this modest description of the antiquarian activities that took place at that time did not presage the marvellous discoveries of the years just before the Second World War, when the mound cemetery was shown to be the last resting place of pagan East Anglian kings from the seventh century* AD.

In 1938, the landowner of the site, Mrs Edith Pretty, decided to indulge her long-held interest in archaeology by engaging Basil Brown, an experienced East Anglian archaeologist, to investigate the burial mounds that graced her estate. Over the next two years, four of the mounds were opened. Finds from the mounds demonstrated that the burials were Anglo-Saxon in date. But it was the discovery in 1939 of the outline of a clinker-built rowing boat, some 27 m long, beneath the largest mound, Mound 1, that captured the British archaeological imagination. The British Museum was alerted and over a mere ten days of excavation, a distinguished team of archaeologists recovered more than two hundred and sixty objects from the burial. These items included a helmet, a shield, a sword, clothing, silverware, fine drinking horns, the remains of a bucket and a splendid cauldron, and the regalia of the long-dead king.

Research at Sutton Hoo began again from 1966 to 1971, and latterly in the 1980s under the auspices of the Sutton Hoo Research Trust. Excavation ended in 1992. These campaigns discovered and mapped the remains of an extensive prehistoric settlement, on top of which was a pagan Anglo-Saxon cemetery consisting of a series of inhumations beneath burial mounds, including ship burials, cremations and flat graves, whose occupants are preserved as shadows in the soil, so-called sand-bodies. In the western part of the site two grave pits were excavated that contained the sand-bodies of a horse and a young, high-status prince, buried in a coffin with a harness of leather, iron and gilt-bronze. The eastern sector of the site included the remains of a mound from which a small silver buckle, silver chain and chatelaine were recovered, indicative of the first demonstrably female grave from

Above: DRINKING HORNS, MADE FROM THE NOW EXTINCT AUROCHS, DECORATED WITH INTRICATE SILVER FITTINGS.

the site. In the eastern cemetery twenty-three graves, contemporary with the great rich burials, appear to be those of sacrificial victims, some of whom had their limbs tied or necks broken.

The treasure from Mound 1 was recovered from a burial chamber, about 5.5 m long, originally located in the centre of the ship. Within a century of the burial taking place, the chamber had given up beneath the weight of the mound, and sand had poured in, preserving the goods within. The chamber contained the burial of a man, possibly placed on a slightly raised dais. Against the east wall of the chamber was a tub made out of yew, held together with iron hoops, within which was placed a smaller bucket. Nearby lay a large silver dish, partly covering a couple of silver bowls, three bone combs, a set of bone-handled iron knives, and a wooden box with iron mountings. The remains of four leather shoes, pieces of leather clothing, a cap made of otter skin and a selection of buckles lay near the bowl, along with a mass of textiles. These carefully folded woollen textiles were dyed with indigo and woad and included a variety of forms, wall hangings, cloaks and linen cushion covers. Other objects were carefully wrapped up before burial using rolls of woven tape, traces of which are preserved on the coat of iron mail and sword. A total of twenty-seven different textiles have been recovered from the tomb.

Utensils for feasting included two bronze hanging bowls, drinking horns and six drinking bottles of maple with silver gilt mounts. The dead king's weapons and regalia included spears, an iron axe-hammer and a fine, pattern-welded iron sword in the remains of a decayed scabbard that would once have hung from an elaborate sword belt, decorated with buckles adorned with gold and semi-precious stones. Gold and garnet clasps were found that would have held together the two halves of a leather cuirass, long

Below: MILLEFIORI GLASS AND CLOISONNE GARNETS ADORN THIS MAGNIFICENT GOLD SHOULDER-CLASP.

since decomposed. Nearby lay the crushed remains of an iron helmet with a face mask, now restored to its full glory, and a wooden shield with gilt-bronze decorations. From the west end of the chamber were recovered a weighty bronze bowl from Egypt and a wooden lyre in a beaver-skin bag. Other objects that reflected the prestige and status of this East Anglian ruler included a huge whetstone decorated with faces that once possibly formed a sceptre, capped by the bronze statue of a stag atop a rotating iron ring.

This king's burial was adorned with sixteen pieces of silver. Most of the objects were of Mediterranean origin and may have come into the possession of the king as a gift of diplomacy from Merovingian Gaul. The most impressive is a large decorated dish, over 70 cm in diameter. The foot of the dish bore the stamp of the Byzantine emperor Anastasius (491–518). Other silverware included small cups, a fluted bowl bearing the design of a woman's head, a nest of silver bowls with cruciform decoration, ladles and spoons inscribed with Greek names. The bronze bowl from Coptic Egypt is further evidence of contact with the Mediterranean world.

The rich burials at Sutton Hoo span about a century, and may well be those of the family of Wuffa, a lineage that ruled over East Anglia with a spirit of defiant paganism in the face of the spread of Christianity through other parts of England. Despite the presence of objects of Mediterranean origin bearing Christian symbols, the great ship burials of Sutton Hoo recognize allegiance to gods across the North Sea, and yet they appear to come late in the sequence at Sutton Hoo, maybe a last stand by kings whose names we know from Saxon chronicles, such as Raedwald and Ecgric, against the arrival of new beliefs.

Medieval Buried Treasure at Środa Śląska

In May 1988, construction workers in the town of Środa Śląska in south-west Poland discovered a container with gold and silver coins. Unfortunately, they had not noticed that they had already dug up other pieces of gold jewellery, which had been carted away to a suburban landfill site. When these were discovered, a gold rush of sorts ensued, and it took several months for the authorities to recover many of the artefacts from treasure hunters, although others had probably fallen into the hands of private collectors. When the recovered objects were finally pieced together, the Środa Śląska find constituted one of the most marvellous medieval hoards in central Europe.

The major element in the Środa Śląska treasure is a woman's gold crown topped by seven eagles and originally decorated with 193 precious stones. Those recovered include garnets, sapphires, emeralds, aquamarines and pearls. Analogies to other crowns suggest that it was made in France early in the fourteenth century, although it is equally possible that it was made in Prague, since French and Italian goldsmiths also worked there.

Another important artefact in the Polish find is a circular fibula (safety pin) with a cameo of an eagle cut from blue chalcedony and set with garnets, emeralds, sapphires and pearls. At 12.9 cm in diameter, the Środa Śląska fibula is one of the largest known and was probably made in Italy during the second half of the thirteenth century, while the cameo was probably made by a Sicilian jeweller around 1240. Other jewellery found at Środa Śląska includes several pendants set with precious stones, a bracelet and three rings, also decorated with precious stones. Finally, a band of gold sheet was of the type used for decorating the covers of reliquaries and books.

Left: THE LARGE CIRCULAR FIBULA SET
WITH PRECIOUS STONES.
Below: THE GOLD CROWN IS THE
CENTREPIECE OF THE ŚRODA ŚLĄSKA
TREASURE.

The coins found in this hoard date from the second half of the thirteenth and the first half of the fourteenth centuries. Nearly four thousand of them are silver Prague pennies of John of Luxembourg and Vaclav II. Other coins can be traced to Venice, Vienna, Burgundy, Florence and Hungary. These finds testify to the connections across the Sudeten mountains between Bohemia and Silesia during this period, as well as to the involvement of these kingdoms in trade throughout Europe. The town of Środa Śląska was an important trade centre and was especially connected to the Prague court, since the chancellor of Carl IV of Bohemia (1346–78) came from Środa. One possibility is that the treasure was collateral for a loan from the merchants of Środa to the Prague court and was hidden during the Black Death in the mid-fourteenth century.

Treasures
of
North
and
Central
America

The Richey-Roberts Clovis Cache

The earliest inhabitants of the North American continent are only fleetingly known. The few remains of the camping sites and hunting stations give us information on their diet and the other necessities of survival, but of the rest of their life, ritual, art, spiritual comforts and enjoyments, we know almost nothing. And so when a find like the Richey-Roberts projectile point cache comes to light, archaeologists are given a rare glimpse into the life of Paleo-Indians.

The Clovis Culture (named after the site of Clovis in New Mexico) is the earliest known culture on the continent for which we have good and widespread evidence. Although there is clear evidence for earlier occupation, it is only with the Clovis Culture that archaeologists have many sites of different types and enough evidence to build up a decent picture of their life. Clovis hunters and gatherers are found throughout most of the continent and are dated to between 11,500 and 11,000 years ago. Their archaeological remains tell us that they hunted now extinct mammoth and bison, camels and horses. Of their reliance on other animals – or on plants – we have much less evidence.

The Clovis peoples are best known for their skills in making magnificent stone projectile points. These points were beautifully carved, and show a level of craftsmanship that went way beyond what was necessary to make the point a functioning tool, whether it was used as a thrusting spear point or as a dart to be propelled from a throwing stick. Many Clovis points were small, perhaps only 5 cm long, but – occasionally – extraordinarily large points are found, such as those at the Richey-Roberts site.

This site, like many other archaeological treasures, was found by accident in 1987, when an apple farmer in central Washington state recovered a large stone point eroding out of an irrigation ditch. Sensibly, he contacted professional archaeologists, and over the course of the next few years excavations recovered fourteen exquisitely carved stone points, along with an assortment of other stone tools like scrapers and bifaces. Some of these points were definitely used as functioning tools for they contained evidence of wear along the edges; some had even been broken in use.

Above: THESE BEAUTIFULLY FLAKED CLOVIS POINTS SUGGEST THAT HUNTING WAS A SYMBOLICALLY PRESTIGIOUS ACTIVITY.

What made this cache significant, besides the actual number of the points, was their size.

One matched pair of points measured nearly 23 cm long, for example. And although at least some of these points were perhaps used functionally, all of them were so beautifully made as to suggest some other purpose. When in doubt, archaeologists call such finds 'ritual', but, of course, this term does not really help us understand them much. Some Paleo-Indian archaeologists think that perhaps the lovely stone work of Clovis and later Folsom points is indicative of some form of hunting ideology, as much concerned with prestige as with providing food for the group.

Whatever their ultimate purpose, we can only look in awe at the beauty of these points, tantalizing testimony to a life rich in ways that may always be beyond our ability to discern.

The Olmec 'Fort Knox'

In the United States, Fort Knox is the repository of the national gold reserve, where millions of gold bars form the symbolic foundation of the economic system. The Olmec people (c. 1200–700 BC) also used precious bricks – of imported jade – as a symbolic 'treasury' of a different sort.

The Olmec, located in the tropical lowlands of Mexico's southern Gulf Coast, are often considered the 'mother culture' of Mesoamerica, as many of their political and religious traits became fundamental parts of the generalized Mesoamerican civilization. Rulers and/or shamans claimed special affiliation with jaguars, the most powerful creatures of the Mesoamerican environment, to the extent that artistic representations often depicted 'were-jaguars' – humans with jaguar traits. Caves were stylized as the open mouths of earth jaguars, and monumental stone sculptures depict rulers emerging from jaguar caves. Another pan-Mesoamerican symbol that originated with the Olmec was the use of jade to symbolize the life-force.

The site of La Venta was one of the major centres of the Formative period Olmec Culture (*c.* 1000–700 BC). The rulers of La Venta engaged in long-distance trade to obtain vast quantities

of jade, which they used for ornamentation, small sculptures or beautifully decorated celts. Another use of jade was in underground caches of jade bricks.

One of the most remarkable of these caches is located beneath the main plaza, where thousands of jade bricks were carefully placed in a mosaic pattern to represent an earth jaguar with an open mouth. The mosaic was then ritually buried using coloured clays that were also exotic imports. In this way the Olmecs of La Venta created an *axis mundi*, or world axis, making it the symbolic centre of the Olmec cosmos. The creation of symbolic landscapes within ceremonial centres became a common theme in later Mesoamerican capitals, such as Teotihuacán, Cholula and Tenochtitlán.

Just as the gold of Fort Knox is sequestered in vaults deep beneath the earth, so the jade caches of La Venta were buried out of sight, but never out of mind. And just as Fort Knox is a symbolic foundation for the American way of life, so the La Venta jade mosaic served as a focus for the cosmic significance of the centre as a world axis.

Below left: BASALT MONOLITHS SUCH AS THIS WERE PROBABLY USED AS THRONES FOR NOBLE AUDIENCES. THIS EXAMPLE DEPICTS A DIVINE ANCESTOR EMERGING FROM A CAVE, THE SYMBOLIC MOUTH OF THE JAGUAR EARTH.

Below: THE GROUPING OF JADE FIGURES WAS FOUND INTENTIONALLY BURIED AT THE SITE OF LA VENTA. IN THE CENTRE OF THE CLUSTER OF GREEN JADE FIGURES IS ONE MADE OF A COARSER STONE, PERHAPS INDICATING A STATUS OR ETHNIC DIFFERENCE. IT IS LIKELY THAT THE ARRANGEMENT REPRESENTS SOME CULTURALLY MEANINGFUL EVENT.

Tomb 7:
Shrine of a Mixtec
Earth Goddess

When Mexican archaeologist Alfonso Caso first entered through the roof of Tomb 7 at Monte Albán in 1932, he must have been amazed at the richness of the exposed remains. Gold, crystal, jade and shell objects of exquisite manufacture shimmered in the light after 500 years of darkness. Awed by the beauty and wealth of the assemblage, Caso was particularly intrigued by a collection of thirty-four carved bones bearing motifs relating to the Mixtec pictographic writing system. These bones, in addition to the other precious objects, provide an important clue for interpreting the functional context of the tomb as a shrine dedicated to the Mixtec earth goddess known as Lady 9 Grass.

Monte Albán was the hilltop capital of the ancient Zapotecs (*c.* 500 BC–AD 800). In accordance with the worship of semi-divine ancestors, tombs were built beneath the floors of houses, particularly of the elite. These were filled with the skeletons of the deceased, around which were placed ceramic urns representing costumed ancestors and other offerings, and the walls were decorated with murals depicting ritual themes. Caso explored over a hundred of these ancestral shrines during the 1930s and 1940s.

Tomb 7 was unique in several ways. First, it was by far the richest in terms of exotic offerings, with more than five hundred objects. Second, it was reused long after its initial construction by a different cultural group, the Mixtec, providing archaeological support for ethnohistoric accounts of Mixtec intervention in the Zapotec Valley of Oaxaca. Finally, the burial context of the Late Postclassic (*c.* AD 1300–1530) tomb provides iconographic hints of the function of the deposit.

Nine partial skeletons were found in the tomb, the most intact being Skeleton A located against the far west wall facing east while seated in a foetal, mummy-bundle position. Osteological evidence for the sex of the incomplete Skeleton A remains ambiguous, with some characteristics such as the mandible indicating a biological female, while other evidence suggests male traits – future genetic testing of the bones may resolve this issue.

The offerings buried with Skeleton A suggest a female identity, as they relate to spinning and weaving. Small clay spindle whorls may have been used to spin fibre into thread, but pictorial manuscripts also depict them worn as part of a perishable headdress of goddesses and their priestesses. Tiny onyx and crystal bowls were found that also would have been used for spinning fibre. The elaborately carved bones resembled miniature weaving battens and picks, though their delicate nature suggests that they may have been effigies rather than functional tools. Thus many of the objects comprised a toolkit that was symbolic of female gender based on sixteenth-century sources.

Yet the burial assemblage provides even more information on Skeleton A's identity and the rituals that took place in the tomb. Several of the associated skeletons were buried with mandibles that had been painted red and perforated so that they could be worn as a mask, just as was commonly depicted in pre-Columbian Mixtec manuscripts, or codices, especially in reference to earth/fertility deities. A golden pectoral from the tomb depicts one such skeletal figure. An altar found in the tomb featured an incense brazier made from a human skull decorated with inlaid shell eyes and mosaic plaques made of turquoise, and with remnants of a knife blade protruding from the nasal passage – again identical to objects illustrated in the Mixtec codices with earth/fertility deities. Obsidian earspools and weaving tools, such as a turquoise inlaid pick, parallel costume elements used by the Aztec goddess Cihuacoatl, the complement to the Mixtec Lady 9 Grass.

The evidence supports an interpretation of Tomb 7 as a shrine dedicated to an incarnation of the Mixtec earth/fertility goddess 9 Grass. The Mixtec Codex Selden depicts Lady 9 Grass, or her mortal impersonator, consulting with Mixtec lords and ladies while seated at her shrine at the 'Temple of Skull'. Tomb 7 at Monte Albán may have been a similar oracular shrine where attendants of the goddess consulted with a mummified representation of Lady 9 Grass. The exotic objects in the tomb may have been left as offerings in return for messages from the supernatural, and provide detailed information on the iconography of Mixtec religion. From an archaeological perspective, the clues about past beliefs far surpass the value of the objects themselves.

Left: THIS GOLD
PECTORAL IS
CONSIDERED ONE
OF THE MASTER-
PIECES OF
MESOAMERICAN
METALWORK
SINCE IT
COMBINES
SEVERAL
TECHNIQUES IN A
SINGLE PIECE. IT
DEPICTS A DEITY
WITH A SKELETAL
JAW AND AN
ELABORATE
SERPENT
HEADDRESS WITH
FLORAL ROSETTES
THAT IS TYPICAL
OF THE MIXTEC
FERTILITY
GODDESS 13
FLOWER. THE
FLANGED BREAST
OF THE FIGURE
FEATURES
CALENDRICAL
DATES IN THE
MIXTEC WRITING
SYSTEM,

Ancient Treasures of Florida

Generally, archaeologists get just a few pieces of the vast prehistoric puzzle with which to work. However, under certain circumstances – when environmental conditions are just right – they are allowed a greater glimpse into the rich world of the past. So it is with two areas in the American states of Florida and Washington (see p.218), both of which have provided wonderfully preserved archaeological sites because of the waterlogged ground in which the sites were immersed.

The swamps and wetlands of Florida do not immediately spring to mind as the home of spectacular archaeological treasures. Yet over the past few years, scholars, taking advantage of the latest scientific preservation techniques, have begun to uncover a treasure trove of ancient wooden artefacts and pieces of art. Until about six thousand years ago, Florida was still a rather dry environment, but at about that time environmental changes began to increase the amount of water in lakes and rivers, and also to create the organic deposits that allow wooden materials to survive. And it is from that time right through to the historic period that archaeologists have uncovered thousands of wooden objects that otherwise would have been lost forever.

The most spectacular finds are the canoes, the oldest of which dates back over five thousand years. More than a hundred and eighty canoes have been found, preserved well enough to show the different styles of construction used on them. Most of them were made of hollowed-out pine logs, up to 6 m in length. Sometimes the cypress tree was used, too. These canoes served a vital purpose in prehistoric Florida, giving Indians access to the rich and varied resources of the waterways and allowing them to trade over long distances. Indeed, it has been found that between about seven thousand and four thousand years ago, there was a shift to a much greater reliance on aquatic resources; the canoe must have been an

Right: LATE PREHISTORIC
FELINE FIGURE IN WOOD
FROM KEY MARCO, FLORIDA.

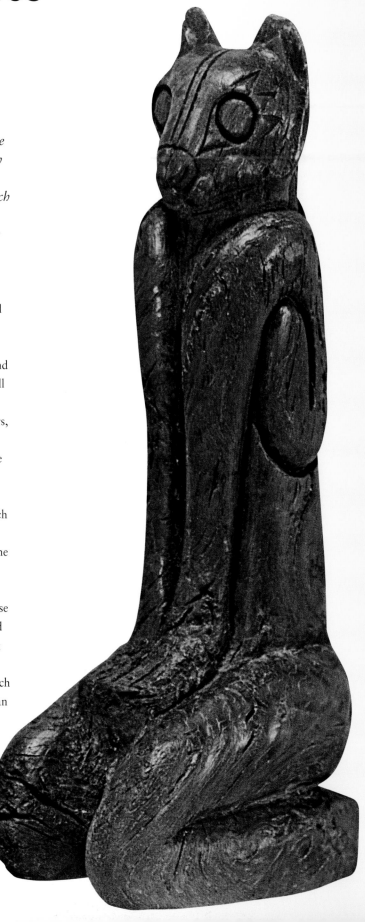

important part of this shift. The Florida canoes are the oldest in the western hemisphere and provide the best body of knowledge on prehistoric water travel in the world.

Other sites provide a unique look into Florida's prehistoric art world. The site of Key Marco is a good example. Located in a swamp in Collier County on the state's south-west coast, it was excavated in 1895-6 by Frank Hamilton Cushing, an anthropologist best known for his pioneering work on the Zuni tribe of the American Southwest. The site, which has been dated between AD 500 and 1000, provides the most comprehensive range of material from any site on the Gulf Coast including wooden cups, bowls, toy canoes, stools, buttons, boxes and knife handles, to name just a few. The site also produced a remarkable array of wooden masks and painted wooden boards.

Besides the spectacular finds described above, the Florida wetland sites have produced valuable information on all aspects of prehistoric human life. A site, like Windover, which dates back 8,000 years, is the location of over a hundred and sixty human remains, many of which still contain human brain tissue. Their preserved DNA has provided major clues for our understanding of the peopling of the New World thousands of years ago. In other sites, simply the mass of material has allowed archaeologists to put flesh on to the dry remains that most often make up the typical archaeological site, revealing new insights into prehistoric lives.

Left: EAGLE TOTEM OF PINE WOOD FROM FORT CENTER, FLORIDA. THE CARVING IS 66 CM HIGH AND DATES TO ABOUT AD 200–600.

The Funerary Mask of Pacal

On Christmas Eve 1985, thieves entered the National Museum of Anthropology in Mexico City and, within half an hour, stole 124 pre-Columbian treasures. After the loss was discovered, the police rushed to the scene only to be baffled by the lack of evidence. Speculation ran wild. At the time, authorities believed the thieves to be 'experts', possibly a gang of professional thieves. It was suggested that 'foreigners', probably from Colombia or Guatemala, could have been the culprits. It was even suggested, though quickly dismissed, that the museum guards might have been in on the heist. None of these hypotheses was ever borne out by the facts and, after months of fruitless leads, the government was still puzzled by the robbery. Sadly, most Mexicans came to believe that the artefacts were no longer in the country and had been sold on the black market. Few people believed that the artworks would ever be seen again.

The stolen objects had a number of things in common. They were all small pieces and so were easily transportable. They were all made of precious materials such as obsidian, gold, jade and turquoise. Finally, and perhaps as baffling as the robbery itself, many of the pieces were priceless, and all were so well known as to be almost impossible to sell.

Certainly the most famous of the stolen objects was the funerary mask of Lord Pacal, the great seventh-century Maya king of Palenque. The mask was first encountered in the 1950s during excavations headed by Mexican archaeologist Alberto Ruz Lhuillier. After years of painstaking archaeology on the Temple of the Inscriptions, Ruz finally cleared the rubble-filled stairway that led down to the crypt containing the sarcophagus and remains of the king. Along the way, the archaeologists had found a cist (stone chest or container) containing ceramic, jade, shell and pearl offerings – but nothing had prepared them for the discovery of the treasures inside the tomb. These were of such abundance and high quality that the discovery would later be compared to that of Tutankhamen's tomb in Egypt (see p. 30).

In the summer of 1952, Ruz's men removed the lid of the huge, monolithic limestone sarcophagus and found the skeleton of a tall male. Besides the ornate jade diadem and earplugs worn by the individual, he held a large jade bead in each hand and had one bead in his mouth. The life-size jade mosaic mask had been carefully placed over his face. Eyes of shell and obsidian stared out at the startled excavators. Eventually, this treasure was removed to the Museum of Anthropology in Mexico City.

In the years following Ruz's discovery, the importance of the mask grew as scholars came to understand more about the symbolism of ancient Maya ritual and kingship. It was realized, for example, that the Mayas' choice of materials had been deliberate. In the past, jade was valued because it symbolized moisture and the breath that is an indicator of life. By placing the mask over Pacal's face, the Maya believed that they were guaranteeing the king life in the afterworld. The obsidian, used in the mask's pupils was material prized by ancient Mesoamericans for its reflective qualities. It is probable that many of the obsidian mirrors found in archaeological contexts throughout the region were used in ritual as aids for shamans (medicine men) in their negotiations with other-worldly powers. Because these mirrors acted as windows to a supernatural realm, it is appropriate that volcanic glass, rather than another dark stone, was chosen for the eyes of Pacal.

Other facial characteristics of the mask are also of importance. The T-shaped tooth appearing between its parted lips is characteristic of Maya deities and so is an indication of the ruler's supernatural qualities of the mask's wearer. Since Maya kings were likened to the offspring of deities, they took on some of the attributes of these supernaturals. Finally, the mask is of paramount

Above: THE LIFE-SIZE JADE MASK OF PACAL THE GREAT IS BELIEVED TO BE AN ACCURATE LIKENESS OF THE DEIFIED KING.
Right: THE TEMPLE OF THE INSCRIPTIONS HOUSES THE TOMB OF THE GREATEST OF PALENQUE'S RULERS, PACAL.

importance because of its similarity to the king himself. Pacal's image is known from sculpted reliefs and from two stucco heads located within the tomb. The mask's prominent nose, close-set eyes and narrow chin compare favourably with these other examples. The mask is, therefore, not a generic representation of the ruler, but rather a specific portrait of the individual for whom it was constructed.

Given the historical significance of Pacal's mask and the other works stolen from the museum, the relief felt by officials on their recovery was immense. All but thirteen of the artworks were found undamaged three and a half years after the robbery. Working on an informants hunch, police raided the Mexico City home of Carlos Percher Trevino in June 1989. There, on the top shelf of his wardrobe, they found a canvas bag containing the stolen artefacts. The treasure had never left the country.

According to Percher's statement after the arrest, both he and his accomplice, Ramón Sardina Garela, had carefully planned the theft. Over a six month period, the pair visited the museum about fifty times to study its layout and to take photographs. In the process, they were able to observe the behaviour and movements of the security guards. Around 2 am on Christmas Day, Percher

and Sardina entered through an air-conditioning duct. Since the museum had no alarm system at the time, it took no more than thirty minutes to go through three exhibition halls and to stuff the chosen pieces into their bag. During this time, the pair never saw any of the museum's nine security guards.

Eventually, Percher and Sardina moved to Acapulco. There, they fell in with drug traffickers and tried to exchange the treasures for cocaine. After a drug trafficker was arrested by the police, he told the authorities about Percher and the artefacts. The police put Percher under surveillance for forty-five days, and finally arrested him.

The mystery of the robbery had been solved. Rather than a foreign gang of professional thieves, the culprits turned out to be two young Mexican veterinary students obsessed by wealth and the artworks themselves. Mexico's president and tens of thousands of citizens welcomed the pieces back to the museum in an official ceremony. The recovered artefacts were put on public display in heavily guarded cases while conservators busily designed the new security cases that would be their future home.

The Sacred Cenote of Chichén Itzá

The sixteenth-century bishop of the Yucatán, Diego de Landa, described rituals at the Sacred Cenote of Chichén Itzá in which sacrificial victims were thrown into the water along with 'precious stones and things which they prized'. Cenotes are sink-holes through the porous limestone bedrock characteristic of northern Yucatán in Mexico, allowing access to the fresh ground water beneath. Cenotes are a prerequisite to human occupation in this area where fresh water is a limited resource. They also provided direct access to the watery underworld of Maya cosmology, and so had important religious significance.

Chichén Itzá, which flourished *c.* AD 800–1100, was the last great city of the Maya, transforming customs of the Classic Maya into a new international style that linked the ruling elite to traditions of central Mexico, particularly the Toltecs of Tula. The vanguard of this international style was provided by the cult of the Kukulkan, the 'feathered serpent' god known in central Mexico as Quetzalcoatl. Chichén Itzá was one of several pilgrimage sites dedicated to this deity, as indicated by carved architectual façades throughout the city as well as offerings found in the Sacred Cenote. Consequently, the offerings come from a wide geographical range, including gold from Panama, Costa Rica and Oaxaca, jade from Guatemala and onyx from southern Puebla.

On 5 March 1904, American archaeologist Edward H. Thompson, whose work was sponsored by the Antiquarian Society of Worcester, Massachussetts, began a programme of retrieving the treasures that the Maya had hurled into the cenote. First by dredging, and later by actually descending into the water, Thompson recovered vast quantities of precious objects of gold, copper and jadeite, as well as offerings of perishable materials that have rarely been preserved archaeologically, such as textiles, wood

Left: THE SACRED CENOTE OF CHICHÉN ITZÁ IS A SINKHOLE THROUGH THE LIMESTONE CRUST TO THE FRESH WATER BELOW. EXCAVATIONS OF THE CENOTE HAVE RECOVERED BOTH PRECIOUS AND PERISHABLE OBJECTS RELATING TO THE RELIGIOUS PRACTICES OF THE ANCIENT MAYA.

and rubber. These precious artefacts attest to the artistic abilities of
the ancient Maya, and reveal patterns of religious practice that
allow keen insight into their ideological system.

One of the most remarkable finds from the cenote was a set of
golden face ornaments, including round eyepieces with feathered
serpent 'eyebrows,' and a mouthpiece decorated with profile
serpent eyes. Carved panels from the Lower and Upper Temples of
the Jaguars at Chichén Itzá depict individuals wearing similar
ornaments.

A feathered serpent also appears as a prominent feature on a
gold disc. The hammered gold depicts a Mexican Toltec who
performs a heart sacrifice on a captive with Maya characteristics.
A serpent with feathers or cut shells (another diagnostic attribute
of Quetzalcoatl) hovers in the sky above the scene.

In addition to treasures of precious metals, however, there are
materials that are seldom preserved in the archaeological record,
such as wood, cloth, copal incense and rubber. A wooden
sceptre carved in the shape of an *atlatl* (spearthrower)
features an anthropomorphic figure with a
jade/turquoise mosaic mask. A tripod ceramic bowl
contains copal resin in which shell and jade beads
are embedded, as well as a blue-painted piece
of rubber.

The Sacred Cenote of Chichén Itzá
presents a unique window on to the ritual life
of the ancient Maya, preserving offerings of
scarce and exotic materials that relate to the
religious practices of a dynamic period in
Mesoamerican history. The excellent
condition of perishable materials offers a
glimpse of the range of objects that may have
been present, but have not survived, in other
contexts with less favourable conditions.

Treasures of the American Desert

The American Southwest is one of the most spectacular archaeological regions in the whole of the North American continent. With a backdrop of towering buttes and majestic desert vistas, ancient Americans developed a series of fascinating cultures based on the cultivation of maize, beans and squash. Although the remarkable Anasazi pueblos of Mesa Verde and Chaco Canyon, with their finely made, black-on-white painted pottery, are the best known, elsewhere ancient Native Americans demonstrated even greater artistic talent.

The most beautiful pottery found in the prehistoric Southwest belongs to the Mimbres culture of south-western New Mexico. This culture is a regional variant of the Mogollon Tradition, one of the three major cultural traditions that archaeologists have identified in the American Southwest (the other two being Anasazi and Hohokam).

The culture derives its name from a small river, whose valley they occupied (*mimbre* is Spanish for willow).

The Mimbres Culture first emerges as a distinct entity around AD 200 as a series of sedentary horticultural villages. Over the next 800 years, archaeologists have identified a series of cultural periods within the overall time frame, each one marked by changes in house architecture (from semi-subterranean pit houses to above-ground stone and adobe pueblo structures), increasing sophistication in pottery technology (from undecorated plain ware to well-executed painted designs) and also an increasing dependence on agriculture compared to hunting and gathering. By the time of the Classic Mimbres period (AD 1000-1150), Mimbres people were living in well-constructed villages and, because of a well-documented population increase, were changing their farming techniques by using marginally arable areas, and intensifying their agricultural methods with the building of check dams and even perhaps irrigation canals. There is evidence that during this period Mimbres people were trading their own turquoise, cotton and buffalo hides for Mexican parrots, macaws and copper bells.

It is during the Classic Mimbres period that there evolved the most impressive ceramic tradition of the prehistoric Southwest. The Mimbres ceramics of this period are best known for their figurative designs. The images, so exquisitely reproduced on the bowls, are geometric, anthropomorphic and zoomorphic. Animals that are represented include dogs, cats, turkeys, ducks, cranes, rabbits, insects and fish. The designs show an overall symmetry of style and conception that perhaps indicates a true artistic school, and, unusually for North American art, perspective is employed.

Understanding what these designs mean is extremely difficult. It is possible that they represent the symbols of individual clans or other social units important to Mimbres

Left: MIMBRES BOWL SHOWING TWO FIGURES THAT PERHAPS RESPRESENTED MALE AND FEMALE, OR LIFE AND DEATH.

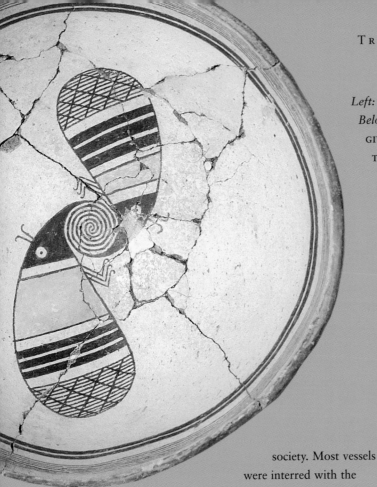

Left: A MIMBRES BOWL DEPICTING INSECTS.
Below: A MIMBRES-STYLE BOWL SHOWING A FIGURE
GIVING BIRTH. THE BOWL WAS A BURIAL OFFERING AND
THE PUNCTURE RELEASED THE VESSEL'S SPIRIT.

expansion of the trading culture based at the town of Casas Grandes. Casas Grandes-related villages appear in the Mimbres Valley towards the end of the twelfth century, probably to exploit the local resources. Mimbres populations may have been displaced or simply been amalgamated into the Casas Grandes nexus.

Unfortunately, Mimbres sites have not fared well over the centuries. Perhaps because they never demonstrated the technically well-executed architectural designs of Anasazi sites to the north, serious archaeological research was slow in coming to the Mimbres Culture, although sites were known to scholars by the 1880s. Moreover, their beautiful pottery has drawn pot hunters to these sites like needles to a magnet, and as a result many sites have been severely damaged. In order to advance our knowledge of this remarkable culture and to try to purchase sites to keep them out of the hands of unscrupulous looters, the privately endowed Mimbres Foundation was established in 1974.

society. Most vessels were interred with the dead, rather than being found in the pueblo rooms themselves. Interestingly, more children are buried with figurative bowls than are adults. Hopi Indians, when consulted, have claimed that some of the designs represent actual implements used by the ancient Mimbres people. They also believe that where two animals are represented on a bowl, some sort of a relationship between different clans is being represented. Such consultation can only improve our understanding of the bowls' meanings.

Archaeologists are still unclear who made such exquisite pottery; whether it was men, women or both is still uncertain. It has been suggested that the figurative designs were produced by a relatively small number of artists, with the geometric and utilitarian vessels being produced by individual households. If one estimates that an individual artist could produce up to a hundred vessels a year, a single artist could complete over two thousand pots in a twenty-year working life. It has also been estimated that a maximum of twenty thousand bowls were buried with the dead over the one hundred and fifty-year period of production, and therefore a total of only ten artists – or two to three artists per generation – could have produced the complete corpus of work.

The climax of Mimbres artistic life was rapidly eclipsed by more mundane events. The Classic Mimbres period is contemporary with the rise of the Chaco Culture in north central New Mexico. This culture had extensive trading ties with Mexico, but around 1130 both of these cultures may have been engulfed by the

Ancient Treasures of Ozette

Ozette, located at the north-western tip of the Olympic peninsula in America's Washington state, is one of the five major villages of the Makah tribe who still live in the vicinity. The location of the site, sheltered from the full harshness of the North Pacific, made it an attractive place to live for thousands of years. It was abandoned in the early part of this century when the families were moved by the Bureau of Indian Affairs. After that the village site was used only seasonally for hunting and fishing. Whales, fur seal, sea otters, salmon, cod and halibut were also caught by fishermen living at the village, and the bountiful rain forest immediately behind the village provided elk, deer and a variety of plants for food, medicine and other purposes.

Below: AN ANTHROPOMORPHIC WOODEN BOWL.

Like other tribes on the resource-rich Pacific Northwest coast of America, the Makah had a socially ranked society, consisting of chiefs, commoners and slaves. The tribe practised the potlatch, a ceremony in which a chief gave away masses of food and other goods to the rest of the village as a means of validating his own power and prestige. Archaeological investigations of sites like Ozette, added to tribal history, allow for a very full knowledge of traditional Makah ways.

Archaeological investigations began at the site in 1966, but were intensified in 1970 when heavy winter storms began to wash it away. At the request of the Makah Tribal Council, Richard Daugherty and his crew of archaeologists worked at the site until 1981. What makes the site of Ozette such a treasure is that during its 2000 years of occupation, it was at different times covered by mudslides. The mud covered sections of the village almost immediately, and consequently the aerobic fungi that normally eat away at the perishable materials died. Preservation was so good that some of the leaves that were found were still green.

The amount of material that the archaeologists recovered was staggering. They excavated eight houses, whose remains comprised wall planks, upright support poles, roof support timbers and sleeping benches. The houses were built on specially constructed earthen platforms and the largest house measured 21 x 11.5 m. The archaeologists found over fifty thousand artefacts, of which close to thirty thousand were made of perishable materials, like wood and fibre. Many of the tools were made of composite materials, and because they were found in different stages of manufacture, archaeologists were given a wonderful opportunity to view the full range of industries practised in the village. These objects included clothing, hide, pieces of nets, cedar-bark matting, wooden loom uprights, canoe paddles, carved wooden boxes, clubs for killing seals, harpoons, fishing hooks and bows (of different sizes for different ages). The art displayed on some of these pieces was magnificent, with anthropomorphic, zoomorphic and geometric designs all represented.

In addition, the archaeologists recovered over four hundred thousand mammal, bird and fish bones, over three hundred thousand pieces of shell and almost half a million seeds. These gave the scientists an amazing amount of detailed information about prehistoric and historic diets in the area.

Following page: WELL PRESERVED WOODEN CLUBS FROM OZETTE, WASHINGTON.

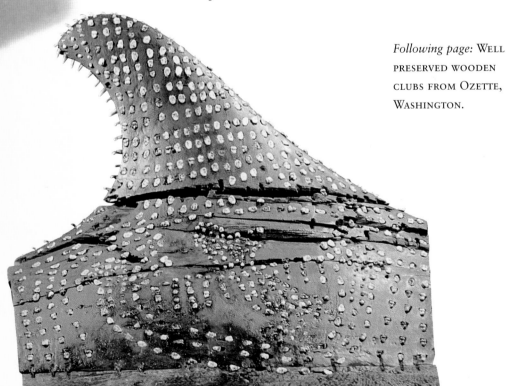

Right: A WHALE-FIN EFFIGY MADE FROM RED CEDAR, INLAID WITH SEA-OTTER TEETH.

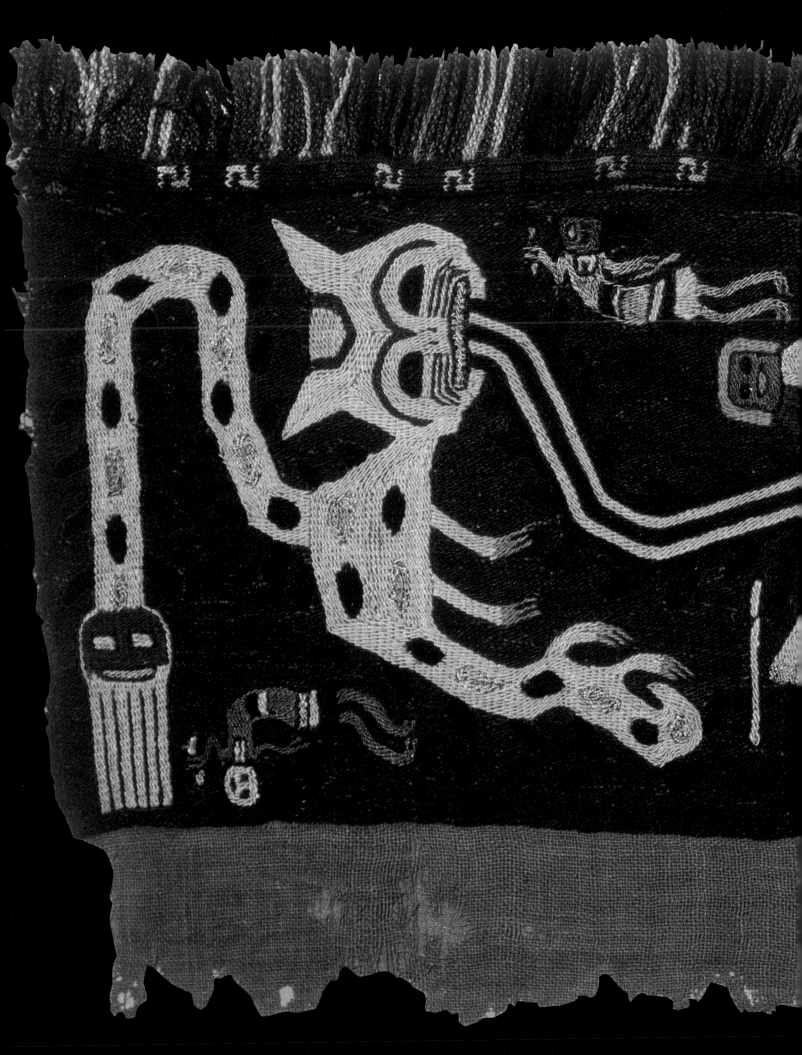

Treasures
of
South
America

Ancient Textiles of the Andes

One of the true treasures of the Andean world is the rich cloth woven by skilled artisans for the wealthy rulers of ancient South America. By the time the Spanish arrived in Peru in the sixteenth century, the tradition of Andean textile manufacture was thousands of years old, and cloth and the clothes made with it were some of the most important cultural objects in the Andean world. Skilled weavers produced the finest cloth for the state, and strict sumptuary rules, as well as laws forcing all residents of the Inka empire to wear only the costumes identified with their own village and area, gave textiles an important role in all aspects of life.

Under the Inka, many of the finest textiles were produced by *mamakuna*, women given to the Inka as beautiful young girls who lived in separate communities within important cities. Other cloth was provided to the state as tribute, gifts, and as a medium for paying taxes. By the time the Spanish arrived in Peru, the Inka held vast storehouses filled with cloth, including relatively plain textiles that could be used by people of many classes, and other cloth with more specific uses. The finest and most distinctive cloth, finely woven wool with decorative symbols that only people of the highest status were allowed to wear, was produced in highly controlled, centralized textile production areas.

Left: DETAIL OF A
PAINTED DESIGN FROM
A MOCHICHA VESSEL,
SHOWING TWO WEAVERS
USING BACKSTRAP
LOOMS, AN ANCIENT
TECHNIQUE STILL IN
USE TODAY
THROUGHOUT THE
ANDEAN REGION.

Left: MANTLE
FRAGMENT, CHANCAY
BROCADE, PERU,
AD 1000–1476.

Because textiles are perishable, relatively little ancient cloth survives from most areas of the world. Along the Andean coast, however, and in a few dry cave sites from the highlands, the arid conditions have allowed the preservation of textiles for hundreds, sometimes thousands, of years. Because of the extraordinary preservation of materials along the Andean coast, we know that decorated cloth, made by the relatively simple techniques of twining (twisting together by passing two threads around another), knotting and looping appeared as much as five thousand years ago, and weaving soon followed. It quickly developed into one of the most important art forms in the Andes.

It is clear that Andean peoples have long invested a great deal of time and effort in the manufacture of their most elaborate textiles. All of the major civilizations of the Andes had distinctive and beautiful textiles, and cloth was an important indicator of wealth and status in all these societies. It is probable that women made most of the cloth in pre-Inka cultures, as they did under the Inka, but much of the most finely wrought clothing is found with male skeletons in archaeological excavations. Most of our best information on textiles comes from excavations of tombs, as clothing was often buried with its owners, only to be rediscovered as much as several thousand years after it was interred.

Paracas Textiles

Late in 1925, after nearly a decade of searching, Peruvian archaeologist Julio C. Tello found the source of the spectacular ancient textiles that were to become known as 'Paracas style'. His excavations of large tombs containing mummies bundled in layer upon layer of finely made and fancily decorated textiles revealed to the world the amazing skill and technique of the ancient artisans of the Paracas Culture. The well-preserved Paracas embroidered textiles found buried in the remote deserts of the Peruvian coast are some of the most stunning in the world, but much has still to be learned about the people who made them.

The scientific discovery of the mummy bundles of Paracas was as fraught with controversy and drama as any archaeological find anywhere. Extraordinary embroidered textiles depicting cat-like figures and humans dressed as fish, birds and other animals had generated illegal looting and smuggling that began early this century. By the 1920s, Paracas textiles had become the prize possessions of local and foreign collectors, appearing for sale and in museums around the world. Tello searched the Peruvian coast for the source of these textiles, eventually convincing a local *huaquero*, or looter, to lead him to the site on the wind-swept Paracas peninsula where the textiles were found. The arrival of Tello and his team on the sites allowed the more systematic excavation of Paracas tombs, as well as the scientific study of these important remains, but looters returned as soon as they could, and the sacking of Paracas sites continues to this day.

Paracas textiles are some of the most impressive examples of ancient cloth ever seen. Their finely spun cotton and wool fibres, elaborate embroidered images and fantastic techniques are unparalleled. Wool and cotton fibres were spun and respun to form the finest threads, and then woven into cloth. The threads and cloth were dyed in bright blues, reds, blacks and other colours, and woven, braided and embroidered with designs of geometric patterns, images of plants and animals, as well as supernatural beings or humans dressed as such beings. Most incredible is the remarkable preservation of these ancient textiles in their bundles, made possible by the arid climate of the Peruvian coast.

The finest of the Paracas bundles can include multiple embroidered mantles, braided, woven and tied headbands, turbans, wigs, ponchos, tunics, skirts, loincloths, bags, and other woven and embroidered items. In addition, jewellery such as necklaces and bracelets, hammered gold pieces, leather capes and bags, feather fans, gourd bowls, and items such as shells, food offerings, unspun camelid wool and raw cotton were placed with the dead.

Complicated designs are found on the embroidered mantles of Paracas. These images feature bipedal creatures with elaborate masks and costumes looking like supernatural or ceremonial incarnations of cat-like animals, sharks or killer whales, snakes and several kinds of birds. There are also depictions of costumes that appear to have features of more than one kind of animal, such as cats with bird tails. In addition, many different animal and plant forms are depicted in the embroidered and woven textiles, including felines, birds, serpents, fish and beans. Geometric motifs, as well as stylized felines, human heads and other items are also found on many Paracas textiles.

Recent study of the textiles of several of the bundles unwrapped by Tello indicates that the textiles found within each bundle form a coherent set. Specific iconographic themes are repeated in different textiles within the set found in each mummy bundle. It must have taken the weavers, who were most likely women, years to complete some of the most intricate mantles and cloaks. The finest items may have been part of costumes worn in rituals during the life of each individual, but they seem to have been buried with their owners, and not used again.

The cemeteries on the Paracas peninsula were the final resting grounds of the leaders and other members of a society that lived on Peru's South Coast between roughly 400 BC and AD 200 or 300. The centre of Paracas civilization lies to the north of the peninsula, in several river valleys on the South Coast of Peru. There, sites built on artificial mounds served as the major monuments of Paracas civilization. Paracas people farmed the river valleys where they lived, but apparently took their important dead to be buried on the windswept desert along the sea, where their remains, including some of the finest textiles ever made, were preserved to the present day.

Right: DETAIL OF A CHARACTERISTICALLY COMPLEX PARACAS-STYLE TEXTILE, EMBROIDERED FROM ALPACA WOOL. THE CENTRAL FIGURE WEARS A GOLDEN DIADEM, AND MAY REPRESENT THE FREQUENTLY DEPICTED 'OCULATE BEING'. IT IS SURROUNDED BY SMALLER FIGURES, HEADS AND SERPENTS.

The Tombs of Sipán

One of the most remarkable archaeological discoveries of recent years was made only a decade ago, when archaeologist Walter Alva was woken by police in the small hours of the morning to examine metal and other items captured in a raid on the home of some local huaqueros, or looters. During the weeks and months that followed, Alva would discover important artefacts from the looted tomb at Sipán, known as the Huaca Rajada, and eventually make the first of what was to become a series of discoveries of intact tombs of Moche rulers and priests, who had ruled the North Coast of Peru nearly two thousand years ago.

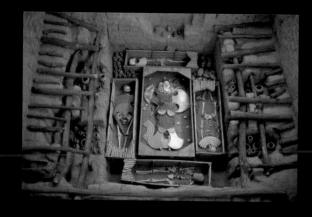

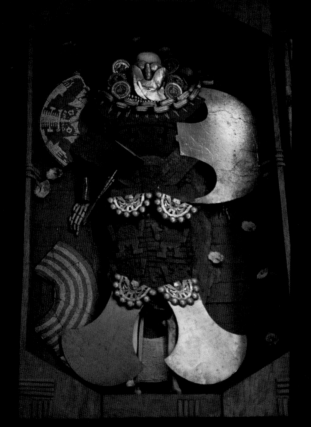

The Moche, who lived on the North Coast of Peru from roughly AD 1 to 750, have been known for years for their extraordinary pottery, metalwork, stone and shell crafts, and other fine artefacts. Until recently, however, most of the known assemblages of fancy Moche objects had come from looted contexts, and little was known about the context of use or burial of most items. No important Moche tombs had been excavated scientifically, and virtually the only information on the ancient Moche rulers came from iconography found on the richly painted walls of Moche temples and mounds, and on pieces of pottery painted with ceremonial scenes (much of it looted and often smuggled out of Peru into European and North American collections).

Researchers had been studying Moche iconography for years. Analysing designs on the pottery, as well as wall friezes, they had identified scenes of complex rituals. These rituals were presided over by a series of figures who were identifiable by the clothes they wore, by their distinctive headdresses, and by the staffs, jewellery and other items that each one used. Although many such figures had been identified in drawings on the pottery, there was no way to be sure that the rituals depicted in the paintings and friezes had actually occurred, or to determine whether the personages seen in the iconography had once existed. The discoveries at Sipán were to resolve these questions, and to remind the world of the long-lost riches of the Moche rulers.

After cleaning the looted tomb, Alva and his team began to find intact tombs of some of the most important personages in Moche society. Careful excavations revealed the remains of individuals whom the excavators named the Lord of Sipán, the Old Lord and the Priest, based on the objects found in the tombs. Masks, jewellery, staffs of office and other items made of gold, silver and semi-precious stones served as part of fabulous ceremonial costumes worn by Moche rulers for important rituals. The items found in the tombs corresponded with objects seen in the drawings on pottery and friezes that researchers had been studying for so many years. Distinctive headdresses, staffs of office, ceremonial chalices, cloaks, belts, ornaments and other items identified with figures painted on scenes of sacrifice and other rituals were found in the tombs. The links between the excavated items and the objects seen in the iconography led investigators to surmise that the ceremonies illustrated on the pottery had actually taken place, and that the personages depicted in the paintings had been buried in the tombs at Sipán.

Study of the items found at Sipán is also providing new information on Moche art and technology. Moche metalwork found in the tombs includes gold, silver, copper, gilded copper and

Left: SKELETONS, URNS AND ARTWORK LIE IN THE TOMB OF A
MOCHE WARRIOR, THE LORD OF SIPÁN.
Above: AN ANTHROPOMORPHIC HEAD IN COPPER AND A NECKLACE
IN MOTHER-OF-PEARL FROM SIPÁN.

copper with silver items. Some items were cast, while others were
hammered and some were made using combinations of techniques.
Each tomb contains unique sets of items that seem to have been
made for the individual with whom they are buried. Some of the
more spectacular pieces found in the tombs include necklaces,
bracelets and ornaments of finely worked gold, silver and gilded
copper, breastplates made with inlaid shell and stone, feathered
cloaks and headdresses, metal staffs featuring intricate sculpted
scenes and fine mould-made pottery.

Research at Sipán and now at other important Moche sites has
shown that the Moche leaders were buried in elaborate ceremonies
such as are sometimes depicted on fine line-painted pottery. The
lords of Sipán and the other sites were buried with their
ceremonial goods and hundreds of pottery offerings, as well as
with human attendants including guards and wives or concubines.
Their wooden coffins were decorated with metal and other items
that symbolized their status as important personages, and were
lowered into massive, deep burial crypts that were filled with
offerings and attendants. The burial chambers were roofed and
then sealed and buried with adobe bricks, hidden within the vast
pyramids that the Moche built at Sipán and other important sites.

The discovery of the tombs at Sipán amazed the world and
changed the way archaeologists study the ancient Moche. At the
time of writing, research at Sipán continues, and there is no telling
when the next big discovery of ancient Moche treasures will occur.

Laguna de los Condores and the Chachapoyas

Deep in the Peruvian forests on the eastern side of the Andes, in lands so remote that it can take days of hiking or riding mules to arrive there, lie the ruined ancient cities and tombs of the Chachapoyas. Stone architecture, traces of ancient roads, and tombs placed in caves and overhangs on high cliffs that command views of vast valleys are the last traces of the Chachapoyas, a civilization that flourished before the Inka, beginning around AD 800.

The Chachapoyas were conquered by the Inka in the fifteenth century, and seem to have disappeared after the Spanish conquest, allowing the jungles and forests to reclaim most of what they had built in these remote lands.

One of the most exciting recent discoveries in the Andes was made in the Chachapoyas region, near the Laguna de los Condores, or Lake of the Condors. There, in overhanging rock shelters high above the lake, local ranch hands discovered groups of mummy bundles placed in two-storey ornamented stone structures. The tombs, really more like mausoleums perched on the cliffs, contained pottery, wood and bone flutes, spears, large wooden figures, textiles and other items. In a balcony above the main tombs were mummies of more important personages. These contained finely made pottery and textiles, as well as a number of

quipus, the sets of knotted string that were made and used by a special class of scribes under the Inka. The Inka used *quipus* to record and document quantities of goods and people, as well as other administrative information needed to control the empire.

The discovery of the tombs at Laguna de los Condores has drawn new attention to an area that has remained largely ignored during the past 400-500 years. Known from colonial period documents and Inka oral histories, the Chachapoyas are described as a troublesome and warlike ethnic group who, although conquered by the Inka, caused many problems and often rebelled against their rulers. Archaeologists and explorers have visited and documented the ruined towns and villages of this almost mythical people, but the area is so remote that sustained study has been rare, and even specialists are often unaware of the archaeology of the Chachapoyas. We still know relatively little about this once densely populated region, where the ruins of fortified villages and towns with stone architecture and circular houses are often found at elevations over 3,000 m above sea level, and tombs with large standing sarcophagi are found in high cliffs.

In this remote and forgotten region, the newly discovered tombs promise to provide some of the best information to come to light in recent years about Inka administration of the most far-flung and problematic regions in the Andes. The pottery in the fanciest of the tombs at Laguna de los Condores is related to local traditions, but also to Inka traditions and to Chimu traditions from the North Coast of Peru, which had also been conquered by the Inka. This suggests that the Chachapoyas area may have been administered by governors and bureaucrats brought by the Inka from both the Andean highlands and the coast of Peru. The discovery of *quipus* in the tombs is mysterious, and raises the ongoing question of how they were really used, and by whom. There are very few *quipus* in existence today, and any new find is extremely important to the study of the ancient civilizations of the Andes. Their discovery in an often ignored region that is still very hard to reach should focus new attention on parts of the Andean jungle that have yet to be re-explored.

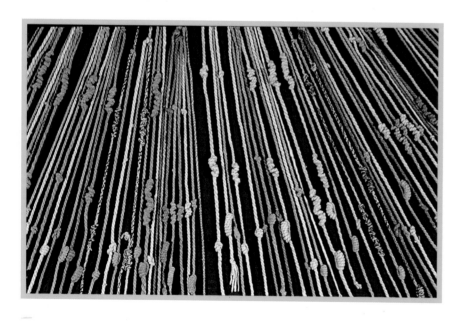

Above: QUIPUS – KNOTTED STRING RECORDING DEVICE.

Left and below:
KARAYA/
PURUNMACHES
CLAY
SARCOPHAGI,
AISPACHACA
RAVINE.

The Gold of El Dorado

Left: ANTHROPOMORPHIC GOLD FIGURE, FROM BOGOTA, COLOMBIA. *Right:* EL DORADO, 'THE GILDED MAN', NEW MUISCA LEADER ANOINTED WITH GOLD DUST ENGRAVED BY DE BRY 1599.

During the sixteenth and seventeenth centuries, legends of cities made entirely of gold flourished throughout the Spanish colonies of the New World. Although none of these exaggerated myths ever proved true, one at least was rooted in the traditions of a little-known ancient chiefdom in the heart of what is now Colombia. This is the legend of El Dorado – 'the Gilded Man' – which told of a golden man who ruled a mountainous interior area of Colombia. This fable, like many others that spread among the Spanish colonists, sparked feverish searches for gold and other treasures that lasted for centuries.

The legend of El Dorado can be traced to early Spanish accounts of an ancient rite practised by the Muisca, a chiefdom that controlled part of the highland basin that surrounds present-day Bogota. According to a seventeenth-century source, Juan Rodriguez, the ceremony took place at a lake called Guatavita, and it marked the ascension of a new chief. Rodriguez states that the new chief's first duty was to make sacrifices to his god (the sun). The chief was covered in powdered gold and golden ornaments; he then climbed aboard a raft that had been decorated with treasure and loaded with gold and emeralds for sacrifice. Accompanied by his retainers, who also wore gold ornaments and feather plumes, he floated out into the middle of Lake Guatavita with incense burning, music playing and his subjects singing loudly. Raising a banner that caused his subjects to stop playing and singing, the new chief threw all the gold and emeralds into the middle of the lake as a sacrifice to the sun. He then returned to shore accompanied by loud playing and singing and was celebrated as the new ruler of the Muisca.

The Muisca not only sacrificed gold, they also used it to make ornaments and votive figures, known as *tunjos*. Gold was an important trade item that moved from the mountains to the coast in Colombia, and some of the main trade routes were controlled

by the Muisca. They, like other groups in the area, buried their important dead with gold and other precious objects. They also placed *tunjos* and valuable items around shrines and sacred spots.

The first Spanish explorers who arrived on the coast of present-day Colombia during the end of the fifteenth and beginning of the sixteenth centuries acquired gold from their trading partners. This led to almost immediate colonization of the area, and the search for the source of the gold began. Beginning with Nuñez de Balboa, Spanish explorers followed native leads and travelled inland in search of the sources of the gold that arrived on the coast. One of the main objectives of Spanish settlement of the region was the acquisition of gold for the royal treasuries. The Spaniards did their best to acquire all of the gold

that local populations, living and dead, might have had. They treated the ancient burial mounds, settlements and sacred sites of present-day Colombia (as well as Peru and other areas of South America) as mines. They looted burial mounds systematically, under licence from the Spanish crown, which claimed its share (one-fifth to a half) of all treasures sacked. They went to great lengths to acquire gold, even granting licences to a series of individuals and companies to drain Lake Guatavita and collect the treasure that had been thrown into it. The Spanish melted down every object they obtained, to send the gold back to Spain in uniform sizes that were demanded by the Spanish king.

Centuries of Spanish looting and mining in Colombia yielded millions of dollars worth of gold, emeralds and other precious metals and stones. It also ensured that archaeologists have very little to work with in their attempts to reconstruct the ancient civilizations of the region, which were on their way to developing into an important native state at the time of Spanish contact. Because of the looting of burial sites and ancient villages, there is not a great deal left to study in the ancient burial mounds of the chiefs of the Muisca and other Colombian chiefdoms. We know relatively little of the lives of these ancient leaders, and much of our information comes from Spanish accounts of native life at the time of contact.

Other information comes from study of the relatively few objects that survived the centuries of legal looting. Ironically, illegal looting continues in Colombia today, but it is looting for the ancient objects themselves, which today have more intrinsic value to collectors than they have as pure gold. Pre-Columbian gold objects from what is now Colombia, almost all of them looted, are now found in private and museum collections around the world. The study of these objects, combined with the Spanish accounts of native technology at the time of contact, has allowed reconstruction of the methods used to mine, process and work gold.

The objects looted by the Spanish were the final products in a system of mining, trade and production of gold objects that linked much of modern-day Colombia and Panama. In mountain regions where gold was found, it was mined using simple techniques that included breaking up the soil with digging sticks, and washing it in shallow wooden trays to expose the gold. Miners also sometimes diverted streams to expose gravel beds that contained gold, and shaft mines were also used in some areas. Mining ranged from part-time, small-scale operations to full-time specialized economies, such as was found among a group known as the Buriticá. Gold was both processed and worked by the mining groups, and traded to other groups in the form of raw material as well as finished products. In Dabeiba an inland centre for goldworking developed, where specialized smiths worked gold that was then traded to the coastal areas.

The Muisca who lived at Guatavita were well-known goldsmiths, who worked gold by casting, using clay pots, crucibles and moulds. They used hammering to finish some cast pieces, as

Right: THE EL DORADO CEREMONY. FIGURES ON A RAFT, MUISCA CULTURE.

well as to make disks and other flat items from gold that had been melted and cast. They also used annealing, reheating and quenching in water, to restore malleability as the objects became harder to work. Pieces of gold were joined together by folding over, soldering, and mechanical methods such as sewing or pinning. Decorations were added using repoussé, or hammering from the underside. Using these and other techniques, they made *tunjos* with human and other figures, effigies, jewellery and some other items.

Some of the most remarkable artefacts made by the Muisca are miniature gold rafts thought to represent the ceremony of El Dorado. One was found in the Laguna de Siecha, in Colombia, in 1856. It featured a circular raft, with a large, highly decorated central figure (apparently the chief) and a series of smaller figures thought to represent the chief's retainers. Taken to Germany, it was apparently lost during the Second World War.

The most elaborate and best known Muisca *tunjo*, which has been displayed around the world, was found in 1969 inside a pottery vessel in a cave south of Bogota. This object, believed to represent the ceremony of El Dorado, depicts a number of human figures on what appears to be a raft. One figure, much larger than the rest, is seated and wears elaborate ornaments including a nose piece. Two figures near the main personage carry what are thought to be lime gourds and dippers, and two more figures carry rattles and wear masks. Six simpler figures surround the others. If this model represents the El Dorado rite, then it is a perfect symbol of the religious and ceremonial practices of an ancient people that were transformed into a legend that stimulated the looting of Colombia's gold and other treasures.

Treasure Maps of the World

Africa

SOUTHERN NAMIBIA	**1**	Africa's Oldest Dated Rock Art *page 12*
EGYPT; GIZA	**2**	The Hetepheres Treasures *page 14*
EGYPT; SAQQARA	**3**	The Tomb of Hemaka *page 16*
EGYPT; HIERAKONPOLIS	**4**	The 'Main Deposit' from Hierakonpolis *page 18*
EGYPT; GIZA	**5**	The Statues of Menkaure *page 20*
EGYPT; THEBES	**6**	The Tod Treasure *page 24*
EGYPT; THEBES	**7**	The Tomb of Kha *page 26*
EGYPT; AMARNA	**8**	The Amarna Letters *page 28*
EGYPT; VALLEY OF THE KINGS	**9**	Tutankhamen *page 30*
EGYPT; EAST OF NILE DELTA	**10**	Tanis *page 34*
EGYPT; NILE DELTA/RASHID	**11**	The Rosetta Stone *page 36*
NIGERIA	**12**	Nigerian Sculpture *page 38*
SOUTH AFRICA; MPUMALANGA	**13**	The Lydenburg Heads *page 44*
SOUTH AFRICA	**14**	Gold from Mapungubwe *page 46*
ZIMBABWE	**15**	Birds from Great Zimbabwe *page 48*
SOUTH AFRICA; KRUGER NATIONAL PARK	**16**	The Royal Graves of Thulamela *page 50*

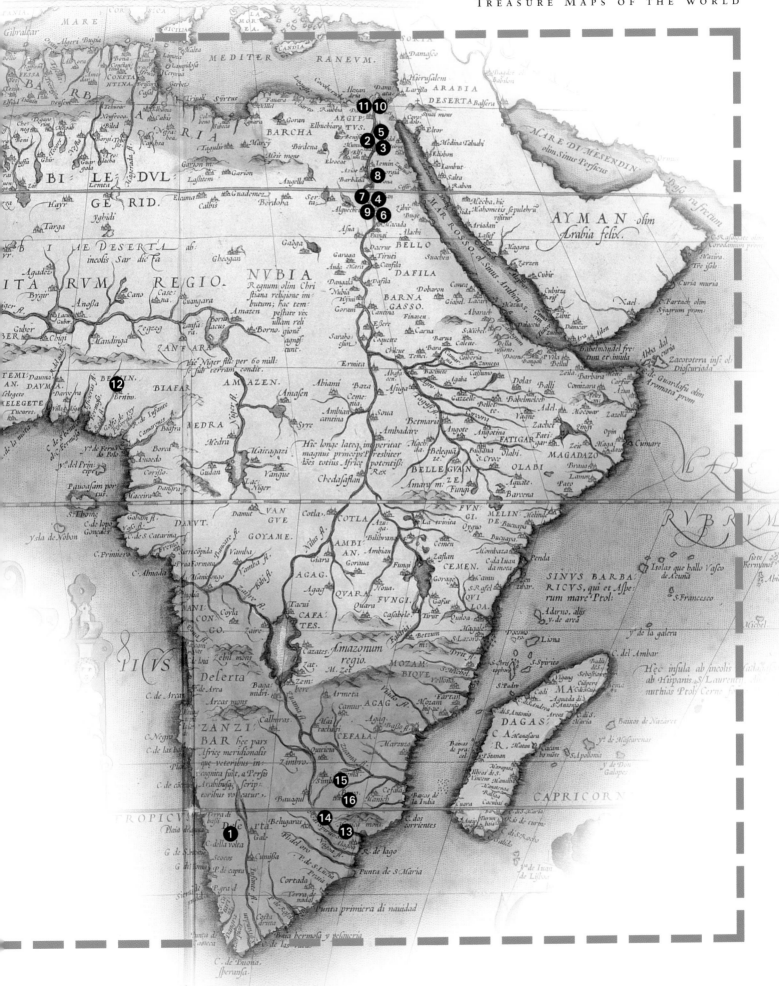

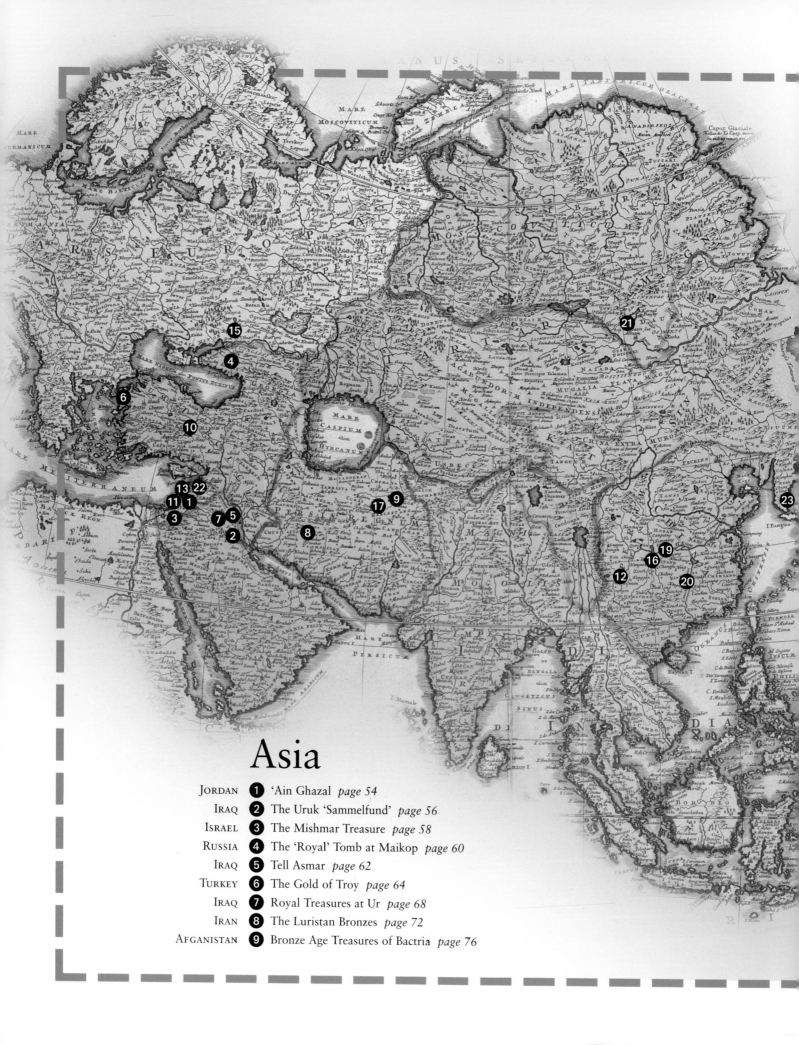

Asia

Jordan	❶	'Ain Ghazal *page 54*
Iraq	❷	The Uruk 'Sammelfund' *page 56*
Israel	❸	The Mishmar Treasure *page 58*
Russia	❹	The 'Royal' Tomb at Maikop *page 60*
Iraq	❺	Tell Asmar *page 62*
Turkey	❻	The Gold of Troy *page 64*
Iraq	❼	Royal Treasures at Ur *page 68*
Iran	❽	The Luristan Bronzes *page 72*
Afganistan	❾	Bronze Age Treasures of Bactria *page 76*

TURKEY **10** Alaca Höyük *page 80*

PALESTINE **11** The Gold from Tell el-Ajjul *page 82*

CHINA **12** The Burial Pits at Sanxingdui *page 84*

PALESTINE **13** The Megiddo Ivories *page 88*

JAPAN **14** The Splendours of Prehistoric Japanese Pottery *page 90*

UKRAINE/RUSSIA **15** Scythian Treasures of the Steppes *page 92*

CHINA **16** Musical Treasures from Ancient China *page 96*

AFGHANISTAN **17** The Golden Hoard of Tillya Tepe *page 98*

JAPAN **18** Bronze Bells of Yayoi *page 100*

CHINA **19** Treasures of Zhongshan *page 102*

CHINA/JAPAN **20** Ancient Scripts from East Asia *page 106*

SIBERIA **21** The Funeral Masks of Tashtyk *page 108*

ISRAEL **22** The Dead Sea Scrolls *page 110*

KOREA **23** Treasures from Early Korean Royal Tombs *page 112*

JAPAN **24** The Treasure House of Ancient Japan *page 114*

JAPAN **25** *Ikor* and the Ainu Bear Ceremony *page 116*

Australasia

AUSTRALIA **1** Valuable Goods in Australia and the Pacific *page 120*

NEW ZEALAND **2** Wooden Combs from Kauri Point Swamp *page 122*

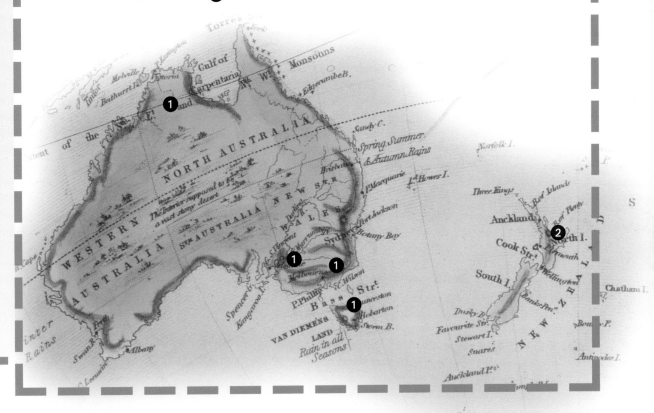

Europe

AUSTRIA/GERMANY **1** Early Ice Age Masterpieces *page 126*

AUSTRIA/CZECH REP./RUSSIA **2** Art Treasures of the Ice Age Steppe *page 128*

BULGARIA **3** Power, Prestige and Gold at Varna *page 130*

CRETE **4** Prepalatial Jewellery from Mochlos *page 134*

BRITAIN/DENMARK **5** Amber and Jet: Treasured Accessories from Prehistoric Europe *page 136*

BRITAIN **6** Bush Barrow and the Treasures of Bronze Age Goldwork *page 138*

HUNGARY/SLOVAKIA/ROMANIA **7** Bronze Age Hoards of the Carpathian Basin *page 140*

GREECE **8** The Aegina Treasure *page 142*

GREECE **9** Mycenae 'Rich in Gold' *page 146*

IRELAND **10** Dowris and the Irish Goldsmiths *page 148*

FRANCE **11** Vix and Treasures of the European Iron Age *page 150*

GREECE/ITALY/TURKEY **12** Ancient Classical Sculptures *page 152*

GERMANY **13** Celtic Prince *page 158*

BRITAIN **14** Celtic Torcs *page 159*

SPAIN **15** The Lady of Elche *page 160*

BULGARIA **16** The Panagyurishté Treasure *page 162*

BULGARIA **17** The Rogozen Treasure *page 164*

ITALY **18** Etruscan Tombs *page 166*

GERMANY **19** The Hildesheim Treasure *page 168*

ITALY **20** Hoards from Pompeii *page 170*

ITALY **21** The Boscoreale Treasure *page 176*

BRITAIN **22** Mosaics from Roman Britain *page 178*

BRITAIN **23** Vindolanda: Letters from Rome *page 182*

GERMANY **24** The Treasure of the Spring at Bad Pyrmont *page 186*

ITALY **25** The Portland Vase *page 188*

BRITAIN **26** The Water Newton Hoard *page 190*

BRITAIN **27** The Mildenhall Treasure *page 192*

ITALY **28** The Esquiline Treasure *page 194*

BRITAIN **29** The Hoxne Treasure *page 196*

SWEDEN **30** The Golden Age of Scandinavia *page 198*

BRITAIN **31** Sutton Hoo *page 200*

POLAND **32** Medieval Buried Treasure at Środa Śląska *page 202*

North and Central America

USA; WASHINGTON STATE **1** The Richey-Roberts Clovis Cache *page 206*

MEXICO **2** The Olmec 'Fort Knox' *page 208*

MEXICO **3** Tomb 7: Shrine of a Mixtec Earth Goddess *page 210*

USA; FLORIDA **4** Ancient Treasures of Florida *page 212*

MEXICO **5** The Funerary Mask of Pacal *page 214*

MEXICO **6** The Sacred Cenote of Chichén Itzá *page 216*

USA; NEW MEXICO **7** Treasures of the American Desert *page 218*

USA; WASHINGTON STATE **8** Ancient Treasures of Ozette *page 220*

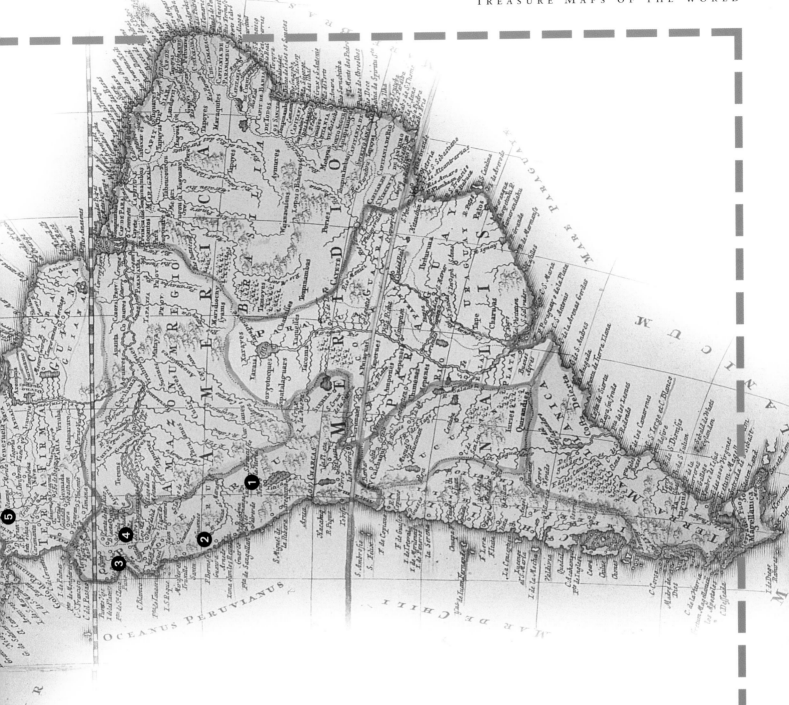

South America

PERU **1** Ancient Textiles of the Andes *page 226*

PERU **2** Paracas Textiles *page 228*

PERU **3** The Tombs of Sipán *page 230*

PERU **4** Laguna de los Condores and the Chachapoyas *page 232*

COLOMBIA **5** The Gold of El Dorado *page 234*

Bibliography

AFRICA

AFRICA'S OLDEST DATED ROCK ART
Lewis-Williams, J. D. 1990. *Discovering Southern African Rock Art*. David Philip: Cape Town.
Solomon, A. 1996. 'Rock Art in southern Africa', *Scientific American* 275,5:86-93.
Wendt, W. E. 1975. '"Art mobilier" aus der Apollo 11-Grotte in Sudwest-Afrika: Die ältesten datierten Kunstwerke Afrikas', *Acta Praehistorica Archaeologica* 5 (1974): 1-42.
Wendt, W. E. 1976. '"Art mobilier" from the Apollo 11 Cave, South West Africa: Africa's oldest dated works of art', *South African Archaeological Bulletin* 31: 5-11.

THE HETEPHERES TREASURES
Edwards, I. E. S. 1947. *The Pyramids of Egypt*. Penguin Books: Harmondsworth.
Reisner, G. A. and Smith, W. S. 1955. *A History of the Giza Necropolis, vol. 2. The Tomb of Hetepheres, the Mother of Cheops*. Harvard University Press: Cambridge, Massachusetts.

THE TOMB OF HEMAKA
Emery, W. B. 1938. *The Tomb of Hemaka*. Government Press: Cairo.
Emery, W. B. 1961. *Archaic Egypt*. Penguin Books: Harmondsworth.

THE 'MAIN DEPOSIT' FROM HIERAKONPOLIS
Hoffman, M. A. 1980. *Egypt Before the Pharaohs*. Routledge & Kegan Paul: London.
Quibell, J. E. and Green, F. W. 1902. *Hierakonpolis II*. Egyptian Research Account: London.

THE STATUES OF MENKAURE
Edwards, I. E. S. 1947; reissued 1991. *The Pyramids of Egypt*. Penguin Books: Harmondsworth.
Reisner, G. A. 1931. *Mycerinus*. Harvard University Press: Cambridge, Massachusetts.

THE TOD TREASURE
Bisson de la Roque, F. 1937. *Tod*. Institut Français d'Archéologie Orientale du Caire: Cairo.
Chapouthier, F. 1953. *Le Trésor de Tod*. Documents de Fouilles de l'Institut Français d'Archéologie Orientale du Caire, XI.
Laffineur, R. 1988. 'Réflexions sur le trésor de Tod', *Aegaeum* 2: 17-30.
Kemp, B. J. and Merrillees, R. S. 1980. *Minoan Pottery in Second Millennium Egypt*. Philipp von Zabern: Mainz.
Vandier, J. 1937. 'A propos d'un dépôt de provenance asiatique trouvé à Tod', *Syria* 18: 174-82.

THE TOMB OF KHA
Schiaparelli, E. 1920. *Relazione sui lavori della missione archeologicha italiana in Egitto*. Turin.

THE AMARNA LETTERS
Moran, W. L. 1992. *The Amarna Letters*. John Hopkins University Press.

TUTANKHAMEN
Carter, H. 1923-33. *The Tomb of Tut.ankh.Amen*, vols. 1-3. Cassell: London.
Reeves, N. 1990. *The Complete Tutankhamun*. Thames & Hudson: London.

TANIS
Coutts, H. (ed.) 1988. *Gold of the Pharaohs*. Edinburgh Museums and Art Galleries: Edinburgh.
Montet, P. 1947-60. *La Nécropole royale de Tanis*, vols. 1-3. Imprimerie Nationale: Paris.

THE ROSETTA STONE
Quirke, S. 1988. *The Rosetta Stone*. British Museum Press: London.

NIGERIAN SCULPTURE
General
Phillips, T. (ed.) 1995-6. *Africa. The Art of a Continent*. Royal Academy of Arts: London. (Entries by Eyo, Fagg and Willett.)
Shaw, T. 1978. *Nigeria. Its Archaeology and Early History*. Thames & Hudson: London.
Willett, F. 1994. *African Art*. Thames & Hudson: London.
Nok
Fagg, A. 1994. 'Thoughts of Nok', *African Arts* 27 (3): 79-83.
Shaw, T. 1981. 'The Nok sculptures of Nigeria', *Scientific American* 244 (2): 154-66.
Igbo-Ukwu
Shaw, T. 1970. *Igbo-Ukwu. An Account of Archaeological Discoveries in Eastern Nigeria*. 2 vols. Northwestern University Press: Evanston, Illinois.
Shaw, T. 1990. 'A personal memoir', in *A History of African Archaeology* (P. Robertshaw, ed.), 205-20. James Currey: London.
Ife
Willett, F. 1967. *Ife in the History of West African Sculpture*. Thames & Hudson: London.
Benin
Connah, G. 1975. *The Archaeology of Benin*. Clarendon Press: Oxford.
Darling, P. J. 1984. *Archaeology and History in Southern Nigeria: the Ancient Linear Earthworks of Benin and Ishan*. British Archaeological Reports: Oxford.

THE LYDENBURG HEADS
Inskeep, R. R. and Maggs, T. M. O'C. 1975. 'Unique art objects in the Iron Age of the Transvaal, South Africa', *South African Archaeological Bulletin* 30: 114-38.

GOLD FROM MAPUNGUBWE
Huffman, T. N. 1996. *Snakes and Crocodiles. Power and Symbolism in Ancient Zimbabwe*. Witwatersrand University Press: Johannesburg.
Meyer, A. 1997. 'Settlement Sequence in the Central Limpopo Valley: The Iron Age sites of Greefswald,' *Research by the National Cultural History Museum* 6:9-42.
Steyn, M. 1997. 'A reassessment of the human skeletons from K2 and Mapungubwe (South Africa)', *South African Archaeological Bulletin* 52: 14-20.
Voigt, E. A. 1983. *Mapungubwe. An Archaeozoological Interpretation of an Iron Age Community*. Transvaal Museum Monograph 1: Pretoria.
Unpublished material kindly supplied by Duncan Miller, University of Cape Town.

BIRDS FROM GREAT ZIMBABWE
Garlake, P. S. 1973. *Great Zimbabwe*. Thames & Hudson: London.
Huffman, T. N. 1985. 'The soapstone birds from Great Zimbabwe', *African Arts* 18 (3): 68-73.
Huffman, T. N. 1996. *Snakes and Crocodiles. Power and Symbolism in Ancient Zimbabwe*. Witwatersrand University Press: Johannesburg.

THE ROYAL GRAVES OF THULAMELA
Miller, S. M. 1996. 'Rebuilding of the walls of sixteenth-century Thulamela', in *Aspects of African Archaeology* (G. Pwiti and R. Soper, eds.). Papers from the Tenth Congress of the Pan-African Association for Prehistory and Related Studies, 837-8. University of Zimbabwe Publications: Harare.
Miller, S. M. 1997. 'From Schoemansdal to Thulamela: thoughts on reconstruction in the conservation process'. *Research by the National Cultural History Museum* (Pretoria) 6: 189-203.
Steyn, M., Miller, S., Nienaber, W. C. and Loots, M. 1998. 'Late Iron Age gold burials from Thulamela (Pafuri region, Kruger National Park)', *South African Archaeological Bulletin* 53:73-85

ASIA

'AIN GHAZAL
Rollefson, G. 1983. 'Ritual and ceremony at neolithic Ain Ghazal (Jordan)', *Paléorient* 9 (2): 29-38.
Tubb, K. and Grissom, C. 1995. ''Ayn Ghazal: a comparative study of the 1983 and 1985 statuary caches', *Studies in the History and Archaeology of Jordan* V, 437-47.

THE URUK 'SAMMELFUND'
Heinrich, E. 1936. *Kleinfunde aus den Archaischen Tempelschichten in Uruk*. Harrassowitz: Leipzig.
Strommenger, E. 1964. *The Art of Mesopotamia*. Thames & Hudson: London.

THE MISHMAR TREASURE
Bar-Adon, P. 1980. *The Cave of the Treasure*. The Israel Exploitation Society: Jerusalem.
Tadmor, M., Kedem, D., Begemann, F., Hauptmann, A., Pernicka, E. and Schmitt-Strecker, S. 1995. 'The Nahal Mishmar hoard from the Judean Desert: technology, composition, and provenance', *'Atiquot* 27: 95-148.

THE 'ROYAL' TOMB AT MAIKOP

Chernykh, E. N. 1992. *Ancient Metallurgy in the USSR*. Cambridge University Press: Cambridge.

Kuzhnareva, K. K. and Markovin, V. I. (eds.) 1994. *Arkheologiya. Epokha Bronzy Kavkaza i Srednei Azii. Rannyaya i Srednyaya Bronza Kavkaza*. Nauka: Moscow.

Nekhaev, A. A. 1992. 'A burial of the Maikop Culture from the Krasnogvardeisk village mound', *Soviet Anthropology and Archaeology* 30: 29-34.

Tallgren, A. M. 1927. 'Maikop', in *Reallexikon der Vorgeschichte* (M. Ebert, ed.), 347-8.

TELL ASMAR

Frankfort, H. 1939. *Sculpture of the Third Millennium BC from Tell Asmar and Khafajah*. University of Chicago Press: Chicago.

THE GOLD OF TROY

Antonova, I., Tolstikov, V. and Treister, M. 1996. *The Gold of Troy. Searching for Homer's Fabled City*. Thames & Hudson: London.

Schliemann, H. 1880. *Ilios: The City and Country of the Trojans. The Results and Discoveries on the Site of Troy and Throughout the Troad in the Years 1871-72-73-78-79*. London.

ROYAL TREASURES AT UR

Woolley, L. 1934. *Ur Excavations II: The Royal Cemetery*. 2 vols. British Museum Press: London.

Woolley, L. and Moorey, P. R. S. 1982. *Ur 'of the Chaldees'* (revised and updated edn). Cornell University Press: Ithaca, New York.

THE LURISTAN BRONZES

Moorey, P. R. S. 1974. *Ancient Bronzes from Luristan*. British Museum Press: London.

Muscarella, O. 1988. 'The background to the Luristan bronzes', in *Bronze-working Centres of Western Asia, c. 1000-539 BC* (J. Curtis, ed.), 33-44. Kegan Paul: London.

BRONZE AGE TREASURES OF BACTRIA

Dupree, L., Gouin, P. and Omer, N. 1971. 'The Khosh Tapa hoard from north Afghanistan', *Archaeology* 24 (1): 28-34.

Ligabue, G. and Salvatori, S. (eds.) 1988. *Bactria, an Ancient Oasis Civilization from the Sands of Afghanistan*. Erizzo: Venice.

Pittman, H. 1986. *Art of the Bronze Age*. Metropolitan Museum of Art: New York.

ALACA HÖYÜK

Arik, R. 1937. *Les fouilles d'Alaca Höyük*, 1935. Turk Tarih Kurumu: Ankara.

Kosay, H. 1944. *Ausgrabungen von Alaca Höyük*. Turk Tarih Kurumu: Ankara.

Lloyd, S. 1967. *Early Highland Peoples of Anatolia*. Thames & Hudson: London.

THE GOLD FROM TELL EL-AJJUL

Kempinski, A. 1993. 'Ajjul, Tell el-', in *The New Encyclopedia of Archaeological Excavations in the Holy Land* (E. Stern et al, eds.). Israel Exploration Society: Jerusalem.

Negbi, O. 1976. 'The hoards of goldwork from Tell el-Ajjul'. *Studies in Mediterranean Archaeology* 25, Göteborg.

Petrie, F. 1931-4. Ancient Gaza I-IV. British School of Archaeology in Egypt: London.

THE BURIAL PITS AT SANXINGDUI

Rawson, J. (ed.) 1996. *Mysteries of Ancient China*. British Museum Press: London.

THE MEGIDDO IVORIES

Barnett, R. 1982. *Ancient Ivories of the Middle East*. Insititute of Archaeology, Hebrew University: Jerusalem.

Crowfoot, J. and Crowfoot, G. 1938. *Samaria-Sebaste II: Early Ivories from Samaria*. Palestine Exploration Fund: London.

Loud, G. 1939. *The Megiddo Ivories*. University of Chicago Press: Chicago.

THE SPLENDOURS OF PREHISTORIC JAPANESE POTTERY

Doi, T. (ed.) 1982. *Jomon Jidai [Jomon Period]. Nihon no Bijutsu 3 [Arts of Japan 3]*. (Agency for Cultural Affairs, Tokyo National Museum). Shibundo: Tokyo.

Kobayashi, T. 1981. *Jomon Doki [Jomon Pottery]. Nihon no Bijutsu 6 [Arts of Japan 6]*. (Agency for Cultural Affairs, Tokyo National Museum). Shibundo: Tokyo.

Pearson, R. (ed.) 1992. *Ancient Japan*. Arthur M. Sackler Gallery (Smithsonian Institution): Washington, DC.

SCYTHIAN TREASURES OF THE STEPPES

Chochorowski, J. and Skoryi, S. 1997. 'Prince of the Great Kurgan', *Archaeology*, September/October, 50: 32-9.

Rolle, R. 1989. *The World of the Scythians*. Batsford: London.

MUSICAL TREASURES FROM ANCIENT CHINA

Qian Hao, Chen Heyi and Ru Suichu. 1981. *Out of China's Earth. Archaeological Discoveries in the People's Republic of China*. Frederick Muller Ltd: London/China Pictorial: Beijing.

Rawson, J. 1996. *Mysteries of Ancient China*. British Museum Press: London.

THE GOLDEN HOARD OF TILLYA TEPE

Sarianidi, V. I. 1985. *The Golden Hoard of Bactria*. Abrams: New York.

BRONZE BELLS OF YAYOI

Hudson, M. 1992. 'Rice, bronze, and chieftains: an archaeology of Yayoi ritual', *Japanese Journal of Religious Studies* 19: 139-89.

TREASURES OF ZHONGSHAN

Qian Hao, Chen Heyi and Ru Suichu. 1981. *Out of China's Earth. Archaeological Discoveries in the People's Republic of China*. Frederick Muller Ltd: London/ China Pictorial: Beijing.

ANCIENT SCRIPTS FROM EAST ASIA

Qian Hao, Chen Heyi and Ru Suichu. 1981. *Out of China's Earth*. Frederick Muller Ltd: London/China Pictorial: Beijing.

Rawson, J. 1996. *Mysteries of Ancient China*. British Museum Press: London.

Tsuboi, K. (ed.) 1987. *Recent Archaeological Discoveries in Japan*. UNESCO and the Centre for East Asian Cultural Studies: Paris and Tokyo.

THE FUNERAL MASKS OF TASHTYK

Vadetskaya, E. B. 1992. 'Tashtyk Culture', in *Archaeology of the USSR*. Vol. on 'Asian steppes of the USSR in Scythian-Saramatian times', 236-46 (in Russian). Nauka: Moscow.

THE DEAD SEA SCROLLS

Fitzmyer, J. A. 1977. *The Dead Sea Scrolls*. Scholars Press: Missoula.

Moorey, P. R. S. 1991. *A Century of Biblical Archaeology*. Lutterworth Press: Cambridge.

TREASURES FROM EARLY KOREAN ROYAL TOMBS

Kim Won-Yong. 1983. *Recent Archaeological Discoveries in the Republic of Korea*. The Centre for East Asian Cultural Studies and UNESCO: Tokyo and Paris.

Goepper, R. and Whitfield, R. 1984. *Treasures from Korea*. British Museum Press: London.

THE TREASURE HOUSE OF ANCIENT JAPAN

Hayashi, R. 1975. *The Silk Road and the Shoso-in*. Weatherhill: New York.

IKOR AND THE AINU BEAR CEREMONY

Utagawa, H. 1992. 'The 'sending-back' rite in Ainu culture', *Japanese Journal of Religious Studies* 19: 255-70.

Ohnuki-Tierney, E. 1974. *The Ainu of the Northwest Coast of Southern Sakhalin*. Holt, Rinehart & Winston: New York.

AUSTRALASIA

VALUABLE GOODS IN AUSTRALIA AND THE PACIFIC

Flood, J. 1995. *Archaeology of the Dreamtime* (3rd edn). Angus and Robertson: Sydney.

WOODEN COMBS FROM KAURI POINT SWAMP

Shawcross, W. 1979. 'Kauri Point Swamp: the ethnographic interpretation of a prehistoric site', in *Problems in Economic and Social Archaeology* (G. de G. Sieveking, I. H. Longworth and K. E. Wilson, eds.), 277-305. Duckworth: London.

Trotter, M. and McCulloch, B. 1989. *Unearthing New Zealand*. GP Books: Wellington.

EUROPE

EARLY ICE AGE MASTERPIECES
Bahn, P. G. and Vertut, J. 1997. *Journey Through the Ice Age*. Weidenfeld & Nicolson: London/University of California Press: Berkeley.
Hahn, J. 1986. *Kraft und Aggression. Die Botschaft der Eiszeitkunst im Aurignacien Süddeutschlands?* Verlag Archaeologica Venatoria, Institut für Urgeschichte der Universität Tübingen.
Hahn, J. 1993. 'Aurignacian art in Central Europe', in *Before Lascaux: the complex record of the Early Upper Paleolithic* (H. Knecht et al, eds.), 229-41. CRC Press: Boca Raton, Florida.
Neugebauer-Maresch, C. 1995. 'La statuette du Galgenberg (entre Stratzing et Krems-Rehberg) et les figurines féminines d'Autriche', in *La Dame de Brassempouy* (H. Delporte, ed.), 187-94. ERAUL 74: Liège.

ART TREASURES OF THE ICE AGE STEPPE
Abramova, Z. 1995. *L'Art Paléolithique d'Europe Orientale et de Sibérie*. Jérôme Millon: Grénoble.
Bahn, P. G. and Vertut, J. 1997. *Journey Through the Ice Age*. Weidenfeld & Nicolson: London/University of California Press: Berkeley.
Delporte, H. 1993. *L'Image de la Femme dans l'Art Préhistorique* (2nd edn). Picard: Paris.
Kozlowski, J. K. 1992. *L'Art de la Préhistoire en Europe Orientale*. CNRS: Paris.

POWER, PRESTIGE AND GOLD AT VARNA
Fol, A. and Lichardus, J. (eds.) 1988. *Macht, Herrschaft und Gold. Das Gräberfeld von Varna (Bulgarien) und die Anfänge einer neuen europäischen Zivilisation*. Moderne Galerie des Saarland-Museums: Saarbrücken.
Renfrew, C. 1978. 'Varna and the social context of early metallurgy', *Antiquity* 52: 199-203.
Renfrew, C. 1980. 'Ancient Bulgaria's golden treasures', *National Geographic* 158 (1), July: 112-29.
Renfrew, C. 1986. 'Varna and the emergence of wealth in prehistoric Europe', in *The Social Life of Things* (A. Appadurai, ed.), 141-8. Cambridge University Press: Cambridge.

PREPALATIAL JEWELLERY FROM MOCHLOS
Davaras, C. 1975. 'Early Minoan Jewellery from Mochlos', *Annual of the British School at Athens* 70: 101-14.
Higgins, R. 1980. *Greek and Roman Jewellery* (2nd edn). University of California Press: Los Angeles and Berkeley.
Seager, R. B. 1912. *Explorations in the Island of Mochlos*. American School of Classical Studies at Athens: Boston and New York.

AMBER AND JET: TREASURED ACCESSORIES FROM PREHISTORIC EUROPE
Clarke, D. V., Cowie, T. G. and Foxon, A. 1985. *Symbols of Power at the Time of Stonehenge*. National Museum of Antiquities of Scotland: Edinburgh.

Hvass, S. and Storgaard, B. 1993. *Digging into the Past*. Aarhus University: Aarhus.

BUSH BARROW AND THE TREASURES OF BRONZE AGE GOLDWORK
Clarke, D. V., Cowie, T. G. and Foxon, A. 1985. *Symbols of Power at the Time of Stonehenge*. National Museum of Antiquities of Scotland: Edinburgh.
Eogan, G. 1994. *The Accomplished Art: Gold and Goldworking in Britain and Ireland during the Bronze Age*. Oxbow Books: Oxford.
Kinnes, I. A., Longworth, I. H., McIntyre, I. M., Needham, S. P. and Oddy, W. A. 1988. 'Bush Barrow gold', *Antiquity* 62: 24-39.
Shell, C. and Robinson, P. 1988. 'The recent reconstruction of the Bush Barrow lozenge plate', *Antiquity* 62: 248-60.
Thom, A. S., Ker, J. M. D. and Burrows, T. R. 1988. 'The Bush Barrow gold lozenge: is it a solar and lunar calendar for Stonehenge?', *Antiquity* 62: 492-502.

BRONZE AGE HOARDS OF THE CARPATHIAN BASIN
Coles, J. M. and Harding, A. F. 1979. *The Bronze Age in Europe*. Methuen: London.
Cunliffe, B. (ed.) 1994. *The Oxford Illustrated Prehistory of Europe*. Oxford University Press: Oxford.
Jażdżewski, K. 1984. *Urgeschichte Mitteleuropas*. Ossolineum: Wrocław.

THE AEGINA TREASURE
Higgins, R. 1957. 'The Aegina treasure reconsidered', *Annual of the British School at Athens* 52: 42-57.
Higgins, R. 1979. *The Aegina Treasure*. British Museum Press: London.

MYCENAE 'RICH IN GOLD'
Dickinson, O. T. P. K. 1977. 'The origins of Mycenaean civilisation'. *Studies in Mediterranean Archaeology* 49, Göteborg.
Schliemann, H. 1878. *Mycenae: A Narrative of the Researches and Discoveries at Mycenae and Tiryns*. London.

DOWRIS AND THE IRISH GOLDSMITHS
Cone, P. (ed.) 1977. *Treasures of Early Irish Art, 1500 BC-1500 AD*. Metropolitan Museum of Art: New York.
Eogan, G. 1994. *The Accomplished Art: Gold and Goldworking in Britain and Ireland during the Bronze Age*. Oxbow Books: Oxford.
Herity, M. and Eogan, G. 1977. *Ireland in Prehistory*. Routledge & Kegan Paul: London.
Neill, K. 1993. 'The Broighter Hoard', *Archaeology Ireland* 7 (2).
Raftery, B. 1994. *Pagan Celtic Ireland*. Thames & Hudson: London.
Waddell, J. and Shee Twohig, E. 1995. 'Ireland in the Bronze Age', *Proceedings of the Dublin Conference*, April 1995. Stationery Office: Dublin.

VIX AND TREASURES OF THE EUROPEAN IRON AGE
Joffroy, R. 1979. *Vix et ses Trésors*. Librarie Jules Tallandier: Paris.

ANCIENT CLASSICAL SCULPTURES
Greenhalgh, M. 1989. *The Survival of Roman Antiquities in the Middle Ages*. Duckworth: London.
Haskell, F. and Penny, N. 1981. *Taste and the Antique: the Lure of Classical Sculpture 1500-1900*. Yale University Press: London and New Haven, Connecticut.
Jenkins, I. 1992. *Archaeologists and Aesthetes in the Sculpture Galleries of the British Museum 1800-1939*. British Museum Press: London.
Stewart, A. 1990. *Greek Sculpture: an Exploration*. Yale University Press: London.

CELTIC TORCS
Brailsford, J. W. and Stapley, J. E. 1972. 'The Ipswich torcs', *Proceedings of the Prehistoric Society* 38: 219-34.
Stead, I. M. 1991. 'The Snettisham treasure: excavations in 1990', *Antiquity* 65: 447-65.

THE LADY OF ELCHE
1997. *Cien Años de una Dama*. Ministerio de Educación y Cultura: Madrid.
Ramos Fernández, R. 1995. *El Templo Ibérico de La Alcudia. La Dama de Elche*. Ediciones Ajuntament d'Elx: Elx.
Ramos Folques, A. 1965. *La Dama de Elche*. Peñiscola: Barcelona.
Vives Boix, F. and Sáez, J. A. 1997. 'Interpretación de la vestimenta de la Dama de Elche', *Revista de Arqueología* XVIII, 199, November: 6-15.

THE PANAGYURISHTÉ TREASURE
Exhibition catalogue. 1976. *Thracian Treasures from Bulgaria*. British Museum Press: London.

THE ROGOZEN TREASURE
Cook, B. F. (ed.) 1989. *The Rogozen Treasure: papers of the Anglo-Bulgarian Conference, 12 March 1987*. British Museum Press: London.
Fol, A., Nikolov, B. and Hoddinott, R. F. 1986. *The New Thracian Treasure from Rogozen, Bulgaria*. British Museum Press: London.
Exhibition catalogue. 1976. *Thracian Treasures from Bulgaria*. British Museum Press: London.

ETRUSCAN TOMBS
Macnamara, E. 1990. *The Etruscans*. British Museum Press: London.

THE HILDESHEIM TREASURE
Oliver, A. 1977. *Silver for the Gods: 800 years of Greek and Roman Silver*. Toledo Museum of Art: Toledo.

HOARDS FROM POMPEII
Zanker, P. 1988. *The Power of Images in the Age of Augustus*. University of Michigan Press: Ann Arbor.
Strong, D. E. 1966. *Greek and Roman Gold and Silver Plate*. Methuen: London.
Von Bothmer, D. 1984. *A Greek and Roman Treasury*. Metropolitan Museum of Art: New York.

THE BOSCOREALE TREASURE
Strong, D. E. 1966. *Greek and Roman Gold*

and Silver Plate. Methuen: London.

MOSAICS FROM ROMAN BRITAIN
Toynbee, J. M. C. 1962. *Art in Roman Britain*. Phaidon: London.
Toynbee, J. M. C. 1964. 'A new Roman mosaic pavement found in Dorset', *Journal of Roman Studies* 54: 7-14.

VINDOLANDA: LETTERS FROM ROME
Birley, R. E. 1977. *Vindolanda, a Roman Frontier Post on Hadrian's Wall*. Thames & Hudson: London.
Birley, R. E. 1997. 'The Vindolanda bonfire', *Current Archaeology* 13 (9), no. 153, July, 348-57.
Bowman, A. K. 1994. *Life and Letters on the Roman Frontier: Vindolanda and its People*. British Museum Press: London.
Bowman, A. K. and Thomas, J. D. 1983. *Vindolanda: the Latin Writing Tablets*. Britannia Monograph no. 4.

THE TREASURE OF THE SPRING AT BAD PYRMONT
Andraschko, F. M. and Teegen, W-R. 1988. *Der Brunnenfund von Bad Pyrmont und die Ur- und Frühgeschichte des Pyrmonter Tales*. Museum im Schloss Bad Pyrmont: Bad Pyrmont.
Hassler, H-J. 1991. *Ur- und Frühgeschichte in Niedersachsen*. Theiss: Stuttgart.

THE PORTLAND VASE
Harden, D. B. 1987. *Glass of the Caesars*. Olivetti: Milan.

THE WATER NEWTON HOARD
Painter, K. S. 1977. *The Water Newton Early Christian Silver*. British Museum Press: London.

THE MILDENHALL TREASURE
Lethbridge, T. C. 1997. 'The Mildenhall Treasure: a first-hand account', *Antiquity* 71: 721-8.
Painter, K. S. 1977. *The Mildenhall Treasure: Roman Silver from East Anglia*. British Museum Press: London.

THE ESQUILINE TREASURE
Shelton, K. 1981. *The Esquiline Treasure*. British Museum Press: London.
Kent, J. P. C. and Painter, K. S. (eds.) 1977. *Wealth of the Roman World: Gold and Silver AD 300- 700*. British Museum Press: London.

THE HOXNE TREASURE
Bland, R. and Johns, C. 1993. *The Hoxne Treasure: an Illustrated Introduction*. British Museum Press: London.

THE GOLDEN AGE OF SCANDINAVIA
Hauck, K. 1985. *Die Goldbrakteaten der Völkerwanderungszeit*. Wilhelm Fink Verlag: Munich.
Knape, A. 1994. *The Magic of Gold in Life and Legend*. Museum of National Antiquities: Stockholm.
Randsborg, K. 1990. 'Beyond the Roman Empire: Archaeological Discoveries in Gudme on Funen, Denmark', *Oxford Journal of Archaeology* 9, 355-66.

SUTTON HOO
Bruce-Mitford, R. 1978. *The Sutton Hoo Ship-Burial, Volume 2*. British Museum Press: London.
Bruce-Mitford, R. (Evans, A. C., ed.) 1983. *The Sutton Hoo Ship-Burial, Volume 3*. British Museum Press: London.
Evans, A. C. 1994. *The Sutton Hoo Ship-Burial*. British Museum Press: London.

MEDIEVAL BURIED TREASURE AT ŚRODA ŚLĄSKA
Gajewska-Prorok, E. 1996. *Skarb Sredzki [The Treasure of Środa Śląska]*. Muzeum Narodowe: Wrocław.

NORTH AND CENTRAL AMERICA

THE RICHEY-ROBERTS CLOVIS CACHE
Mehringer Jr., P. J. 1988. 'Weapons Cache of Ancient Americans', *National Geographic*, October, 174 (4): 500-3.

THE OLMEC 'FORT KNOX'
Coe, M. D. and Diehl, R. A. 1980. *In the Land of the Olmec*. University of Texas Press: Austin.

TOMB 7: SHRINE OF A MIXTEC EARTH GODDESS
Caso, A. 1969. *El Tesoro de Monte Albán*. Memorias del Instituto Nacional de Antropología e Historia 3: Mexico City.
McCafferty, S. D. and McCafferty, G. G. 1994. 'Engendering Tomb 7 at Monte Albán: respinning an old yarn', *Current Anthropology* 35: 143-52.

ANCIENT TREASURES OF FLORIDA
Purdy, B. A. 1991. *The Art and Archaeology of Florida's Wetlands*. CRC Press: Boca Raton, Florida.
Purdy, B. A. 1996. *Indian Art of Ancient Florida*. University Press of Florida: Gainesville.

THE FUNERARY MASK OF PACAL
Branigan, W. 1989. 'Robbery, recovery, and relief: behind Mexico's archaeological near-catastrophe', *The Washington Post*, final edn, 31 July 1989, Style Section c1.
Miller, M. 'Museum's priceless pre-Columbian artifacts recovered. Mexico miracle: stolen art found', *Los Angeles Times*, home edn, 15 June 1989, Section 1, 7.
Robertson, M. G. 1983. *The Sculpture of Palenque*. 3 vols. Princeton University Press: Princeton.

THE SACRED CENOTE OF CHICHÉN ITZÁ
Chase Coggins, C. and Shane III, O. C. (eds.) 1984. *Cenote of Sacrifice: Maya Treasures from the Sacred Well at Chichén Itzá*. University of Texas Press: Austin.

TREASURES OF THE AMERICAN DESERT
Anyon, R. and LeBlanc, S. A. 1984. *The Galaz Ruin. A Prehistoric Mimbres Village in Southwestern New Mexico*. University of New Mexico Press: Albuquerque.
LeBlanc, S. A. 1983. *The Mimbres People*. Thames & Hudson: London.

ANCIENT TREASURES OF OZETTE
Kirk, R. and Daugherty, R. D. 1974. *Hunters of the Whale*. Morrow: New York.
Pascua, M. P. 1991. 'Ozette. A Makah village in 1491', *National Geographic*, October, 180 (4): 38-53.

SOUTH AMERICA

ANCIENT TEXTILES OF THE ANDES
Morris, C. and Von Hagen, A. 1993. *The Inka Empire and Its Andean Origins*. Abbeville Press: New York, London and Paris.
Rowe, A. P., Benson, E. P. and Schaffer, A-L. (eds.) 1979. *The Junius B. Bird Pre-Columbian Textile Conference*. The Textile Museum and Dumbarton Oaks: Washington, DC.

PARACAS TEXTILES
Paul, A. 1990. *Paracas Ritual Attire*. University of Oklahoma Press: Norman, Oklahoma, and London.
Paul, A. (ed.) 1991. *Paracas Art and Architecture*. University of Iowa Press: Iowa City.
New Discoveries at the Moche Pyramids
Morris, C. and Von Hagen, A. 1993. *The Inka Empire and Its Andean Origins*. Abbeville Press: New York, London and Paris.

THE TOMBS OF SIPÁN
Alva, W. 1988. 'Discovering the New World's richest unlooted tomb', *National Geographic* 174 (4): 510-48.
Alva, W. 1989. 'New tomb of royal splendor', *National Geographic* 177 (6): 2-15.
Alva, W. and Donnan, C. B. 1993. *Royal Tombs of Sipán*. Fowler Museum of Cultural History, UCLA: Los Angeles.

LAGUNA DE LOS CONDORES AND THE CHACHAPOYAS
Bruhns, K. O. 1994. *Ancient South America*. Chapter 16. Cambridge University Press: Cambridge.
Von Hagen, A. 1998. 'A Tomb with a View'. *Archaeology* 51/2:48-54.

THE GOLD OF EL DORADO
Bray, W. 1978. *The Gold of El Dorado*. Times Newspapers Ltd: London.
Emmerich, A. 1984. *Sweat of the Sun and Tears of the Moon. Gold and Silver in Pre-Columbian Art*. Hacker Art Books: New York.

Index

NOTE: References in italics denote illustrations; those in bold figures denote the main treatment of a subject, including illustrations.

Abu (Mesopotamian god) 62
Abydos, Egypt 16
Achaemenid dynasty 99
Adrianov, Alexander 108
Aegina, Greece 242-3
  temple of Aphaia, sculptures 154
  Treasure 142-5
Afghanistan 240-1
  Bactrian culture 76, 79
  Khosh Tapa hoard 76
  Tillya Tepe hoard 98-9
  trade 24, 33, 67, 71, 144
Africa 10-51, 238-9
  see also individual sites and
  countries
agriculture, introduction of 55, 90
Ahab, king of Israel 89
'Ain Ghazal, Jordan; plaster figures 54-5, 240-1
Ainu Culture, Japan 116-17
Ajjul see Tell el-Ajjul
Akhenaten, king of Egypt 28, 30
Akkadian language 28
alabaster jars, Ur 68
Alaca Höyük, Turkey 25, 61, 67, 80-1, 240-1
Albán, Monte, Mexico 210-11
Alexander the Great, king of Macedon 99
Ålleberg, Sweden; gold collar 199
Amarna, Egypt; letters 28-9, 30, 238-9
Amazons 162, 164
amber objects, European 136-7, 139, 146, 148, 242-3
Amen (Egyptian god) 30, 34
Amenemhet II, king of Egypt 24, 25
Amenemope, king of Egypt 34
Amenhotep III, king of Egypt 28
America
  North and Central 204-23, 244-5
  South 224-37, 245
  see also individual sites and
  countries
amethyst beads 57, 144, 135
amphorae
  ceramic 150, 162, 163
  glass 188
Amu Darya (River Oxus) 98
amulets
  Egyptian 24, 33, 33
  Roman bulla 174
  Thulamela 51
Anatolia
  metalwork 25
  see also Alaca Höyük; Troy
ancestor cults 49, 54-5, 132, 210
Andes, textiles from 226-7, 245
Anglo-Saxon era; Sutton Hoo 200-1
Ankan, king of Yamato 115
Apollo, statues of 152, 155
Apollo 11 cave, Namibia; rock art 12-13, 238-9
Arik, Remzi 80
Arles, France 152
armour 115, 200
Artemidorus (Greek traveller in Iberia) 160

Artemision, Cape, Greece 155
Asia 52-117, 240-1
  see also individual sites and
  countries
Asmar see Tell Asmar
Assyria 28, 89
Astana, China 106
Astarte pendants, Tell el-Ajjul 83, 83
Astrabad, Persia 76
astronomy, archaeo- 139
Ateas, king of Scythians 93
Aten (sun's disc, Egyptian god) 28, 30
Athena, statues of
  Pheidias' chryselephantine 156, 162
  from Piraeus 154, 155
Athens, Greece 154, 156, 162
atlatl (spearthrower), Maya 217
Augustus, Roman emperor 172
Aurelius Ursicinus 196
aurochs drinking horns, Sutton Hoo 200, 200
Australasia 118-23, 241
Australia 120-1, 241
Avignon, France 152
awl, copper; Mishmar 58
axes and axeheads, bronze
  Carpathian basin 140
  Dowris hoard, Ireland 148
  Luristan 73
  Wessex Culture 138
Aztecs 210

Babylonia 28
Bactria 78-81, 98-9, 240-1
Bad Pyrmont, Germany; hoard 186-7, 242-3
bag, Egyptian leather tool- 16
Balboa, Vasco Nuñez de 235
Ballindery 2 farmstead, Ireland 148
Ballytegan, Co Laoghais, Ireland 149
Baltic Sea, islands of 198, 199
Bambanyanalo, South Africa 46-7
bamboo strips with writing, China 106, 107
banquets, Roman 174, 179
Barberini, Cardinal Francesco 188
Barberini tomb, Etruria 167
Barca, Slovakia; hoard 140
barrows, Bronze Age 136-7, 138-9
basalt monoliths, Olmec 208
basketry; Mishmar 58
Bath, Avon 179
baths, Roman 180
beads
  bronze, Troy 67
  semi-precious stones: Maikop 60; Mishmar 58; Mochlos 135; Nigeria 41; Tod Treasure 24; Troy 67; Uruk 57
  glass: Indian, in Thulamela 51; Nigeria 41
  gold: Aegina 144; Maikop 60; Troy 67
  ostrich eggshell, Thulamela 51
  silver, Troy 67
bear ceremony, Japan 116-17
beds, Egyptian 14, 15, 33
bells, bronze
  China 96-7
  Ireland 148, 148
  Japan 100-1
Benin, Nigeria 42
Berghe, Louis van der 73, 75
Bernardini tomb, Palestrina, Italy 166
Bezing, Dr K.L. von 44
Bielke, Count Nils Adam 198
Bihar, Romania 140
Bilje, former Yugoslavia 140, 141

bird-of-paradise plumes 120
Birley, Robin 182
boats
  canoes, Florida 212-13
  gold models: Colombia 236, 237; Ireland 149, 149
  ship burials, Sutton Hoo 200-1
Bodrum (Halikarnassos), Turkey 155
Bohemia 203
Bonaparte, Lucien, Prince of Canino 166
bone objects
  combs, Anglo-Saxon 201
  flutes, Chachapoya 232
  knives, Anglo-Saxon 201
  see also ivory
bones, genetic testing of 210
Book of Changes (I Ching) 106
Boscoreale, Italy; hoard 170-5, 176-7, 242-3
Boudicca, queen of Iceni 159
bow, Japanese wooden 115
bowls
  bronze: Anglo-Saxon hanging 201; Egyptian, at Sutton Hoo 201
  gold: China 97; Mapungubwe 46, 47
  silver: Etruria 166; Mildenhall 192, 193; Sutton Hoo 201; Water Newton 190, 190-1
  stone, Uruk 56
  wooden, Ozette 220-1
boxes
  copper-bronze, Tod Treasure 24, 25, 25
  inlaid: Egypt 14; Hoxne 196
  ivory, Megiddo 89
bracelets, golden
  Bilje 140, 141
  Hoxne 196
  Thulamela 51, 51
  Varna 130, 131, 133
bracken 182
bracteates, gold 199
brain tissue, Florida wetlands 213
brass sculptures, Nigeria 39, 40, 41, 42, 42-3
braziers, ritual
  Egypt 34
  Mixtec, from skull 210
breastplates
  Scythian bronze 92
  Moche 231
Britain
  amber and jet 136-7
  Anglo-Saxon, Sutton Hoo 200-1
  Roman, see Mildenhall; mosaics; Vindolanda; Water Newton
  see also Wessex Culture;
British Museum, London 36, 154, 155, 159, 172
  and Aegina Treasure 142
  Esquiline Treasure 194
  Etruscan art 166
  Portland Vase 188
  and Sutton Hoo ship burials 200
Brittany 139
Broighter, Ireland; hoard 149, 149
bronze and bronze objects
  alloys 59, 60, 81
  Carpathian Basin hoards 140-1
  Dowris hoard 148-9
  Luristan 72-5
  Sanxingdui 84-7
  Zhongshan 102-3
  see also individual types of
  artefact
brooches 199
  see also fibulae
Brown, Basil 200
Bryaxis 155

buckets, Anglo-Saxon 200, 201
Buddhism 99, 115
bulls head vase, Mycenae 146
bulla, gold, Pompeii 174
Buondelmonti (15th-century traveller) 152
Buret', Russia 129
burials
  Americas 210-11, 219, 227, 228, 230-3
  animals in royal 73, 80, 95, 103, 200
  Australasian 120
  Bactrian princely, Tillya Tepe 98-9
  of bells, Japan 100
  Bulgarian Copper Age 130-3
  Celts 150, 151, 172
  disarticulated, Thulamela 51
  Egypt 14-17, 20-3, 26-7, 30-5
  Etruscan 166-7
  European Early Bronze Age rich 136-7, 138-9
  European Iron Age rich 150-1, 172
  excarnation 51, 54
  Hittite royal see Alaca Höyük
  human sacrifice in 71, 94, 97, 231
  Korean royal 112-13
  Luristan 72, 75
  Maikop, Russia 60-1
  Mallia, communal 145
  Mapungubwe 46-7
  Mishmar 58
  Mochlos, Early Minoan 134-5
  Mycenae 146-7
  Nigerian elite 40-1
  robbing 9, 68, 72, 73, 76, 93, 113, 145; Egypt 14-15, 16, 20, 26, 32, 34
  Scythian 92-5
  secondary or fractional 54, 55
  ship, Anglo-Saxon 200-1
  Tashtyk Culture 108-9
  Thulamela, South Africa 50-1
  Ur 68-71
  Wessex Culture 138-9
  Zhongshan 102-5
burial suit, jade; Zhongshan 103, 104-5
braziers, ritual
Bush Barrow, Wilts 138-9, 242-3
Byres, James 188

Calvert, Frank 64
camel, jar in shape of 77
cameo
  medieval Sicilian, in Poland 202, 203
  Roman glass 188-9
Campello Esclápez, Manuel 160
Cancong, Chinese mythical ruler 87
Canning, Sir Stratford 155
canoes, Florida wetlands 212-13
canopic jars and boxes 14, 33, 34
canopy frames
  Egypt 14, 15
  Maikop 60
cape, golden; Mold, North Wales 139
Carnarvon, 5th Earl of 32, 33
carnelian jewellery
  Maikop 60
  Minoan 135, 142, 144
  Nigeria 41
  Tod Treasure 24
  Troy 67
  Ur 70, 71
  Uruk 57
Carpathian Basin; hoards 140-1, 242-3
Carter, Howard 32-3, 32
Carthage, North Africa 166
Casas Grandes, New Mexico 219

casket, Esquiline silver 194-5, 195
Caso, Alfonso 210
Caucasus mountains 93
cauldrons, bronze
  Anglo-Saxon, Sutton Hoo 200
  Celtic 151
  Dowris Phase, Ireland 148, 148
Celts 242-3
  hillforts 150, 151
  rich burials 150-1, 172, 242-3
  stone statue of 'prince' 158, 242-3
  torcs 159, 242-3
cenotaphs, Bulgarian Copper Age 130, 132
cenote of Chichén Itzá 216-17, 244
Cerveteri, Etruria 166-7
Chachapoyas of Peru 232-3, 245
Chaco Culture 219
chairs, Egyptian 14, 15, 25
chalcedony jewellery 135, 202, 203
chalcolithic period 58-9
Champollion, Jean-François 36, 36
Chang'an, China 106
Changsha, China 106
Charioteer sculpture, Delphi 155, 156
charred objects, Tashtyk Culture 109
Chedworth Roman villa, Glos 180
Cheops (Khufu), king of Egypt 14, 15
Chephren (Khaefre), king of Egypt 20, 20
Chesterholm see Vindolanda
Chichén Itzá, sacred cenote of 216-17, 244
chimes, Chinese stone 96-7
Chimu people 232
China
  glass 112
  Han empire 106
  influence on Japan 115
  and Korea 112, 113
  Liang Dynasty 113
  lost wax technique 97
  musical instruments 96-7
  porcelain 51
  Sanxingdui sacrificial deposits 84-7
  Tang dynasty 106, 112
  trade 51, 106, 112
  Warring States period 96-7, 102-5
  writing 106
  Zhongshan 102-5, 240-1
chi-rho monogram in Britain 180, 180-1, 190, 190-1, 193, 196
Chiusi, Etruria; sarcophagus 166
Cholula 209
Christianity in Britain 180, 180-1, 190, 190-1, 193, 196, 201
Chrysolakkos, 'Pit of Gold'; communal tomb, Mallia, Crete 145
church plate; Water Newton hoard 190
Cigarrelejo, El, Murcia 160
Cihuacoatl (Aztec goddess) 210
Cirencester, Glos 179, 180
Clandon, Dorset 137, 139
Clarke, E.D. 154
Classical sculpture 152-7, 242-3
Claudia Severa, letter from 184, 185
clay objects
  Jomon jewellery 90
  Venus figurines 129
  see also masks; pottery
cloisonné technique 82, 83, 89, 201

Clonfinlough crannog, Ireland 148
clothing
  Anglo-Saxon, Sutton Hoo 200, 201
  Japanese 115
  Korean royal tombs 113
  Lady of Elche as evidence on 160
  preservation, Ozette 221
  see also textiles
Clovis Culture 206-7
clubs, wooden; Ozette, USA 220-3, 222-3
Cockerell, C.R. 154
coffin, golden, of Tutankhamen 32
Cogidubnus, king of the Atrebates 180
coin hoards
  medieval 202, 203
  Roman 159, 186, 186, 187, 196-7
Coke, Thomas, 1st Earl of Leicester 154
collar, gold; Möne, Sweden 198
Colombia 234-7, 244-5
combs
  bone, Anglo-Saxon, Sutton Hoo 201
  ivory, Megiddo, Israel 88
  wooden, Maori, Kauri Point Swamp 122-3
conservation 139, 183
  see also preservation
Cooma, Australia 120, 120
Copper Age see Mishmar; Varna
copper alloys 41, 59, 81
  see also bronze; copper-bronze
copper objects
  Alaca Höyük 81
  Egypt 18
  Maikop 60
  Mishmar 58
  Moche 230
  Mycenae 146
  Nigeria 41
  Thulamela 51
  Ur 68, 71
  Varna 130, 132
copper-bronze boxes, Tod Treasure 24, 25, 25
coprolites 9
cosmetic items
  Bactria 77
  Egypt 14, 26
  Ireland 149
  Megiddo 88
  South Africa 45
  Tillya Tepe 99
  Ur 71
couch, Eberdingen-Hochdorf wheeled 151
cowrie shells 47
crania, plastered, 'Ain Ghazal 54, 55
crannogs 148, 149
cremation
  Anglo-Saxon 200
  Tashtyk Culture 108-9
Crete
  Early Minoan (pre-palatial) phase 134-5
  Minoan civilization 24, 25;
    contacts abroad 33, 134, 144, 146
crotals, bronze; Dowris hoard 148
crowns, gold and silver
  Alaca Höyük 80
  Korea 112, 113, 113
  medieval, Šroda Śląska 202, 203
  Mishmar 58, 59
  see also diadems
cult objects, Tell Asmar 62-3
cuneiform script 28, 71

Cunnington, William 138
Cuo, king of Zhongshan 102-3
cups
  amber 137
  gold: Aegina 144; Carpathian Basin 140; Mycenae 146
  shale 137
  silver: 'jelly-mould', Tod Treasure 24, 25; Mochlos, Crete 134; Roman 169, 169, 170, 171, 172; Scythian 94
Cushing, Frank Hamilton 213
Cyclades 135
Cyprus 28

Dabeiba, Colombia 236
daggers
  Alaca Höyük 81
  Carpathian Basin hoards 140
  Wessex Culture 138
Dalboki, Bulgaria 162
Damasus, Pope 194
Darling River area, Australia 120
Daugherty, Richard 221
Dead Sea Scrolls 110-11, 240-1
Deir el-Medina, Egypt 26-7
Delos, Greece 152
Delphi, Greece 155, 156, 156
Demeter, Greek goddess 154
Denmark
  amber hoards 136
  Hoby elite burials 172
Dennis, George 166
diadems
  gold: Aegina 144; Maikop 60;
    Mochlos 134-5, 135;
    Mycenae 146; Tillya Tepe, Afghanistan 99; Troy 64, 66, 67
  jade, Maya 214
  see also crowns
Dickens, Charles 152, 154
Didykaimos (name on cup) 164
diet 90, 221
dinner services 24, 168-9
Dio Cassius 159
diplomacy 132, 201
discs
  gold, Chichén Itzá 217
  gold-covered soapstone, Bactria 77
  steatite, Egypt 16, 17
dishes, large silver
  Mildenhall 172, 192-3
  Sutton Hoo 201
Djerty see Tod
DNA 213
dolls, Tashtyk funerary 108-9
Dolní Věstonice, Moravia 129
Domitius Polygnos, M. (silversmith) 174
Dorchester mosaicists 180
dotaku (Japanese bronze bells) 100-1
Dowris, Ireland 148, 148, 242-3
Dowris Phase, Ireland 148-9, 242-3
drinking sets
  Mycenaean plate 146
  Roman silver 168-9
  Sutton Hoo Anglo-Saxon 201
drum, Leigudun, China 97
duck, Mycenaean rock crystal vase in shape of 146
Dunboyne, Co Meath, Ireland 149
Durobrivae (Water Newton) 190-1
Duvanli, Bulgaria 162

earplugs, Maya jade 214
earrings, gold
  Aegina 142, 144, 145
  Tell el-Ajjul 82-3, 82, 83
  Troy 65

earth goddess, Mexico 210-11
Eberdingen-Hochdorf, Germany 151
eggcups, Roman silver 174
Egypt 14-37, 238-9
  overseas contacts 24, 33, 82, 89, 144, 166
Elamite art 73
Elche, Spain; Lady of 160-1, 242-3
El Dorado, gold of 234-7, 245
electrum objects
  Mycenaean masks 146
  Sumerian helmet 71
elephant tusks, Sanxingdui 85
Eleusis, Greece 154
Elgin Marbles 154
Elizavetinskaya Scythian tomb 92
emblemata, Roman 174, 176, 177
emeralds
  Colombia 234, 235, 236
  Šroda Śląska 202, 203
Emery, Walter 16
enamelled Roman ladle 186-7, 186
En Gedi, Israel 59
Essenes 110
Etruscans 150, 151, 166-7, 242-3
Europe 124-203, 242-3
  Early Bronze Age rich burials 136-7, 138-9
  Ice Age 126-7, 128-9, 242-3
  Iron Age elite burials 150-1, 172
  see also individual sites and countries
Evans, Sir Arthur 134, 142
ewer, Syrian glass 112-13
excarnation 51, 54
exchange 24, 25, 120, 132, 139, 164, 174
Extremadura 160
Eye, Suffolk 196

Fagg, Angela 40
Fagg, Bernard 38, 40
faience objects 135, 166
Farway Broad Down barrow 137
feast, mortuary; Alaca Höyük 80
feathered headdresses, Moche 231
fibre objects; Ozette 221
fibulae
  bronze 150, 186, 186, 187
  gold circular, medieval 202, 203
Fifehead Neville Roman villa, Dorset 181
figures and figurines
  Benin ivory 42, 42
  Chachapoya wooden 232
  Colombian votive 234, 235
  Mapungubwe gold-covered 46, 47
  Olmec jade 209
  Roman silver 197, 197
  Trojan anthropomorphic 67
  Sumerian wooden 69, 71
  Zhongshan jade 103
filigree technique 67, 142, 160
Fishbourne Roman villa, Sussex 18-9, 180
Flame-style pottery, Japan 90
flint objects
  arrowheads, Maikop 60
  tools: Egypt 16; Varna 130
Florida, USA 212-13, 244
flutes, Chachapoya 232
foils, ornamented Scandinavian gold 198, 199
Folsom projectile points 207

Frampton Roman villa, Dorset 181
Fukui Cave, Japan 90
furniture
  Cretan work in Mycenae 146
  Egyptian funerary 14, 14, 15, 33
  ivory plaques for, Megiddo 88, 89
  Japan 115
  Korean funerary 113

Gagarino, Don region 129
Galgenberg, Dancing Venus of 127, 127
gaming items
  Egypt 16, 17
  Japan 115
  Megiddo 88
  Ur 69, 71
Gandhara sculpture 99
Gardner, Captain Guy 47
Gaul, Dying (sculpture) 159
Gaymanova, Russia 93
Gaza, ancient 82-3
Geissenklösterle Cave, Germany 126
genetic testing 210, 213
gift exchange 24, 164, 199, 201
Giza, Egypt 14-15
glass and glass objects
  African imports 41, 48, 51
  Anglo-Saxon millefiori 201
  cloisonné work, Megiddo 89
  Egyptian 26
  in Japan 115
  Korean imports 112-13
  Persia cut 115
  Roman cameo 188-9
Glauberg, Germany; Celtic statue 158
Goddess, Great 164
Gold Crown Tomb, Korea 112
gold objects
  Aegina 142-5
  African trade 46, 47, 48
  Alaca Höyük 80-1
  Carpathian Basin 140-1
  Chichén Itzá 216, 217
  Eberdingen-Hochdorf rich burial 151
  Egyptian 14, 15, 24-5, 32, 33
  El Dorado 234-7
  Etruscan 167
  Hoxne 196-7
  Ireland, Dowris Phase 148-9
  Khosh Tapa 76
  Korean royal tombs 112, 112, 113
  Leigudun 97
  Maikop, Russia 60
  Mapungubwe, South Africa 46-7
  Mixtec 210, 211
  Moche 230
  Möne, Sweden 198
  Mochlos, Crete 134-5
  Mycenae 122-3, 146-7
  Panagyurishté, Bulgaria 162
  Paracas Culture 228
  Pompeii 173, 174
  Šroda Śląska 202-3
  Sanxingdui 84
  Scandinavian hoards 198-9
  Scythian 92-4
  Snettisham 159
  Sutton Hoo 201
  Tell el-Ajjul 82-3
  Thulamela 50-1
  Tillya Tepe 98-9
  Tod Treasure 24-25
  Troy 64-7
  Ur 69, 70, 71
  Varna 130-3
  Vix burial 150

Wessex Culture 138-9
  see also individual types of object
gongs, iron; Thulamela 51
Gournia, Crete 24
Graan, E.S.J. van 47
Grand Tour 154, 179
Graniceri, Romania 140
granulation techniques 67, 82, 83
Greece
  pottery 150, 150, 162, 166
  sculpture 152-7
  silver vessels 162
  writing 36, 37
greenstone objects 120-1
greywacke sculpture 21, 21
Guatavita, Lake, Colombia 234, 235, 236
gypsum objects
  sculptures, Tell Asmar 63
  vase, Uruk 56-7

Hadjúsámson hoard, Hungary 140
Hadrian, Roman emperor
  mausoleum of 152
  Villa at Tivoli 154
Hadrian's Wall, Britain 182-5
Halikarnassos, mausoleum of 155
Hamilton, Gavin 154
Hamilton, Sir William 188
hammer-axes
  copper, Varna 132
  stone, Troy 67
harpoons, iron; Thulamela 51
Hathor (Egyptian goddess) 21, 21, 83, 83
heads
  bronze sculptures, Sanxingdui 84, 85, 85, 87
  ceramic sculptures, Lydenburg 44-5
  plastered crania, 'Ain Ghazal 54, 55
  vases shaped as, Panagyurishté 162
Heavenly Horse, Tomb of, Kyongju 112
Heian period, Japan 114-15
Heijo palace archive, Nara, Japan 106, 107
hei tiki and hei matau pendants 121
Helgö, Sweden; gold foils 198
Hellenistic art 99
helmets
  Anglo-Saxon, Sutton Hoo 200, 201
  Sumerian, Ur 71
Hemaka, tomb of, Saqqara, Egypt 16-17, 238-9
Herculaneum, Italy 170
Hercules 152, 164, 169, 197
Herodian (Greek historian) 183
Hetepheres Treasure, Egypt 14, 15, 238-9
Heuneburg, Germany 151
Hierakonpolis, Egypt; Main Deposit 18-19, 238-9
hieroglyphs 36, 37, 89
Higashi-kushiro, Japan 116
Higgins, Reynold 142
Hildesheim, Germany; silver hoard 168-9, 242-3
hillforts, Celtic 150, 151
Hinton St Mary, Dorset; Roman mosaic 180-1, 180-1
Hisarlik, Turkey 64
Hittites 28, 89
  see also Alaca Höyük
hoards
  amber, European 136
  metals for recycling 83
  see also Aegina; Bad Pyrmont; Boscoreale; Carpathian Basin;

Dowris Phase; Hoxne;
Mishmar; Pompeii;
Scandinavia; Snettisham; Tod
Treasure; Water Newton
Hoare, Sir William Colt 138
Hoby, Denmark; Roman silver
cups 172
Hodder, Cecil 159
Hohlenstein-Stadel, Germany
127
Hokkaido, Japan 116-17
Holkham Hall, Norfolk 154
Hopi Indians 219
horns
Anglo-Saxon drinking 200,
200
Celtic drinking 151
Irish bronze musical 148, 148
horse gear
Esquiline treasure 195
Korean royal tombs 112
Luristan bronzes 72, 74, 75
Vix burial 150
horses
in elite burials 95, 103, 200
Vogelherd mammoth ivory
sculpture 126, 127
Horus (Egyptian god) 18, 20, 83
Hospitaller Knights of St John
155
Hove, Sussex; Bronze Age burial
137
Howitt, A.W. 121
Hoxne, Suffolk; Roman hoard
196-7, 242-3
Huaca Rajada, Sipán, Peru 230
Hui Yang, Prince of Chu 96
Humberside mosaicists 180
Hungary; Bronze Age hoards
140
hunting
Clovis Culture 206-7
Thulamela 51
huts, Mapungubwe 47
Hwangnam-ni, Tomb of,
Kyongju 112-13
Hyksos rulers of Egypt 83

I Ching (Book of Changes) 106
Ice Age 126-9, 242-3
Iceni 159
Idogava, Japan 116
Ife, Nigeria; sculptures 39, 40,
41, 41-2
Igbo-Ukwu, Nigeria; elite burial
40-1
ikor (offerings in Ainu bear
ceremony) 116-17, 240-1
Inanna (Sumerian goddess) 56,
57
Inayoshi, Japan; pottery jar 100
incense
copal, Chichén Itzá 217
Mixtec brazier 210
India 41, 51, 99, 115
Indus Valley civilization 79
ink, Roman 183
Inka empire 226-7
cultures preceding 227, 232-3
inlaid items
Aegina 142, 144
Mycenaean weapons 146
Roman niello, Hildesheim 169
Roman wooden boxes, Hoxne
196
Ur 68, 71, 142
Uruk stone jars 57
Zhongshan 103, 102-3
Inskeep, R.R. 44
iomante (Ainu bear ceremony)
116-17
Iran 76, 79, 112
Iraq; Uruk Sammelfund 56-7,
240-1
Ireland 148-9, 242-3
iron and iron objects
Hittite empire 81

Ireland 149
Korea 112
Luristan 75
meteoric, Alaca Höyük 81
sub-Saharan Africa 40, 44,
46-7, 48, 51
Troy 67
Isaiah, Book of 110
Isis tomb, Vulci 166
Israel see Megiddo
Iulius Verecundus (Roman
military commander) 185
ivory and ivory objects
Africa 42, 42, 46, 47, 48, 51
Bactria, Tillya Tepe 99
China 85
Near and Middle East 58, 59,
88-9

jade objects, ritual and funerary
Leigudun 96-7
Maya 214-15, 216
Olmec 208-9, 109
Sanxingdui 84, 85
Zhongshan 103, 104-5
jaguars, Olmec 208, 209
Japan 240-1
Ainu Culture 116-17
bronze bells 100-1
Jomon period 90-1, 116
Nara Shosoin 114-15
writing 106, 107
Jemaa, Nigeria 38
Jemdet Nasr 57
Jericho 55
jet objects 61, 136-7, 242-3
jewellery
Aegina 142-5
Alaca Höyük 81
Australia 120, 129
Carpathian Basin 140, 141
Egypt 14, 24, 32, 33, 33
Jomon Japan 90
Koszider type hoards 140
Luristan 75
Maikop 60
Mapungubwe 47
Moche 230, 231
Mochlos 134-5
Mycenae 146
Paracas Culture 228
Roman 174, 196
Środa Śląska 202-3
Scythian 94
Silla royal tombs 112
Tell el-Ajjul 82
Thulamela 51, 51
Troy 64, 65, 66, 67
Ur 68, 71
Varna 130, 131, 132, 133
Vix 150
Zhongshan 103
see also individual types
Joffroy, René 150
Jomon period, Japan 90-1, 116,
240-1
jugs, precious metal
head-shaped: Esquiline treasure
194; Panagyurishté 162
Rogozen 164
Julius II, Pope 152

K2 settlement site, South Africa
46-7
Kamo Iwakura, Japan; bells 100
kantharoi, Roman silver 171,
172, 174
Karakhoja, China 106
Kauri Point Swamp, New
Zealand 122-3, 241
Kaya, Korea 112
Ken Hill, Snettisham, Norfolk
159
Keramopoullos, A. 142
Kerseblreptes (Thracian king) 164
Key Marco, Florida 213
Kha, tomb of, Egypt 26-7, 238-9

Khaefre (Chephren), king of
Egypt 20, 20
Khamerernebty II, queen of
Egypt 21, 22-3
Khosh Tapa, Afghanistan; hoard
76
Khufu (Cheops), king of Egypt
14, 15
Kimmeridge shale 137
Kinai region of Japan 100
Kings, Valley of the, Egypt 30-3
knives
Anglo-Saxon 201
Chinese 115
Knowes of Trotty, Orkney 137
Koguryo, Korea 112, 113
Komyo, Empress of Japan 114
Korea
bronze bells 100
royal tombs 112-13, 240-1
Kosay, Hamit 80
Kostenki, Don region 129
Kosziderpadlás and Koszider
type hoards 140
Kotys (Thracian king) 164
kouros found off Piraeus 155
kraters
bronze, Vix 150-1, 151
silver, Hildesheim 169
Kuban region, Russia 60-1, 93
Kukulkan (Maya deity) 216
kurgans 60-1
Kuril Islands 116
Kushan dynasty 99
Kyongju, Korea; royal tombs
112-13

La Alcudia (Elche), Spain 160-1
La Venta, Mexico 208-9
lacquer objects 97, 103, 116-17
ladles, Roman
enamelled bronze, Bad
Pyrmont 186-7, 186
silver Hildesheim 169; Hoxne
197
Laguna de los Condores, Peru
232-3, 245
Laguna de Siecha, Colombia 236
lampstands
Roman silver, Hildesheim 168
Zhongshan bronze 103
Landa, Diego de 216
landscapes, symbolic 209
languages, decipherment 36-7
Lao Zi 106
Laocoön (sculpture) 152, 154
lapis lazuli, worked
Aegina 142, 144
Tod Treasure 24, 25
Ur 68, 69, 70, 71, 142
Uruk Sammelfund 57
Larthia Seianti, tomb of, Chiusi
166
Lassois, Mont, France 150
lathe turned shale objects 137
lazurite hammer-axe, Troy 67
lead isotope analysis 24-5
leather objects
Mishmar 58
Ozette 221
Paracas Culture 228
Saqqara, Egypt 30
Sutton Hoo 201
Vindolanda 182
Leigudun, China; tomb of
Marquis Yi, musical
instruments 96-7
Lelang, Korea; Chinese
commandery 112
lenses, rock crystal, from Troy
67
Leochares (Greek sculptor) 155
Leopards, tomb of the,
Tarquinia 166
letters from Vindolanda 106,

182-5
Li Cang, marquis of Da 106
Liang Dynasty of China 113
Libya 34
limestone sculptures, Tell Asmar
63
linen cloth, Mishmar 58
Lingshan, China; royal burials
103, 104-5
Lingshuo, China 102
lions
silver, Tod Treasure 24
vase in shape of head of,
Mycenae 146
Liu Sheng, Prince Jing of
Zhongshan 103, 104-5
locks, Roman silver; Hoxne 196
loess soil, Venus figurines of
fired 129
looms, wooden 58, 221
looting
Europeans in South America
228, 235-6
theft from museum 214-15
lost wax method 41, 59, 81, 97
Louvre museum, Paris 24, 160,
172
Low Ham Roman villa,
Somerset 180
lozenges, Wessex Culture gold
138, 138, 139
Ludwig I, king of Bavaria 154
Lullingstone Roman villa, Kent
179-80
Lundeborg, Fryn, Denmark 199
Luristan bronzes 72-5, 240-1
lutes, Nara Shosoin 115
Lydenburg, South Africa;
ceramic heads 44-5, 238-9
lyres
Sutton Hoo 201
Ur 68, 71

maceheads
Alaca Höyük 67, 81
Egypt 18-19, 67
Mishmar 59, 59
Troy 67
Varna 132
Maikop, Russia; royal burials
60-1, 240-1
Makah tribe 220-3
Mal'ta, Siberia 129, 129
Mallia, Crete; Chrysolakkos
communal tomb 145
mamakuna (Inka weavers) 226
mammoth ivory sculptures 126,
126-7, 128, 129, 129
Manchuria 116, 117
Manuoris 120-1
greenstone pendants 121
wooden combs 122-3
maps, Far Eastern 106, 115
Mapungubwe, South Africa;
gold grave goods 46-7, 238-9
Marcellus (governor of Britain)
185
Marseilles (Massilia), France
150
Maskhuta, Tell el-, Egypt 162
masks
Bulgarian gold-ornamented
clay 130, 132
Chinese bronze 85, 86-7, 87
Egyptian gold funerary 32, 33,
34, 35
Japanese 115
Maya funerary, of Pacal 214-
15
Moche gold and silver 230
Mycenaean gold and electrum
funerary 122-3, 146
Tashtyk funerary 108-9
mastabas 16
Mauch, Carl 48
mausolea
of Hadrian 152

at Halikarnassos 155
Mawaki, Japan 116
Mawangdui, China 106
Maya civilization 214-16
cenote of Chichén Itzá 216-17
mask of Pacal 214-15
Megiddo, Israel; ivories 88-9,
240-1
Melos, statue of Venus from
152, 154-5
Memphis, Egypt 16, 30
Menkaure, king of Egypt 20-3,
238-9
Meshoko, Russia 61
Meskalamdug, helmet of 71
Mesoamerican culture,
generalized 208
Mesopotamia
and Bactria 79, 99
Early Dynastic III phase 61
Luristan bronzes influenced by
73
Minoan trade with 144
see also Tell Asmar; Ur; Uruk
metal-detectorists 8, 159
metallurgy
alloys 59, 60, 81
annealing 148
casting 82, 100, 103, 148,
236; lost wax technique 41,
59, 81; moulds 59, 81, 97,
148
China 97, 103
control of high temperatures
130, 132
Hittites 81
Ireland 148
Japan 100
Moche 231
Muisca 236
Near East 59
Nigeria 41
reuse of metals 9, 24, 25, 67,
83, 155, 235
Tell el-Ajjul 82
Troy 67
see also granulation; repoussé
Mexico 210-11, 214-15, 244
Mildenhall, Suffolk 172, 192-3,
242-3
Miller, Sidney 51
Mimbres culture 218-19
mining, South American gold
236
Minoan civilization 24, 25
contacts abroad 33, 134, 144,
146
prepalatial phase 134-5
Minusinsk Basin, Siberia 108
mirrors
Bactrian metal 76, 79
Japanese 115
Korean bronze 113
Mesoamerican obsidian 214
Roman silver 172, 174, 175
Mishmar Treasure, Israel 58-9,
240-1
Mitanni 28
Mixtec people 210-11, 244
Moche people 230-1
Mochlos, Crete 134-5, 242-3
models, gold
Colombian rafts 236, 237
Irish ship 149, 149
Mogollon tradition 218
Mohammed Dib 110
mokkan (writing tablets) 106,
107
Mold, North Wales; gold cape
139
Möne, Sweden; gold collar 198
monoliths, Olmec basalt 208
Montefortino, Italy; Celtic burial
172
Montet, Pierre 34
Monthu (Egyptian god) 24
Mooghaun, Co Clare, Ireland

148-9
Morse, Edward S. 90
mosaics
    Olmec jade, La Venta 209
    Roman Britain 178-81, 242-3
Moscow, Pushkin Museum 67
mother-of-pearl
    inlay, Ur 71
    necklace, Pompeii 173
mudslides, items preserved
    under 221
Muisca people 234-7
mummies
    Chachapoyas, Peru 232-3
    Egypt 32, 33, 34
    Paracas Culture 228
    Tashtyk Culture 108
Munyong, king of Paekche 113
museums
    rise of European 154-5
    theft from 214-15
musical instruments
    China 96-7
    Ireland 148, 148
    Japan 100-1, 115
    Maoris 122
    Ur 68, 71
Mutnodjmet, queen of Egypt 34
Mycenae, Greece 122-3, 137,
    146-7, 242-3
Mycenaean civilization 142-5
    see also Mycenae
Mycerinus, king of Egypt see
    Menkaure

nacre inlay, Ur 71
Nahal Mishmar Cave, Israel
    58-9, 240-1
Nalchik, Russia 61
names, ownership, on vessels
    164
Namibia; painted slabs, Apollo
    11 cave 12-13
Napoleon I, emperor of France
    36
Nara, Japan
    Heijo palace archive 106, 107
    Shosoin of Todaiji temple 114-
    15
Narmer, king of Egypt 19
Natsushima, Japan; shell mound
    90
Navan Fort, Ireland 148
necklace
    Cretan gold 135
    Roman gold and mother-of-
    pearl 173
    Scottish jet 137, 137
    Wessex Culture amber 136,
    136
Nefertiti, queen of Egypt 28
Nekhbet (Egyptian goddess) 33
Nekhen, Egypt, see
    Hierakonpolis
nephrite objects, Maori 120-1
Nero, Roman emperor 156
Nestor's cup, Mycenae 146
nets, fishing; Ozette 221
New Guinea 120
New Mexico 218-19
New Zealand 120-1, 122-3, 241
Newby Hall, Yorkshire 154
Newton, Charles 155
Ngilipitji quarry, Australia 121
niello
    Mycenaean 146
    Roman 169, 196
Nienaber, Coen 50
Nigerian sculpture 38-43, 238-9
Nîmes, France 152
Nok Culture, Nigeria 38, 38-9,
    40, 42
Normanton Down, Wilts 138-9
Novosvobodnaya, Russia 61

obsidian
    Maori 122

Mesoamerican 214
ochre, red; in burials 60
Odrysian royal family of Thrace
    164
Okhotsk Culture 116
Olmec people 208-9, 244
Olympia, Greece 156
Olympic peninsula, USA 220-3
Oman 71
Omori, Japan; shell mounds 90
Onatas of Aegina (Greek
    sculptor) 156
onyx objects, Maya 216
organic materials
    East Asian writing materials
    106
    Mishmar 58
    Kauri Point Swamp, New
    Zealand 122
    Vindolanda 182
Orkney Islands 137
Orpheus mosaics 180
Osorkon I and II, king of Egypt
    34
Ostia, Italy 154
ostrich eggs
    asphalt-inlaid, Ur 71
    beads, Thulamela 51
    carved, Etruscan 166
Ostrovul Mare hoard, Romania
    140
Otford Roman villa, Kent 180
Ovcharovo, Bulgaria 132
Oxus river 98
Ozette, USA 220-3, 244

Pacal, king of Palenque: funerary
    mask 214-15, 244
Pacific region 120-1
Paekche, Korea 112, 113
painting
    Etruscan tombs 166
    sculptures 87, 160
    Stone Age slabs, Apollo 11
    cave, Namibia 12-13
Pakistan 76, 79
Palenque, Mexico 214-15
Palestine 82
    see also Mishmar; Tell el-Ajjul
Palestrina, Etruria; Bernardini
    tomb 166
palettes, Egyptian slate 19, 19
Panagyurishté, Bulgaria 162-3,
    164, 242-3
Panama 236
papyri 16, 184
Paracas Culture 228, 245
Paris, Pierre 160
Parthenon, Athens 154, 156
Pasiteles (Roman craftsman) 174
Paterno, Sicily 172
Patras, Greece 156
Pausanias (traveller) 156
pearls
    Środa Śląska jewellery 202,
    203
    Tillya Tepe hoard 99
pectorals, gold
    Minoan, Aegina 144-5
    Mixtec, Monte Albán 210, 211
pen case, ivory; Megiddo 89
pendants
    Astarte, Tell el-Ajjul 83, 83
    bronze 'ivy-leaf', Koszider type
    hoards 140
    gold, Aegina 143, 144, 144-5
    greenstone, Maori 120-1, 121
pens, Roman 'fountain' 183
'pepper pots', Roman silver;
    Hoxne 197
Percher Trevino, Carlos 215
Pergamon, Asia Minor 152, 153,
    154
Persia 99, 115
Peru 228-33
Peter I the Great, Tsar of Russia
    93

Petrie, Sir William Matthews
    Flinders 28, 82
Pfalzfeld, Rhineland, Germany
    158
Pheidias; statue of Athena
    Parthenos 156, 162
phialai, silver
    Boscoreale, silver 176, 177
    Panagyurishté, gold 162, 164
    Rogozen, silver 164, 165
Philip II of Macedon 93
Phoenicians 89, 142, 166
Piggott, Stuart 138-9
pins
    Bactrian 79
    Cretan gold 135
    Irish gold-clad 149
    Luristan bronze 75
    Mycenaean rock-crystal headed
    146
    toggle, Tell el-Ajjul 82, 83
Piraeus, Greece 155
Pi-Ramesses, Egypt 34
pitcher, gold, Alaca Höyük 81
plaques
    Megiddo, ivory 88, 89
    Tillya Tepe, precious metals 98,
    99
    Varna, gold 130
    Water Newton, silver 190, 190
plaster figures and plastered
    crania, 'Ain Ghazal 54-5
platters, Roman silver;
    Mildenhall 192-3, 193
Pliny the Elder 152, 155, 174
points, North American
    projectile 206-7
Poland see Środa Śląska
Polyanitsa, Bulgaria 132
Polybius 159
Polyzalos, tyrant of Gela 155
pommel, Trojan iron 67
Pompeii, Italy 170-5, 188, 242-3
porcelain, Ming, at Thulamela
    51
Porticello, Straits of Messina 155
Portland Vase 188-9, 242-3
Portugal 48
possum-skin cloaks 120, 121
potlatch 221
pottery
    Chachapoya 232
    Chinese 51, 103, 113
    and cooking 90
    Greek 150, 150, 162, 166
    Japanese 100, 115; Jomon 90-1
    Lydenburg ceramic heads 44-5
    Maikop Culture 60, 61
    Mimbres Culture 218-19
    Minoan, early 134
    Moche 230, 231
    Mycenaean 142
    Zimbabwean 48, 50
    see also amphorae
Prague 202, 203
prepalatial civilization, Crete
    134-5
preservation of items
    in arid conditions 227, 228
    in mudslides 221
    in wetlands 212, 213, 216, 217
Pretty, Edith 200
Priam's treasure, Troy 64-7
Psusennes, king of Egypt 34
pyramids
    Egyptian 14-15, 20-1
    Moche 231
Pyrenees, French 129
Pyrmont, Bad 186-7, 242-3

Qoco (Turpan, China) 106
quartz jewellery, Tod Treasure
    24
Quetzalcoatl (Maya deity) 216,
    217
quipus (record-keeping devices)
    232, 232

Qumran, Palestine 110

Rachmanli, Thrace 162
radiocarbon dating
    Africa 12, 40, 44
    Jomon pottery, Japan 90
    Venus figurines 129
rafts, model gold 236, 237
rams caught in thickets, Ur 69,
    71
Rathtinaun, Co Sligo, Ireland
    149
rattles, bronze; Dowris, Ireland
    148, 148
records
    South American quipus 232,
    232
    see also writing
recycling
    metals 67, 83, 155, 235
regalia
    Silla royal tombs 112
    Sutton Hoo 200, 201
Regolini-Galassi tomb, Cerveteri
    166
Reisner, George 14, 20, 21
Reliefs, tomb of the, Cerveteri
    166-7
repoussé technique
    European Bronze Age 140, 141
    Mochlos, Crete 135
    Tell el-Ajjul 82, 83
    Muisca 236
    Mycenae 146
    Silla 113
rhinoceros, gold; Mapungubwe
    46, 47
rhyta, Panagyurishté 162, 162
Riace Marina, Italy; bronze
    statues found off 156, 157
rice agriculture 90
Richey-Roberts Clovis cache,
    USA 206-7, 244
rings
    finger-: Roman, Bad Pyrmont
    186, 186; swivel signet, Tell
    el-Ajjul 82; Trolleberg,
    Sweden 198
    lock, Ireland 149
ritual objects
    Hittite 'standards' 80-1, 81
    Japanese bells 100-1
    Jomon pottery 90
    Lydenburg ceramic heads 44,
    44-5
    Maya 217
    Mishmar 59
    Mycenae 146
    Nigeria 41
    Sanxingdui 84-7
    Venus figurines 129
rituals
    El Dorado 234-7
    Megiddo 89
    Moche 230
rock art, African 12-13
rock crystal objects
    jewellery 57, 135, 144, 146
    lenses and maceheads, Troy 67
    vase, Mycenaean duck-shaped
    146
Rockefeller, John D. 88
Rodriguez, Juan 234
Rogozen, Thrace 164-5, 242-3
Roman empire see Bad Pyrmont;
    Boscoreale; Esquiline Treasure;
    Hildesheim; Hoxne;
    Mildenhall; mosaics, Roman;
    Pompeii; Portland Vase;
    Vindolanda; Water Newton
Romania 140
Rome
    Esquiline treasure 194-5
    Greek sculptures in 152, 155
    Museo Pio-Clementino 152
    Palace of Titus 152
    San Martino ai Monti, church

of 194
Rosetta Stone 8, 36-7, 238-9
rubber 216, 217
Russia 240-1
    Scythian art 92-5
    Tashtyk Culture 108-9
    Venus figurines 129
Ruz Lhuillier, Alberto 214
Ryzhanovka, Ukraine 94

Sabinus (Greek silversmith) 172
sacrifice
    American deposits in water
    216-17, 234, 235
    human 71, 94, 97, 201, 231
    heart, Maya 217
    Roman scene 172
Sanxingdui 84-7
St Petersburg, Russia; Hermitage
    Museum 93
Sakhalin 116, 117
Samaria 88, 89
sand-bodies, Sutton Hoo 200
San el-Hagar (Tanis), Egypt 34-5
Sannai Maruyama, Japan 90
Sanxingdui, China; sacrificial
    deposits 84-7, 240-1
Saqqara, Egypt; tomb of
    Hemaka 16-17, 238-9
sarcophagi
    Chachapoya standing 232, 233
    Etruscan 166
Sardina Garela, Ramón 215
Sarianidi, Viktor I. 98
Satokos (Thracian king) 164
Satsumon Culture 116
sauceboat, Trojan gold 67, 67
'saucepans', Roman silver 172,
    174, 194
scabbard hook, Wessex Culture
    gold 138, 139
Scandinavian gold hoards 198-9,
    242-3
scarabs, Egyptian; Tell el-Ajjul
    83
sceptres
    bronze, Luristan 73
    gold: Mapungubwe 46, 47;
    Varna 130, 132, 132
    jade, Sanxingdui 84
    Maya spearthrower, in shape of
    217
Schiaparelli, Ernesto 26
Schliemann, Heinrich 64, 67,
    146
Schliemann, Sophia 64, 64, 67
Schroda, South Africa 46, 47
Scorpion Macehead,
    Hierakonpolis 18-19
screens, Shosoin of Nara 114-
    15, 115
sculpture
    'Ain Ghazal plaster figures
    54-5
    Bactrian seated figures 76, 79,
    79
    Celtic 'prince' from Glauberg
    158
    Classical world 152-7, 160-1
    Egyptian 18, 20-3, 27, 33
    European Ice Age 126-7
    Gandhara 99
    Great Zimbabwe soapstone
    birds 48-9
    Lydenburg heads 44-5
    Nigeria 38-43
    Sanxingdui 84, 85, 87
    Tell Asmar 63-3
Scythians 92-5, 99, 240-1
Seager, Richard 134
seals
    Akkadian, in Egypt 34
    Bactrian 76, 77
    cylinder: Maikop 61; Susa 79;
    Tod Treasure 24; Ur 71; Uruk
    57
    metal stamp 79

sea-otter teeth, Ozette *221*
seeds 221
Sennedjem, tomb of, Deir el
  Medina 26
Sevso treasure 172
shale objects 137
shamanism 13, *13*, 214
Shang state, China 85
Shannon valley, Ireland **148-9**
Shaw, Thurstan 40-1
Shawcross, Wilfred 122
shells
  mounds, Japan 90
  Spondylus artefacts, Varna
    130, 132
  see also ostrich eggs
Shepseskaf, king of Egypt 20
Shibarghan oasis, Bactria 98
shield, Anglo-Saxon 200, 201
ship burials, Anglo-Saxon **200-1**
ships, gold model
  Colombia 236, *237*
  Ireland 149, *149*
shipwrecks 155
shoes
  gilt-bronze, Korea 112
  gold, Tillya Tepe 99
  leather, Sutton Hoo 201
Shomu, emperor of Japan 114
Shona-speaking peoples 46-7,
  48-9
Shoshenq II and III, kings of
  Egypt 34
Shosoin, Nara, Japan **114-15**
shoulder-clasp, Anglo-Saxon
  gold, Sutton Hoo *201*
shrine, Monte Albán, Mexico
  210-11
Siberia **108-9**, 129, *129*, **240-1**
Sicily 166
Silesia 203
silk
  Chinese writing on 106
  Korean crown 113
Silk Road 106, 115
Silla, kingdom of **112-13**, **240-1**
silver objects
  Alaca Höyük 81
  Bactria *78*
  Boscoreale 170, *171*, 172,
    172-3
  Esquiline **194-5**
  Etruria 166
  Extremadura 160
  Hildesheim **168-9**
  Hoxne **196-7**
  Khosh Tapa 76
  Korea 113, *113*
  Maikop 60
  Mildenhall **192-3**
  Moche 230
  Mochlos 134, 135
  Mycenae 146
  Panagyurishté **162-3**
  Pompeii **170-5**
  Rogozen **164-5**
  Scythian **92-4**
  Snettisham *159*
  Sutton Hoo 200, 201
  Tell el-Ajjul 83
  Tod Treasure **24-25**
  Troy *67*
  Ur 68, *70*, 71
  Uruk 57
  Water Newton **190-1**
  weight inscriptions 169, 174
  *see also individual types of
    object*
Sipán, Peru **230-1**, *245*
'skillet', silver, Boscoreale 172,
  174
Skopas (Greek sculptor) 155
skull, Mixtec incense brazier
  made from human 210
skyphos, Roman silver, Pompeii
  172
slate objects, Egyptian

palettes 19, *19*
  sculpture 21, *21*
slave trade, Iron Age 151
Slovakia 140
Smig, Romania 140
Sneferu, king of Egypt 14, *15*
Snettisham, Norfolk; hoard **159**
soapstone objects
  gold-covered disc, Bactria *77*
  jars, Ur 68
  sculptures, Great Zimbabwe
    48-9
  statuette, Bactrian *76*
social organization
  Africa 40, 41, 47, 48, 50
  amber trade affects 137
  Bulgarian Copper Age 132
  Early Minoan 135
  European Early Bronze Age
    elites 136, 137
  Japan 100
  Luristan, and gender 75
  Scandinavia 199
  Silla 112
Sortekoers Mose, Denmark;
  hoard 136
Sorte Muld, Bornholm,
  Denmark 199
Spanish conquest of South
  America 235-6
spearheads
  African iron 51
  Australian stone 121
  Irish bronze 148, *148*
spearthrower, Chichén Itzál 217
specularite 45
Spondylus shell, objects of 130,
  132
spoons, Roman silver 196, *196*,
  197
Środa Śląska, Poland; medieval
  jewellery **202-3**, **242-3**
staffs of office
  Moche 230
  see also sceptres
standards
  Hittite, Alaca Höyük **80-1**, 81
  Luristan bronze 73, *75*
  Mishmar 58, *59*, *59*
  of Ur 71, *71*
Stark, Freya 73
Staromyshastovskaya, Russia 61
Stavropol, Russia 61
steatite objects
  Early Minoan beads 135
  Egyptian discs 16, *17*
steppes 61, **92-5**, **128-9**, **240-1**
Stone Age painted slabs,
  Namibia **12-13**
stone objects
  Australasia 120-1, *121*
  bowls, Uruk 56
  chimes, China **96-7**
  cosmetic jars, Egypt *26*
  tools: Clovis Culture **206-7**;
    Jomon Japan 90
  Venus figurines 129
  vessels: Maikop 60; Uruk *57*
  weapons: Australia 121; Clovis
    Culture **206-7**; Troy 64, 66,
    67
  see also flint; soapstone
Stonehenge, Wilts 139
Strangford Shield 156
straw sieve, Mishmar 58
strings, knotted record-keeping
  see *quipus*
Sulpicia Lepidina, wife of
  Flavius Cerealis *184*, 185
Sumer *see* Ur; Uruk
'sun-discs', Alaca Höyük 81
surveying tool, possible Wessex
  Culture 138, *139*
Susa, Persia 79
Sutton Hoo, Suffolk 200-1, 242-3
swords
  Anglo-Saxon, Sutton Hoo 200

Bronze Age, Carpathian Basin
  140
  Japanese, in Ainu bear
    ceremony 116-17
synchronism, historical 25
Syria 24, 25, 28-9, 89, 112-13

tables
  Japanese sugoroku *115*
  Roman silver folding tripod
    168
tablets, writing
  Amarna clay **28-9**
  Japanese wooden 106, *107*
  Vindolanda wax **182-9**
Tacitus 179, 185, 187
Tang dynasty of China 106, 112
Tanis, Egypt **34-5**, **238-9**
tapu (Maori concept of
  sacrosanctity) 122
Tarquinia, Etruria 166
Taruga, Nigeria 40
Tashtyk, Siberia; funeral masks
  108-9, **240-1**
Tashtyk Culture **108-9**
tattoos 109
teeth, animal
  jewellery, Australia 120, *120*
  Ozette, USA 221
Tell el-Ajjul gold hoards **82-3**,
  240-1
Tell Asmar cult objects **62-3**,
  240-1
Tello, Julio C. 228
Tenochtitlán, Mexico 209
Teotihuacán, Mexico 209
terracotta sculpture
  Etruscan sarcophagus, Chiusi
    166
  Nigeria 38-43
textiles
  Andes **226-7**, *245*
  Chachapoya 232
  Chinese **116-17**
  Eberdingen-Hochdorf burial
    151
  Maya, Chichén Itzá 216, 217
  Mishmar 58
  Mixtec 210
  Paracas **228-9**, *245*
  Sutton Hoo 201
  Vindolanda 182
Thebes, Egypt 30
Thompson, Edward H. 216
Thrace; Rogozen treasure **164-5**,
  242-3
Thucydides 164
Thulamela, South Africa; royal
  burials **50-1**, **238-9**
Tiberius, Roman emperor 172
tiger, Zhongshan inlaid bronze
  102-3, 103
tigress, Roman silver 197, *197*
Tillya Tepe, Afghanistan; hoard
  98-9, **240-1**
Timboholm, Sweden; hoard
  198-9, *199*
Timotheos (Greek sculptor) 155
Titus, Roman emperor 152
Tivoli, Italy; Villa of Hadrian
  154
Tod Treasure **24-5**, **238-9**
toilet items 14, 19, 99
  see also cosmetic items
Tolentino, Treaty of 152
Tolstaya tomb, Russia 93
Toltec people 216
tombs *see* burials
torcs 150, 159, *159*, **242-3**
Townley, Charles 154, *155*
Transylvania 140
tray, Chinese bronze 97
treasury, hoards as tribal 159
trepannation 137
trident, Zhongshan bronze 103
Trolleberg, Sweden; gold ring
  198

Troy 25, **64-7**, **240-1**
trumpets, Irish bronze 148, *148*
Tufalau, Romania; hoard 140
Tula, Mexico 216
tunjos (Muisca votive figures)
  234, *235*, 236
Tureholm, Sweden; hoard 198
Turkey *see* Alaca Höyük; Troy
Turkmenistan 79
Turpan, Xinjiang, China 106
turquoise 60, 210
Tutankhamen, king of Egypt,
  tomb 28, **30-3**, **238-9**
Tuthmose (Egyptian sculptor) 28

Ukraine **92-5**, 129
Unetice Cultures 137
Ungjin 113
Upton Lovell, Wilts 139
Ur **68-71**, 142, **240-1**
Ur-Namma, king of Uruk 56
Uruk Sammelfund, Iraq **56-7**,
  240-1
United States of America **218-
  19**, *244*

Valley of the Kings, Egypt **30-3**
Varna, Bulgaria Copper Age
  cemetery **130-3**, **242-3**
vases
  Early Minoan: pottery 134;
    silver 135
  Mycenaean: metal 142, 146;
    rock crystal 146
  Tod Treasure metal 24-5
  Trojan metal 66, 67
  Uruk gypsum 56-7
Venus, classical statues of *152*,
  152, **154-5**
Venus figurines 127, *128*, 129
Venus of Galgenberg, Dancing
  127, *127*
Veselovskii, N.I. 60
Vestorius Priscus, C. 170
Vesuvius, eruption of 170
Vikings 199
villas, Roman Britain **178-81**,
  242-3
Vindolanda Roman fort,
  Northumberland 106, **182-5**,
  242-3
Virgil 179-80
Vix rich burial, France **150-1**,
  242-3
Vogelherd Cave, Germany;
  animal sculptures 126, *126*,
  127
votive offerings
  Carpathian Basin 140
  Denmark 136
  Egypt **18-19**
  Ireland **148-9**
  Maya **216-17**
  Muisca, Colombia 234, *235*
  Tell Asmar 62-3
  Water Newton 190, *190*
  watery places **148-9**, **186-7**,
    216-17
Vulci, Etruria 166

Warka *see* Uruk
Washington State, USA *see*
  Ozette; Richey-Roberts cache
waterlogged deposits 122, **212-
  13**, **216-17**, 221
Water Newton, Cambs; hoard
  190-1, **242-3**
weapons
  Bactrian 76
  Carpathian Basin 140
  Irish 148
  Luristan 75
  Maikop 60
  Mycenaean 146
  Sutton Hoo 201
  Tillya Tepe 99
  Troy 64, 66, 67

Ur 71
Wessex Culture 138
  see also individual types
Wedgwood, Josiah 166, 188
Wendjebaendjed (Egyptian
  general) 34
Wendt, Erich 12
Wessex Culture burials 136,
  138-9
whale-fin effigy, Ozette 221
White Di (Chinese people) 102,
  103
wig, hair-moss; Vindolanda 182
Willendorf, Venus of *128*, 129
William, Mount, Victoria 121
Wilsford, Wilts 136, *139*
Winckelmann, Johann 188
Windover, Florida 213
wine jars, Saqqara, Egypt 16
wine sets in Celtic tombs 150,
  151
Woodchester Roman villa, Glos
  180
wooden objects
  Chichén Itzá 216, 217
  figures *25*, 69, 71, 232
  Florida **212-13**
  Ozette, USA **220-1**, **222-3**
  preservation 182, 212, 216,
    217, 221
  slivers with writing 183-5, *183*,
    184
  see also bowls; clubs; combs;
    flutes; looms; tablets, writing
woollen textiles 58, 201
Woolley, Sir Leonard 68
writing
  cuneiform script 28, 71
  Dead Sea Scrolls **110-11**
  East Asian scripts **106-7**
  Egypt **28-9**, **36-7**
  Greek 36, *37*
  Mixtec pictographic 210
  Roman 106, **182-5**
  Sumer 28, 71, 56
  women's 185
Wuffa, king of East Angles 201

Yamato 115
Yayoi, Japan; bells **100-1**, **240-1**
Yi, Marquis, tomb of **96-7**
Young, Colonel Dent 38
Yucatán, Mexico 216-17
Yugoslavia, former 140, *141*

Zapotec people 210
Zeus, statue from Cape
  Artemision 155
Zhongshan, China **102-5**, **240-1**
ziggurats 56
Zimbabwe, Great 46, 47, **48-9**,
  50, **238-9**
Zvornik, former Yugoslavia *141*

Picture credits

p. 1 Ligabue Collection, Venice
p. 2 Sergio Ripoll
p. 5 Muzeum Narodwe, Wroclaw (Photo: Edmund Witecki)
p. 7 The Bridgeman Art Library/ Cecil Higgins Art Gallery, Bedford
p. 11 Werner Forman Archive/ courtesy Entwistle Gallery, London
pp. 12, 13 National Museum of Namibia
pp. 14, 15 Werner Forman Archive/ Egyptian Museum, Cairo
p. 17 e.t. archive
p. 18 e.t. archive
p. 19 The Bridgeman Art Library/ Ashmolean Museum, Oxford
pp. 20, 21 Werner Forman Archive/ Egyptian Museum, Cairo
pp. 22-23 Harvard-Museum Expedition, Museum of Fine Arts, Boston (11.1738 Pair statue of Mycerinus and Queen Kha-merer-nebty II Egypt, Dynasty IV, Giza, Valley Temple of Mycerinus Greywacke H: 54 1/2 in. (1.39 cm) Base 57 x 54 cm)
p. 25 © Photo RMN - Chuzeville
p. 26 AKG London/ Erich Lessing
p. 27 Museo delle Anitchità Egizie, Turin
p. 28 © Photo RMN - Jean Schormans
p. 29 Ancient Art & Architecture Collection
pp. 30-31 Werner Forman Archive/ Egyptian Museum, Cairo
p. 32 (top) Mary Evans Picture Library
pp. 32 (bottom), 33 Ancient Art & Architecture Collection
p. 34 e.t. archive
p. 35 Werner Forman Archive/ Egyptian Museum, Cairo
pp. 36, 37 AKG London
p. 38 Werner Forman Archive/ W. Musterberger Collection
p. 39 Werner Forman Archive/ Museum fur Volkerkunde, Berlin
p. 40 AKG London
pp. 41, 42 (top) Werner Forman Archive/ British Museum, London
p. 42 (bottom) AKG London
p. 43 Werner Forman Archive
pp. 44, 45 © South Africa Museum
pp. 46, 47 University of Pretoria
p. 48 Robert Aberman
p. 49 CORBIS/ Robert Holmes
pp. 50 (top), 51 (both) Marius Loots
p. 50 (bottom) Coen Nienaber
pp. 52-53 Werner Forman Archive/ Hermitage Museum, St. Petersburg
pp. 54, 55 © Alexander Marshack
p. 56 e.t. archive
p. 57 AKG London
pp. 58 Collection of Israel Dept. of Antiquities/ Photo: The Israel Museum
p. 59 The Israel Museum, Jerusalem
pp. 60, 61 The Hermitage Museum, St Petersburg
pp. 62, 62-63 The Oriental Institute of The University of Chicago
p. 64 (both) © Photo Peter Clayton
p. 65 AKG London
p. 66 e.t. archive
p. 67 Novosti (London)
p. 68 The Bridgeman Art Library/ British Museum, London
p. 69 (inset) Ancient Art & Architecture Collection
p. 69 (backdrop) e.t. archive
p. 70 The Bridgeman Art Library/ Ashmolean Museum, Oxford
p. 71 Werner Forman Archive/ British Museum, London
p. 72 The Bridgeman Art Library/ The Louvre, Paris
p. 73 C.M. Dixon
p. 74 The Bridgeman Art Library/ Ashmolean Museum, Oxford
pp. 75, 76 C.M. Dixon
p. 77 (inset) Ligabue Collection, Venice
pp. 77 (backdrop), 78 Galerie Nefer AG
p. 79 C.M. Dixon

pp. 80-81 (backdrop), 80, 81 Hirmer Fotoarchiv
p. 82 Collection of Israel Dept. of Antiquities/ Photo: The Israel Museum
p. 83 Collection of Israel Antiquities Authority (Photo: The Israel Museum/D.Harris)
pp. 84-85 (backdrop), 84, 85, 86-87, Art Exhibitions China
pp. 88, 88-89 The Oriental Institute of The University of Chicago
p. 89 Ancient Art & Architecture Collection
p. 91 Lauros-Giraudon
p. 92 Werner Forman Archive/ Hermitage Museum, St Petersburg
p. 93 e.t. archive
pp. 94-95 Werner Forman Archive/ Hermitage Museum, St Petersburg
p. 95 e.t. archive
pp. 96-97 Art Exhibitions China
pp. 98, 99 The Bridgeman Art Library/ Kabul Museum, Afghanistan
p. 101 CORBIS/Sakamoto Photo Research Laboratory
pp. 102-103, 104-105 CORBIS/Asian Art & Archaeology, Inc.
p. 107 (top left) Art Exhibitions China
p. 107 (right) Nara National Cultural Properties Research Institute
p. 108 Paul G. Bahn
p. 109 V. Stukalov
p. 110 The Israel Museum, Jerusalem
p. 110 (top & bottom) The Israel Museum, Jerusalem
p. 110 (middle) The Israel Museum/ Auraham Hay
p. 111 The Israel Museum, Jerusalem
p. 112 Ancient Art & Architecture Collection
p. 113 Werner Forman Archive/ San Francisco Museum of Asiatic Art
pp. 114-115 The Granger Collection, New York
p. 115 The Bridgeman Art Library/ Shosho-in Treasure House
pp. 116, 117 © British Museum, London
pp. 118-119, 123 Werner Forman Archive/ National Museum of New Zealand, Wellington
p. 120 © NPWS (Photo: Ben Wrigley)
p. 121 (left) The Bridgeman Art Library/ British Museum, London
p. 121 (right) Werner Forman Archive/ British Museum, London
p. 122 The Bridgeman Art Library/ British Library, London
pp. 124-125 C.M. Dixon
p. 126 © Alexander Marshack
p. 127 © Naturhistorisches Museum Wien (Photo: Alice Schumacher)
p. 128 © Alexander Marshack
p. 129 © Alexander Marshack
p. 130 AKG London/ Erich Lessing
p. 131 Ancient Art & Architecture Collection
p. 132 e.t. archive
pp. 133, 134, 135 Ancient Art & Architecture Collection
p. 136 e.t. archive
p. 137 © The Trustees of the National Museums of Scotland
p 138 e.t. archive
p 139 e.t. archive
pp. 140-141, 141 © Naturhistorisches Museum Wien
p. 142 © British Museum, London
p. 143 © British Museum, London
pp. 144-145 C.M. Dixon
p. 147 Ancient Art & Architecture Collection
p. 148 © National Museum of Ireland
p. 149 Werner Forman Archive/ National Museum of Ireland
pp. 150, 151 (inset) AKG London/ Erich Lessing
p. 151 (backdrop) Cliché Musée du Châtillonais - Châtillon-sur-Seine
p. 152 © Photo RMN - Arnaudet; J.Schormans
p. 153 AKG London/ Erich Lessing
p. 154 The Bridgeman Art Library/ Archaeological Museum, Piraeus, Greece
p. 155 The Bridgeman Art Library/ Townley Hall Art Gallery and Museum, Burnley, Lancashire
pp. 156, 157 (both) AKG London/ Erich Lessing
p. 158 © Landesamt für Denkmalpflegs Hessen (Photo: Ursula Seitz-Gray, Frankfurt am Main)
p. 159 AKG London/ Erich Lessing
p. 160 e.t. archive

p. 161 Sergio Ripoll
pp. 162, 163 Ancient Art & Architecture Collection
p. 165 National Museum of History, Sofia, inv. no. 22397 (photo: Ivo Hadjimishev), courtesy NOMA
p. 166 e.t. archive
p. 167 Giraudon
pp. 168, 169 AKG London
pp. 170, 171, 172, CORBIS/Mimmo Jodice
p. 173 e.t. archive
p. 175 CORBIS/Mimmo Jodice
pp. 176, 177 (both) © Photo RMN - Hervé Lewandowski
pp. 178-179 C.M. Dixon
pp. 180-181 © British Museum, London
pp. 183, 184 The Vindolanda Trust
pp. 186, 187 Museum im Schloss Bad Pyrmont
pp. 188, 189 © British Museum, London
pp. 190, 191, 192, 193, 194, 195, 196, 197 © British Museum, London
pp. 198-199 © Statens Historiska Museum, Stockholm
p. 200 © British Museum, London
p. 201 Ancient Art & Architecture Collection
pp. 202, 203 Muzeum Narodwe, Wroclaw (Photo: Edmund Witecki)
pp. 204-205 © Ruth Kirk
pp. 206-207 © Warren Morgan
p. 208 Topham Picturepoint
p. 209 Giraudon
p. 211 South American Pictures
pp. 212, 213 © Barbara Purdy
p. 214 Werner Forman Archive/ National Museum of Anthropology, Mexico City
p. 215 © Dr. Constance Cortez
p. 216 South American Pictures
p. 217 (both) National Geographic Society Image Collection
p. 218 (left) Werner Forman Archive/ Maxwell Museum of Anthropology, Albuquerque
pp. 218-219, 219 Werner Forman Archive/ Peabody Museum, Harvard University, Cambridge MA
pp. 220, 221, 222-223 © Ruth Kirk
pp. 224-225 Ancient Art & Architecture Collection
p. 226 Werner Forman Archive/ British Museum, London
p. 227 Ancient Art & Architecture Collection
p. 229 Werner Forman Archive/ David Bernstein Fine Art, New York
p. 230 (both) CORBIS/ Kevin Schafer
p. 231 AKG London
p. 232 e.t. archive
p. 233 (both) South American Pictures
p. 234 CORBIS/Francis G. Mayer
p. 235 e.t. archive
p. 236 e.t. archive
p. 237 Ancient Art & Architecture Collection
pp. 238-239 The Bridgeman Art Library/ Royal Geographic Society, London
pp. 240-241 The Bridgeman Art Library/ O'Shea Gallery, London
p. 241 The Bridgeman Art Library/ private collection
pp. 242-243 The Bridgeman Art Library/ Royal Geographic Society, London
pp. 244-245 AKG London

List of Contributors

PAUL G. BAHN
General editor and contributor, Hull, England

CAROLINE BIRD
School of Archaeology, La Trobe University,
Melbourne, Victoria, Australia
(Australia and the Pacific)

PETER BOGUCKI
School of Engineering and Applied Science,
Princeton University, USA
(Central and Eastern Europe and ex-USSR)

CONSTANCE CORTEZ
Department of Art and Art History, Santa Clara
University, Santa Clara, California, USA
(Central America)

PHILIP DUKE
Department of Anthropology, Fort Lewis
College, Durango, USA
(North America)

CHRISTOPHER EDENS
Peabody Museum, Harvard University,
Cambridge, Massachusetts, USA
(Near East, Central Asia, India)

DAVID GILL
Department of Classics and Ancient History,
University College, Swansea, Wales
(Classical archaeology)

JOHN HOFFECKER
Institute of Arctic and Alpine Research,
University of Colorado at Boulder,
Colorado, USA
(Early periods, Central and Eastern Europe and
ex-USSR)

MARK HUDSON
Institute of History and Anthropology,
University of Tsukuba, Japan
(Japan)

SIMON KANER
Department of Archaeology, University of
Cambridge, England
(Far East and Western Europe)

GEOFFREY McCAFFERTY
Department of Anthropology, Salve Regina
University, Newport, Rhode Island, USA
(Central America)

STEVEN SNAPE
School of Archaeology, Classics and Oriental
Studies, University of Liverpool, England
(Egypt and Levant)

LOUISE STEEL
British School of Archaeology, Jerusalem, Israel
(Aegean)

ANNE THACKERAY
Department of Archaeology, University of the
Witwatersrand, South Africa
(Africa)

KAREN WISE
Anthropology Section, Natural History
Museum Los Angeles County, Los Angeles,
California, USA
(South America)

First published in the United Kingdom in 1999
by Weidenfeld & Nicolson Illustrated

This paperback edition first published in 2000
by Seven Dials, Cassell & Co
Wellington House, 125 Strand
London, WC2R 0BB

A CIP catalogue record for this book is
available from the British Library

ISBN 1 84188 061 2

Picture research: Caroline Thomas
Printed and bound in Italy by Printer Trento s.r.l.